Zohar
The Book of Enlightenment

TRANSLATION AND INTRODUCTION
BY
DANIEL CHANAN MATT

PREFACE
BY
ARTHUR GREEN

PAULIST PRESS

Cover Art:
MICHAEL BOGDANOW is a native of Houston, Texas. He now lives near Boston and is completing a Juris Doctor degree at Harvard Law School while continuing with his art. "My art is motivated by a desire to communicate with people, to express feelings and ideas that cannot necessarily be captured by word," he says.

Library of Congress
Catalog Card Number: 83-82145

ISBN: 0-8091-2387-8 (paper)
0-8091-0320-6 (cloth)

Published by Paulist Press
545 Island Road, Ramsey, N.J. 07446

Printed and bound in the
United States of America

CONTENTS

CONTENTS

TO MY PARENTS,
TOVAH GITEL AND HA-RAV ZEVI YONAH HA-LEVI,
WHO HAVE NURTURED ME WITH LOVE AND TORAH

ACKNOWLEDGMENTS

I have been blessed with wise teachers and understanding *ḥavrayya*. Here I thank a few who read portions of the manuscript: Pamela Adelman, Alexander Altmann, Michael Fishbane, Arthur Green, Burt Jacobson, Steve Joseph, Ana Massie, Jo Milgrom, Stephen Mitchell, Sara Shendelman, and David Winston.

I am grateful to John Farina and Richard Payne, editors at Paulist Press, for their help and encouragement.

PREFACE

One who delves into the religious literature of some figures and periods can never forget the profound link that exists between spiritual creativity and the poetic imagination. The reader of Solomon Gabirol or Judah Halevi among the medieval Hebrew poets, like the reader of John of the Cross, to limit the consideration to fellow Spaniards, will perforce see how the poetic vehicle and the religious message converge to influence and mediate one another.

This is not so obviously the case with the Zohar, the *magnum opus* of Spanish-Jewish Kabbalah in the late thirteenth century. Here the thicket of symbolism is so dense, and the Aramaic prose in which the work is presented often so obscure, that the sense of the poetic is not immediately apparent. The author of the Zohar was, however, possessed of a truly magnificent literary imagination, and he created out of the emerging kabbalistic tradition a work of masterful poetic scope, though doing so without recourse to those specific literary canons that distinguished "poetry" in his age. Working with an already established system of symbolic correspondences (the *sefirot*, as will be explained below), Moses de León was able to keep the conventionalized religious language in the background, and to sing loftily of lights and sparks, sun and moon, flowing streams and rivers, and, most passionately, of the unending love between the celestial Bridegroom and His Bride.

Such was the fate of this work, however, that it came to be increasingly venerated by generations of devotees who sought to make its poetry transparent, to see beyond the imagery into the "true" religious meaning of the text, exegeting it much as the early rabbis had the Bible, to find in each word or phrase previously unseen layers of sacred meaning. As kabbalistic thought itself developed, particularly after the sixteenth century, a new and infinitely more complicated system of symbols, based on further development of zoharic themes, supplanted the old. Now the purpose of exegesis became a rereading of the Zohar in this later spirit, seeking to find the Lurianic teaching, as it was called, in the more venerable source. Commentaries of the Zohar became increasingly illegible to the noninitiate, and even once deci-

PREFACE

phered had increasingly little to do with the original meaning of the Zohar text.

As moderns have turned their attention once again to the study of Zohar, largely under the inspiration of Gershom Scholem and his Jerusalem school of kabbalistic history, the task of exegesis has turned again to *peshat*, the attempt to reconstruct the symbolic *meaning* of the Zohar's fantasy-laden means of expression. Here too, however, the goal is to some extent one of penetrating beyond the surface content of the work, translating its unique poetic back into the conventional symbol-clusters of kabbalistic tradition.

It is the strength of the work before us that its editor has refused to follow such a generally accepted method. The work you are about to read, both in selection and translation, is an act of daring, the creation of a young scholar undaunted by the conventions of the academy. He seeks to do nothing less than to recover de León the poet, to allow the Zohar to be read, perhaps for the first time since it emerged from the author's mind into the written word, first as a work of poetic imagination, and only second, through a highly competent series of notes, as a textbook of kabbalistic symbolism. It is characteristic of the editor and his intent that he chose to place the notes at a distance from the text itself, so that the reader be left the choice of when—and indeed whether—to consult them.

In both readings, that of translation alone and that of text as explicated in the notes, Matt's *Book of Enlightenment* is one that the Zohar's author would enjoy, and one that the thoughtful reader will find enriching, on more than one level.

Arthur Green

FOREWORD

Sefer ha-Zohar, the Book of Splendor, Radiance, Enlightenment,[1] has amazed and overwhelmed readers for seven centuries. The Zohar is the major text of Kabbalah, the Jewish mystical tradition. It is arranged in the form of a commentary on the Torah, the Five Books of Moses. It is a mosaic of Bible, midrash (see Glossary), medieval homily, fiction, and fantasy. Its central theme is the interplay of human and divine realities. Its language is a peculiar brand of Aramaic that breaks the rules of grammar and invents words.

Who wrote the Zohar? The question has been debated ever since the first hand-written booklets were distributed in Spain late in the thirteenth century. The Introduction below tells the story of the answer.

The Zohar is immense. This volume contains approximately 2 percent of the entire work. It is presumptuous to pick and choose from a mystical corpus, but I have tried to select passages that are spiritually evocative and that demonstrate the uniqueness of the Zohar's encounter with Torah. I have supplied the passages with titles, and occasionally omitted material within a passage, in which case the omission is indicated by ellipsis points. An index at the end of the volume identifies the location of the passages in the Zohar. The translation attempts to convey the lyrical flavor of the original without smoothing away its rough vibrancy.

The Zohar is an esoteric and cryptic work, a commentary that requires a commentary. The notes in the second half of the volume are designed to guide the reader through the maze of kabbalistic symbolism and to identify rabbinic sources and zoharic parallels. Here I have relied especially on *Ketem Paz* by Shim'on Labi; *Or ha-Hammah,* edited by Avraham Azulai; *Nizozei Zohar* by Re'uven Margaliot (printed in his edition of the Zohar); *Mishnat ha-Zohar* by Isaiah Tishby; and the works of Gershom Scholem (*nishmato eden*). I suggest that the reader first encounter each passage on his own, and then go back to study it with the notes, which are unnumbered (except in the Foreword and Introduction) and keyed to a particular Zohar selection.

FOREWORD

The teachings of Kabbalah are profound and powerful. One who hopes to enter and emerge in peace must be careful, persevering, and receptive. Follow the words to what lies beyond and within. Open the gates of imagination. Let Zohar *alef* the Ineffable.

INTRODUCTION

With the light created by God during the six days of
    Creation
Adam could see from one end of the world to the other.
God hid the light away for the righteous in the hereafter.
Where did He hide it?
In the Torah.
So when I open *The Book of Zohar,* I see the whole world.

           —Israel son of Eli'ezer
            the *Ba'al Shem Tov*

The Zohar has kept me Jewish.

           —Pinhas of Koretz
            Hasidic rabbi[1]

1

Seven hundred years ago, a Spanish Jewish mystic named Moses de León began circulating booklets to his friends and fellow kabbalists. These booklets contained teachings and tales that had never been seen or heard. Moses claimed that he was merely the scribe, copying from an ancient book of wisdom. The original had been composed in the circle of Rabbi Shim'on son of Yoḥai, a famous teacher of the second century who lived in the land of Israel and, according to tradition, spent twelve years secluded in a cave. After Rabbi Shim'on's death, so the story goes, the book was hidden away or secretly handed down from master to disciple. Only recently had it been sent from Israel to Catalonia in northeastern Spain. Then it fell into the hands of Moses de León of Guadalajara. He took it upon himself to spread the ancient secrets, copying portions from the original manuscript and offering them for sale.

But history impinged. In 1291 the Mamluks conquered the city of Acre in Israel and massacred most of the Jewish and Christian inhabitants. One of the few who managed to escape was a young man named Isaac son of Samuel. He journeyed to Italy and eventually to Spain, arriving in Toledo in 1305. Isaac, who later became one of the leading kabbalists of the fourteenth century, was amazed at the reports he heard about the newly discovered Midrash of Rabbi Shim'on. The book had supposedly been written in Israel, but Isaac was from Israel and had never heard of it.

According to his diary, Isaac sought out those who possessed the booklets and was informed that the distributor was Moses de León, whom he located in Valladolid. Moses assured him that he owned the original manuscript composed by the ancient sage, and that he would let Isaac see it if he came to Ávila, where Moses now lived. They parted company. Moses set out for his home, but on the way, in the town of Arévalo, he became ill and died. When Isaac heard the news, he went straight to Ávila to see if anyone there knew the truth about the book. He was told that immediately following Moses' death, the wife of Joseph de Ávila, the tax collector of the province, had offered her son

in marriage to the daughter of Moses de León's widow in exchange for
the ancient manuscript. Moses' widow had responded:

> Thus and more may God do to me if my husband ever
> possessed such a book! He wrote it entirely from his own
> head. When I saw him writing with nothing in front of him, I
> said to him, "Why do you say that you are copying from a
> book when there is no book? You are writing from your head.
> Wouldn't it be better to say so? You would have more honor!"
> He answered me, "If I told them my secret, that I am writing
> from my own mind, they would pay no attention to my
> words, and they would pay nothing for them. They would
> say: 'He is inventing them out of his imagination.' But now
> that they hear that I am copying from *The Book of Zohar*
> composed by Rabbi Shim'on son of Yohai through the Holy
> Spirit, they buy these words at a high price, as you see with
> your very eyes!"

Isaac was aghast when he heard this story. He traveled on to make
further inquiries and found support for Moses' claim that the book was
ancient. He heard a report that Rabbi Jacob, a former student of Moses
de León, had sworn that "the Zohar composed by Rabbi Shim'on son
of Yohai . . ." And here the citation from Isaac's diary breaks off.[2]

Moses de León's name faded. The Zohar was gradually accepted as
the ancient wisdom of Rabbi Shim'on and his circle. By the middle of
the sixteenth century, it ranked with the Bible and the Talmud as a
sacred text. While kabbalists delved into its mysteries, Oriental Jews
chanted the strange Aramaic, often unaware of the literal sense. But
both groups, and countless others, were inspired and uplifted by the
Holy Zohar.[3]

Who was Moses de León? Devoted scribe or devious author?

As with many mystics, the facts of Moses' life are scarce. In one of his books, he calls himself "Moses son of Shem Tov from the city of León."[4] The year of his birth is unknown, but by 1264 he was engaged in the study of philosophy, for in that year a Hebrew translation of Maimonides' *Guide of the Perplexed* was copied "for the erudite [*ha-maskil*] Rabbi Moses de León."[5] (The *Guide*, completed about 1200 in Egypt, was a grandiose attempt at a synthesis of Jewish faith and Aristotelian philosophy.) Philosophy, however, was not Moses de León's only undertaking. He immersed himself in rabbinic literature and was also drawn to the teachings of Kabbalah.

Kabbalah means "receiving" and refers to that which is handed down by tradition. For many centuries the word was used quite generally, but by the time of Moses de León, the term Kabbalah denoted esoteric teachings, techniques of meditation, and a growing body of mystical literature. A kabbalistic movement had emerged in Provence and Catalonia toward the end of the twelfth and the beginning of the thirteenth centuries. The famous rabbi Naḥmanides of Gerona explored the teachings and helped Kabbalah gain wider acceptance. The movement spread westward to Castile (central Spain). Wandering south from León, Moses came to know some of the kabbalists and was introduced to the *Bahir* ("Brightness"), the main text of Provençal Kabbalah, to the teachings of the school of Gerona, and to more recent Castilian formulations.[6]

Moses de León did not reject philosophy. Many of his kabbalistic comrades had also studied the *Guide of the Perplexed*, and there were parallels and connections between Maimonides' system and Kabbalah. Both adopted the Neoplatonic scheme; both aimed at contemplative union with higher spheres; both were dissatisfied with the plain, literal meaning of Torah and sought to spiritualize its teaching.

However, Moses and his fellow kabbalists saw the effects of radical rationalism on Spanish Jewry. Maimonides had written his *Guide* in Arabic for an intellectual elite. Once it was translated into Hebrew and transplanted to Spain, rationalism became the vogue among the Jewish upper class. Many of these wealthy, assimilated Jews embraced a rationalistic ideology not for the pursuit of truth but in order to justify their neglect of tradition. In his *Sefer ha-Rimmon* ("Book of the Pomegranate"), Moses de León lashes out at these lazy scoffers:

> When they are alone with one another, they ridicule and mock [the words of the rabbis] and delight in the words of the Greeks and their assistants [the medieval philosophers]. They kiss their words! Furthermore, I have seen them on the festival of *Sukkot* ["Booths"] standing in their places in the synagogue, watching the servants of God circling with palm branches around the Torah scroll in the ark, laughing at them and mocking them, saying that they are fools without any knowledge. Meanwhile, they have no palm branch and no citron. They claim: "Has not the Torah said to take these in order to 'rejoice in the presence of *YHVH* your God for seven days' (Leviticus 23:40)? Do you think these species will make us happy? Silver and gold ornaments and fine clothes make us happier!" And they say, "Do you think we have to bless God? Does He need this? Foolishness!" Eventually there are no phylacteries on their heads. When you ask them why, they answer, "Phylacteries are only meant to be 'a reminder between your eyes' (Exodus 13:9). This is no reminder. It is better to mention the Creator with our mouths several times a day. That is a better and more fitting reminder!" They take those books and see those words and say that this is the Torah of truth![7]

Moses was incensed at this cavalier attitude toward tradition. At the same time, he was dissatisfied with the traditionalists. Having experienced the knowledge of Kabbalah, he was no longer content with mere book learning. In his *Or Zaru'a* ("Sown Light"), Moses writes:

> I have seen some people called "wise." But they have not awoken from their slumber; they just remain where they are. . . . Indeed, they are far from searching for His glorious Reality. They have exchanged His Glory for the image of a

bull eating grass [cf. Psalms 106:20]. For when one of them comes to the case of a bull that is to be stoned [because it gored someone; see Exodus 21:28–32; Mishnah and Talmud, *Bava Qamma*, 4], and he finds out exactly how it should be stoned, he thinks he is a great wise man and has achieved what no one else has. Now indeed, all the words of the rabbis, may their memory be a blessing, are true and perfect; they are all words of the living God! But having reached this case, which is one level, why does he not ascend from wisdom to wisdom, from level to level?

The ancient wise ones have said that there was once a man who engaged in Mishnah and Talmud all his days according to his animal knowledge. When the time came for him to depart from the world, he was very old, and people said that he was a great wise man. But one person came along and said to him, "Do you know your self? All the limbs in your body, what are they for?" He said, "I do not know." "Your little finger, what is it for?" He said, "I do not know." "Do you know anything outside of you, why it is how it is?" He began shouting at everyone, "I do not know my self! How can I know anything outside my self?" He went on, "All my days I have toiled in Torah until I was eighty years old. But in the final year I attained no more wisdom or essence than I attained in those first years when I began studying." The people asked, "Then what did you toil over all these years?" He said, "What I learned in the beginning." They said, "This wise man is nothing but an animal without any knowledge. He did not know the purpose of all his work; just like an animal carrying straw on its back, not knowing whether it is sifted grain or straw!" ... See now how my eyes shine, for I have tasted a bit of this honey! O House of Jacob! Come, let us walk in the light of *YHVH*![8]

Moses settled in the city of Guadalajara and sometime between 1275 and 1280 began to produce a mystical Midrash. The root of *midrash* means "to search." Midrash is the ancient technique of searching for the meaning of passages, phrases, and individual words of the Bible. It includes philology, etymology, hermeneutics, homiletics, and imagination. The earliest Midrashim were edited during the fourth and fifth centuries. Moses called this creation *Midrash ha-Ne'elam*, the Concealed Midrash, the Esoteric Midrash, an ancient composition that had disappeared until now.[9]

Midrash ha-Ne'elam is the earliest stratum of the Zohar. It is a commentary on parts of the Torah and the Book of Ruth. We also possess *Midrash ha-Ne'elam* on the beginning of Lamentations and the beginning of *Midrash ha-Ne'elam* on Song of Songs.[10] The style of these passages reveals that Moses de León is still under the influence of philosophy. He employs philosophical terminology and the technique of allegory. Abram's journey to the land of Canaan, for example, is presented as the journey of the soul into the world.[11] The language of *Midrash ha-Ne'elam* is a mixture of Hebrew and Aramaic, unlike that of the rest of the Zohar, which is completely Aramaic. Aramaic, the language of the Talmud, spoken hardly anywhere in the medieval world, lent an ancient tone to the Zohar and clothed its radical teachings in the garb of tradition.[12]

The figure of Rabbi Shim'on appears in *Midrash ha-Ne'elam*, but he is not the only master. At times Eli'ezer son of Hyrcanus, an earlier rabbi, is the hero. At other times there is no single master. Rather, we meet a whole array of talmudic figures, many of whom lived centuries apart. In the main body of the Zohar the anachronisms are fewer though still striking; Rabbi Shim'on is the undisputed Holy Light.

By the year 1281 Moses de León had already shown parts of *Midrash ha-Ne'elam* to at least one of his kabbalistic colleagues in Guadalajara, Isaac son of Solomon Abi Sahula. In Isaac's *Meshal ha-Qadmoni* ("Fable of the Ancient"), written in that year, there appear one quotation and one paraphrase from *Midrash ha-Ne'elam* and several oblique references to the work. Two years later Isaac completed a mystical commentary on the Song of Songs in which he quotes eight passages from *Midrash ha-Ne'elam*. Apparently Isaac knew the real origin of these citations and was helping to spread the "ancient" teachings.[13]

Between 1280 and 1286 Moses de León produced the main body of the Zohar, a rambling mystical commentary on the Torah containing a number of distinct literary compositions.[14] The language is a pseudo-Aramaic spoken by Rabbi Shim'on and his disciples as they wander through the Galilee exchanging kabbalistic insights. The Zohar refashions the Torah's narrative into a mystical novel. On one level, the biblical heroes are the protagonists, and the rabbis interpret their words, their personalities, and their encounters with holy or demonic forces. The commentary is often far removed from the literal meaning of the biblical text. The words of Torah are a starting point, a springboard for the imagination. At times the commentators become the main characters, and we read about dramatic study sessions with Rabbi Shim'on or about the rabbis' adventures on the road.

In the standard printed editions of the Zohar there is one volume on Genesis, one on Exodus, and one on the remaining three books of the Torah: Leviticus, Numbers, and Deuteronomy. On Deuteronomy, in fact, there are only a few Zohar passages. It is unlikely that significant portions have been lost. Rather, at a certain point Moses de León simply exhausted his creative power or felt that he had done enough and turned his attention elsewhere.[15]

From 1286 until his death in 1305, Moses wrote books in Hebrew under his own name and copied out portions of the Zohar for sale and circulation. His Hebrew writings are filled with the ideas and imagery of the Zohar and serve as a valuable commentary. They were intended to prepare his reading audience for the publication of his pseudepigraphic *magnum opus*. Frequently in these books Moses alludes to the Zohar: "It is expounded in the inner Midrashim"; "They say in the secrets of Torah"; "The pillars of the world have discussed the secrets of their words"; "I have seen a profound matter in the writings of the ancients"; "I saw in the *Yerushalmi*"; "I have seen in the secrets of the depth of wisdom."[16] Moses is tantalizing the reader, hinting that an unknown book of ancient wisdom has been discovered. Soon it will be available.

Moses remained in Guadalajara until at least 1291,[17] and from there he began circulating the Zohar. He did not distribute entire copies of the book, just portions. This is indicated in the diary of Isaac of Acre and accords with the fact that the first authors to quote the Zohar cite only certain sections. No complete manuscript has yet been found. When the Zohar was first printed in Italy in the sixteenth century, the editors had to combine several manuscripts to produce a complete text. Later other manuscripts were located, and an additional volume was printed elsewhere.[18]

Despite Moses' efforts, the Zohar was not accepted by everyone as an ancient work. We have already heard of the investigation of Isaac of Acre. There were other kabbalists who treated the Zohar with restraint, for example, the students of Rabbi Solomon son of Abraham ibn Adret of Barcelona. In 1340 the philosopher and kabbalist Joseph ibn Waqqar warned: "Very many errors occur in the book. Therefore it is necessary to be careful and keep a safe distance from it in order not to make mistakes."[19]

A number of adventurous souls followed Moses' example and produced their own ancient Midrashim. Foremost among these were *Ra'aya Meheimna* ("The Faithful Shepherd") and *Tiqqunei Zohar* ("Embellishments on the Zohar"), written at the end of the thirteenth or the beginning of the fourteenth century. These two imitations were successful enough to become part of the zoharic literature. *Ra'aya Meheimna* is actually printed as part of the Zohar, while *Tiqqunei Zohar* appears in a separate volume.[20] Another kabbalist, David son of Judah the Hasid, wrote *Mar'ot ha-Zove'ot* ("The Book of Mirrors") in the early fourteenth century. This work contains numerous translations of Zohar passages into Hebrew along with rabbinic Midrashim, selections from thirteenth-century kabbalistic literature, and the author's own imitations of Zohar.[21]

3

Gradually the Zohar's antiquity was accepted by kabbalists. However, it was not read or circulated beyond small circles. In the middle of the fifteenth century the Marrano Pedro de la Caballeria stated that few Jews possessed the Zohar.[22] It was not until after the expulsion of the Jews from Spain in 1492 that the Zohar became the Bible of Kabbalah. From 1530 onward, Safed, Israel, was a meeting place for kabbalists. One of them, Moses Cordovero, wrote two systematic books of Kabbalah based on the Zohar and also a long commentary on it. Isaac Luria developed a new system of Kabbalah that drew heavily on certain sections of the Zohar. The mystical-ethical literature that emerged from this circle helped to popularize the Zohar's teachings, while the messianic fervor generated here encouraged the spreading of the secrets. Earlier kabbalists had already made a connection between the dissemination of Kabbalah and the redemption of Israel, but now studying the Zohar was raised to the level of a divine command:

> The decree from above not to engage openly in the wisdom of Kabbalah was meant to apply only for a set time, until 1490. From then on is the time of the last generation [before the Messiah]; the decree is rescinded, and permission is granted to engage in studying *The Book of Zohar*. From 1540 on, the best way to fulfill the *mizvah* [divine command] is to engage in it publicly, young and old.... Since this and nothing else will bring about the coming of King Messiah, do not be negligent![23]

The technology of printing made it feasible for young and old to engage in the Zohar. Between 1558 and 1560 the first two editions appeared in the neighboring Italian cities of Mantua and Cremona. There was a fierce controversy over the printing; among the opponents were kabbalists who felt that it was dangerous and forbidden to reveal such secrets of Torah. They did not agree that the decree from above had been rescinded. Others opposed publication because they suspected that the Zohar was a late work. However, the editors countered these objections, and *The Book of Enlightenment* became available to wider circles.[24]

Even before the Zohar was printed, it had aroused the interest of certain Christians. At the end of the fifteenth century, Pico della Mirandola and Johannes Reuchlin took up the study of Kabbalah. They became convinced that it contained the original divine revelation and that its true, hidden meaning accorded with the secrets of the Christian faith. They tried to identify kabbalistic parallels to the Trinity, Incarnation, the Virgin Mother, the Name of Jesus, and Original Sin. In the first half of the sixteenth century, the Franciscan Francesco Giorgio of Venice used manuscript material from the Zohar extensively in his works, and Guillaume Postel began to translate the Zohar into Latin.[25]

The claims of Christian Kabbalah helped stimulate the first critical work on the Zohar, *Ari Nohem* ("Roaring Lion"), written by the Italian rabbi and scholar Leone Modena in 1639. Modena stated flatly that the Zohar was not composed by Rabbi Shim'on or his circle; that it could not be "more than 350 years old." He praised the Zohar's style and inspirational effect but identified anachronisms to prove its recent origin and impugn its authority.[26] By now, however, the Zohar was too highly venerated to be openly challenged. Modena did not dare to publish *Ari Nohem;* it was printed only in 1840, nearly two hundred years after the author's death. Until then it circulated in manuscript. Certain freethinkers approved, while one kabbalist of the eighteenth century, Moses Ḥayyim Luzzatto, responded to it with a written defense of Kabbalah.[27]

It was not until the second half of the eighteenth century that a major critical work on the Zohar was printed. This book too was written with polemical intent. Sabbatianism, the messianic movement of the seventeenth century, was based on Lurianic Kabbalah and relied heavily on the Zohar for imagery, symbolism, and doctrine. In fact, Shabbetai Ẓevi, the hero of the movement and reputed Messiah, was more influenced by the Zohar than by Luria.[28] In 1666 the royal council of Turkey, alarmed at Shabbetai's growing power and eccentric behavior, offered him the choice of being put to death or converting to Islam. Shabbetai converted, but the movement persisted and was driven completely underground only at the start of the eighteenth century.

One of the most dedicated opponents of the later secret sect was

INTRODUCTION

Jacob Emden, a noted rabbi and halakhic authority. He pursued suspected Sabbatians, including the famous rabbi Jonathan Eybeschuetz, and developed an extraordinary critical ability for uncovering heretical allusions in Sabbatian literature. This led him to a critical reading of the Zohar, the bastion of Sabbatianism. Emden believed firmly in the truth of Kabbalah, and it was difficult for him to publish his radical discoveries. At the beginning of his *Mitpaḥat Sefarim* ("Covering of the Holy Books," 1768), he says that he suppressed his doubts for forty years but now feels compelled to reveal the truth. He then proceeds to list nearly three hundred pieces of evidence culled from the pages of the Zohar that prove the late editing of the book. These include traces of medieval sources, corrupt Aramaic, halakhic mistakes, historical allusions, and anachronisms. Nevertheless, Emden attempted to preserve the sanctity of at least part of the Zohar and concluded that there was an ancient core to the book, though even this was composed hundreds of years after Rabbi Shim'on. Many passages, including the entire *Midrash ha-Ne'elam*, were added in the thirteenth century.[29]

Emden laid the groundwork for modern research on the Zohar. In the nineteenth century, Adolf Jellinek proceeded to compare one of Moses de León's Hebrew writings with the Zohar. He showed that most of the Hebrew book appeared in the Zohar in Aramaic, sometimes with variations. The Hebrew work also quoted zoharic passages, attributing them to ancient sources.[30] Jellinek concluded that Moses de León was, at least, one of the authors of the Zohar. He also detected the influence of thirteenth-century Kabbalah on the Zohar's ideas and terminology.[31]

The historian Heinrich Graetz relied on Jellinek but insisted that the Zohar was written entirely by Moses de León. Graetz worshiped rationalism and saw Kabbalah as a malignant growth in the body of Judaism. He called the Zohar a "book of lies" and claimed that its fantasies and illusions had blinded Jews to the light of rational truth. Accepting the testimony recorded by Isaac of Acre, Graetz charged that Moses de León was nothing but a conniving forger.[32]

The reserach of Gershom Scholem has broken through the rationalistic prejudice of the nineteenth century and demonstrated that Kabbalah is a vital component of Jewish thought and history. Scholem's first lecture at the Hebrew University in Jerusalem in 1925 was entitled: "Did Moses de León Write the Zohar?"[33] The question occupied him for many years. He sifted the writings of kabbalists, critics, and scholars. He examined the Zohar's language, terminology, ideas, and symbolism in the context of early Kabbalah and medieval Hebrew thought and literature. He explored the literary structure of the Zohar, its fictional format, and historical allusions. Scholem demonstrated that the peculiar Aramaic was constructed from literary sources, particularly the Babylonian Talmud and Targum Onqelos; it contains grammatical errors and medieval Hebraisms. The mystical theosophy of the work proved to be pure thirteenth-century Kabbalah, which derives from medieval Jewish Neoplatonism and Gnosticism.

Scholem undertook a detailed analysis of all of Moses de León's extant Hebrew writings, most still in manuscript. Moses draws on the Zohar frequently, quoting it directly as an ancient work, paraphrasing or altering it, combining separate passages. "His method is that of the artist who shapes the material into any form he desires."[34] Moses' Hebrew exhibits characteristics of the Zohar's Aramaic: the same strange syntax, the same new meanings, the same incorrect grammatical forms. These similarities appear not only in Moses' translations of Zohar passages but also when he is writing on his own. Gradually Scholem became convinced that the author was one and the same. But whereas Graetz had condemned Moses de León, Scholem defended his pseudepigraphic venture as a legitimate expression of religious creativity.[35]

Scholem's student, Isaiah Tishby, has further advanced Zohar scholarship. His *Mishnat ha-Zohar* ("The Wisdom of the Zohar") includes extensive analyses and numerous translations arranged by subject.

4

Traditionalists often feel threatened by the findings of critical scholarship. Some still cling to the view that the Zohar is ancient. They suspect that historical research is out to destroy the wonder and mystery of the book. But reality is more amazing than fantasy. Understanding when, how, and by whom the Zohar was written only enhances one's appreciation.

By the end of the thirteenth century, the condition of Spanish Jewry was on the decline. The Jews were still a vital source of revenue for the royal treasury; they remained so until their expulsion in 1492. However, their political power was already weakening. In the height of the *Reconquista* (the Christian reconquest of Spain from the Moslems), the Jews had played an important role in resettling and administering captured cities. But during the reign of Alfonso X of Castile (1252–1284), the *Reconquista* was nearly completed, and the Jews' usefulness as colonizers soon disappeared. The emerging class of Christian burghers saw the Jews as competition. Jewish economic opportunities were gradually restricted.

Officially, the Jews were the property of the king and enjoyed his protection, but even so there was little security. The reign of Alfonso X provides a dramatic example. Called Alfonso the Wise, he was a patron of scholarship and employed several Jewish translators and scientists. He also produced a comprehensive code of law, *Las Siete Partidas*. This code was not enforced until the fourteenth century, but it reflects the attitudes prevailing during Alfonso's reign. The Jews were guaranteed physical security and the right of worship, but they were required to wear a "distinguishing mark upon their heads" in accord with the edict of the Fourth Lateran Council (1215). A judicial procedure was outlined for suspected cases of ritual murder. Following older authorities, the code states that Jews are tolerated as a reminder of their ancestors who crucified Jesus.[36] Toward the end of his reign, Alfonso's attitude toward the Jews worsened. In 1279 he imprisoned all the Jewish tax collectors; in 1281, on a Sabbath, he arrested all the Jews in Castile while they were attending synagogue and demanded a huge ransom in gold.[37]

INTRODUCTION

The picture was not altogether bleak. The Jews lived independently, within their own tradition and legal system. Because of the special relationship the Jews had with the King, the Christian municipalities had no authority over them. Nahmanides, the famous rabbi of Gerona (1194–1270), states in his Commentary on the Torah (Deuteronomy 28:42): "We dwell in countries like the other inhabitants or better." Still, there was an overwhelming sense of *galut*, exile. The Zohar expresses this feeling and offers words of comfort and encouragement.

Once, it is told, Rabbi El'azar encountered a gentile who challenged the chosenness of Israel:

> You say that you are closer to the Supreme King than all other nations. One who is close to the King is always happy, with no pain, fear, or oppression. But you are always in pain and grief, more oppressed than all other people in the world. As for us, no pain, oppression, or grief even comes near. We are close to the Supreme King; you are far from Him!

Rabbi El'azar stared at this man and he turned into a heap of bones. Then the rabbi said:

> The words spoken by that wicked man I once asked the prophet Elijah. He told me that these words were once arranged before the Blessed Holy One in the Academy in Heaven, and this was the response. . . . Indeed we are closer to the Supreme King than all other nations. Indeed it is so! For the Blessed Holy One has made Israel the heart of the whole world. Thus Israel lives among the other nations as the heart among the limbs of the body. Just as the limbs cannot exist even for a moment without the heart, so all the nations cannot exist without Israel. . . . The heart is tender and weak; yet it is the life of all the limbs. Only the heart perceives pain and trouble and grief, for it contains life and intelligence. The other limbs are not close to the King. They have no life; they perceive nothing.[38]

Israel feels the pain of the world. As the heart, they also nourish the world, and their exile enables them to perform this vital function. "Rabbi Ḥizkiyah said, 'The Blessed Holy One placed Israel in exile among the nations only so that the nations would be blessed because of them, for Israel causes blessings to flow from above to below every day' " (Zohar 1:244a).

Christian teaching claimed that Israel's exile was a sign of divine punishment for their rejection of Christ. The Zohar turns this argument upside down and cites biblical verses to indicate that Israel's lowly condition is the result of God's loving, parental discipline, whereas Christianity's rise to power is evidence that God has forsaken them and offers them no correction.[39]

Despite these rationalizations, the Zohar does not gloss over the humiliation of exile. "There is no nation that mocks Israel to their face and spits in their face like the children of Edom."[40] Israel is persecuted and oppressed; the time is ripe for the coming of Messiah. The author of the Zohar offers a number of apocalyptical calculations that set the date of redemption around 1300. Strong yearnings and pleadings are heard: "The exile is drawn out, and still the Son of David has not come." "How long will we be in this exile? . . . When will You deliver us from it?"[41]

God is viewed not only as the transcendent source of deliverance but also as a being who is personally involved in Israel's exile. The Talmud records a teaching by the real Shim'on son of Yohai: "Wherever Israel went in exile, *Shekhinah* [God's Presence] was with them." The Zohar expands this notion into a dramatic theme: the exile of *Shekhinah*. God shares Israel's suffering and yearns along with them for reconciliation and redemption.[42]

Meanwhile, Israel needs strength and hope. Torah offers both, providing a noble way of life and the promise of a better life. "Even when they are among the nations, bowed down among them, they are like a lion with the laws of Torah, the ways of Torah."

> Were it not for all those good things that they look forward to, that they see written in the Torah, they would not be able to endure and to bear the exile. But they go to the houses of study, they open the books and see all those good things they are waiting for. They see in the Torah everything promised to them by the Blessed Holy One, and they are comforted in their exile.[43]

In a revealing passage, the Zohar indicates that kabbalistic creativity is a means of sustaining the people:

INTRODUCTION

> If you do not know how to fortify yourself in exile, how to
> assert the power to protect your own child, then go out, go
> out to be strengthened by following the tracks of the sheep
> [see Song of Songs 1:8]. . . . Rabbi El'azar said, " 'The tracks of
> the sheep' means the students of the Academy who later came
> into the world [i.e., the kabbalists] and discovered Torah by
> following the straight path. The path is open; so they create/
> renew ancient teachings every day. *Shekhinah* rests upon them
> and listens to their words."[44]

By renewing tradition, by discovering and inventing ancient
teachings, the Zohar overcame the degradation of exile and celebrated
the vision of Israel's spiritual destiny.

The Christian environment leaves its mark in other ways as well.
Yitzhak Baer has pointed out the influence of the Spirituals, the radical
wing of the Franciscans, for example, their glorification of poverty as a
religious value.[45] There are also parallels in the Zohar to the Christian
midnight vigil and the four levels of meaning in Scripture.[46]

However, in an era of religious disputations and dogmatism there
was little room for open sharing and tolerance. The Zohar sees Israel
as the heart of the world, God's chosen people. They have sole claim on
truth. The faith of all other peoples is "a faith of foolishness."[47]
Throughout the Zohar there is an implicit rejection of Christian belief
and an affirmation of the faith of Israel. In one passage Rabbi Shim'on
ritualizes these attitudes:

> Rabbi Shim'on said, "When the Torah scroll is taken from the
> ark to be read in public, the heavenly gates of compassion are
> opened and love is aroused above, and a person should say the
> following: 'Blessed be the name of the Master of the world! . . .
> I am a servant of the Blessed Holy One, before whom and
> before whose glorious Torah I bow at all times. I do not place
> my trust in a human being; I do not rely upon a son of
> divinity, but rather, on the God of heaven, who is the God of
> truth, whose Torah is truth, whose prophets are truth, and
> who abounds in deeds of goodness and truth. In Him do I
> trust; to His holy and glorious name I utter praises!' "[48]

Without naming Jesus directly, the Zohar makes it clear that Israel
does not need him. All Jews are the sons of God. "Out of His love for

them, He called them 'My first-born son, Israel' (Exodus 4:22)."[49] The role of atoning for the sins of the world is assigned by Rabbi Shim'on to the righteous, and Isaiah 53 is cited as the proof text:

> When the righteous are seized by disease or affliction, it is in order to atone for the world. Thus all the sins of the generation are atoned for. When the Blessed Holy One wants to bring healing to the world, He strikes one righteous human among them with disease and affliction; through him He brings healing to all. How do we know this? As it is written: "He was wounded because of our sins, crushed because of our iniquities . . . by his bruises we were healed" (Isaiah 53:5).[50]

Two Zohar passages contain mythical descriptions of the Son of God:

> The Blessed Holy One has one son who shines from one end of the world to the other. He is a great and mighty tree, whose head reaches toward heaven and whose roots are rooted in the holy ground. (Zohar 2:105a)

The son is the cosmic tree, the trunk of the body of the *sefirot* (see chart in §6). Another passage reads:

> The mystery of the word is written concerning the mystery on high: "What is His name? What is the name of His son, if you know?" (Proverbs 30:4). That name is known: *YHVH Zeva'ot* is His name. The name of His son? Israel is his name, as it is written: "My first-born son, Israel." All the keys of faith hang from Israel. He praises himself, saying: "*YHVH* has said to me: 'You are My son' " (Psalms 2:7). Indeed it is so, for Father and Mother have crowned him and blessed him with countless crowns; they have commanded everyone: " 'Kiss the son!' (Psalms 2:12). Kiss the hand of this son!" As if it were possible, He has given him power over all, for all will worship him. "Lest he turn angry" (Ibid.). For he has been crowned with judgment and compassion. Judgment for one who deserves judgment; compassion for one who deserves compassion. All the blessings of above and below belong to this son.[51]

19

INTRODUCTION

The son is not earthly Israel but its divine archetype, the central *sefirah* called Beauty of Israel. Of course the theme of the Son of God is not original to Christianity; its ancient mythological derivation is well known. However, the use of such language and imagery by a Jewish mystic in Christian Spain is remarkable. The author of the Zohar is translating Christological formulations into the language of kabbalistic myth.

Similarly, Trinitarian formulae appear occasionally in descriptions of the *sefirot*. Graetz, the great Jewish historian who maligned Kabbalah, was shocked to find that "the Zohar even contains utterances which seem favorable to the Christian dogma of the Trinity of the Godhead."[52] Christian kabbalists adduced such passages as proof that Kabbalah accorded with the Catholic faith. Here too we are dealing with an ancient mythological image adopted and transformed by Christianity and imitated by the author of the Zohar, who no doubt rejected the Christian formulation. That it is possible to reject the Trinity and yet be influenced by its terminology is demonstrated dramatically by a contemporary of Moses de León, Abraham Abulafia. A prophetic kabbalist, he calls the Trinity "a lie and a deception" in one composition, but elsewhere refers to the three aspects of the intellect as God, Son of God, and Holy Spirit.[53] The Zohar is more subtle in its borrowings.

There are certain similarities between the Trinity and the *sefirot*. The Trinity consists of three persons of God, all coequal, coeternal, and indivisible. It is considered a profound mystery of faith. The *sefirot* are ten manifestations of the Infinite, ten aspects of the divine personality. "It is they and they are It" (Zohar 3:70a). They are called "the mystery of faith," *raza di-meheimanuta*.[54] Abulafia offers this revealing criticism:

> The masters of the *kabbalah* of *sefirot* intended to unify the Name and flee from the Trinity, but they have made it ten! As the gentiles say, "He is three and the three are one," so certain kabbalists believe and say that Divinity is ten *sefirot* and the ten are one.[55]

The term *sefirot* first appears in the early cosmogonic text *Sefer Yezirah* ("The Book of Creation"), written between the third and sixth centuries. There the word means "numbers, ciphers" and refers to metaphysical potencies that are stages of creation. Gradually Gnostic elements were assimilated, and in the *Bahir*, the first kabbalistic text (edited in the twelfth century), the *sefirot* constitute a mythical scheme. The Spanish kabbalists adopted this scheme and expanded it.[56]

The ten *sefirot* are sometimes grouped in three triads. The last *sefirah, Shekhinah*, the Divine Presence, includes them all. Near the beginning of the Zohar (1:32b) appears this cryptic description of the emanation of the *sefirot:*

> Three emerge from one; one stands in three;
> enters between two; two suckle one;
> one suckles many sides.
> Thus all is one.

The Oneness of God was a vital issue. The traditional Jewish declaration of God's unity is the *Shema*, Deuteronomy 6:4: "Hear O Israel! *YHVH*, our God, *YHVH* is one." Christian interpreters adduced the threefold mention of God in the verse as proof of the Trinity, and as early as the twelfth century, Jewish commentators countered this interpretation.[57] The Zohar (2:43b) has this to say:

> The unification [recited] every day is the unification of the verse in the Bible: "Hear O Israel! *YHVH*, our God, *YHVH* is one." They are all one; therefore He is called One.
> But there are three names! How are they one? Even though we say "One," how are they one?
> Through the vision of the Holy Spirit it is known. In the vision of the eye that is closed these three are revealed as one.... "*YHVH*, our God, *YHVH*" are one. Three colors, and they are one.

The passage is cryptic. Closing the eye and rotating the eyeball is described elsewhere in the Zohar as a technique for attaining a vision of the colors of the *sefirot*.[58] In the *Shema*, "*YHVH*, our God, *YHVH*" designates the middle triad of *sefirot*, which linked together, demonstrates the unity of God.[59]

In another passage (Zohar 3:162a), two rabbis on a mystical journey to the Garden of Eden hear a voice saying: "They are two; one is joined to them, and they are three. When they become three, they are one." The rabbis are confounded, but the guardian of the Garden explains the meaning: "These are the two names in the *Shema:* '*YHVH*,

YHVH.' 'Our God' joins them. . . . When they join together, they are one in one union."

It was a kabbalistic custom to correlate individual words of the liturgy to specific *sefirot.* However, in his specific wording with regard to the *Shema,* the author of the Zohar appears to be responding to the Christological interpretation. Appropriating the Trinitarian theme, he transposes it into a kabbalistic key. The structure of the *sefirot* offers ready-made triads, and the result is a curious harmony. An element of parody may also be involved. In several narrative passages of the Zohar such an element can be detected.[60]

The Zohar's emphasis on faith and belief is colored by the Christian environment, but its prime motivation was provided by the contemporary rationalistic trends. The kabbalists perceived these trends as a threat to tradition, and as we have seen (above, §2), Moses de León was deeply concerned. He felt called upon to defend traditional belief and practice, and he indicates in one of his Hebrew works that this was his purpose in revealing the ancient secrets: "God knows that my intention is good: that many may become wise and strengthen their faith in God."[61]

Despite Moses' critical attitude toward the effects of philosophic rationalism, the Zohar's theology is influenced by philosophy. Kabbalah grew out of philosophy, or as some kabbalists would say, outgrew it: "Their heads reach the point where our feet stand."[62] The kabbalists drew on Jewish Neoplatonic and Aristotelian teaching but were not confined to it. Their name for the ultimate reality of God is *Ein Sof,* the Infinite. *Ein Sof* is inaccessible to thought and has no attributes. This accords with Avicenna's and Maimonides' conception. In the Zohar, however, *Ein Sof* is rarely mentioned.[63] The focus of theological discussion is the *sefirot,* the manifestations of *Ein Sof,* Its mystical attributes. Here God thinks, feels, responds, and is affected by the human realm. He and She comprise the divine androgyne; their romantic and sexual relationship is one of the most striking features of the Zohar. Though ultimately God is infinite and indescribable, the *sefirot* are real "from our perspective."[64] They provide the human being with a way to know the Unknowable. "Through these gates, these spheres on high, the Blessed Holy One becomes known. Were it not so, no one could commune with Him."[65] The human need to contact God informs the Zohar's theology. Its emphasis on a living, dynamic faith is a reaction against the pure, cold logic of the philosophers. The critique is expressed by the poet Meshullam Da Piera (first half of the thirteenth century): "Those who deny the proper attributes of God speak out until faith has been drained."[66] In the Zohar Rabbi Yohanan exclaims: "We must not destroy the faith of all; we must maintain it!" (Zohar 1:136a [*Midrash ha-Ne'elam*]). The kabbalists are called "sons of faith."[67]

Some of the radical rationalists questioned the divine origin of the Torah. The Zohar responds by saying that not only does the Torah come from God; her words and letters are permeated with God. Study flowers into revelation.[68]

The Zohar is also capable of employing philosophical terminology and techniques for its own purposes. In the early stratum, *Midrash ha-Ne'elam*, where Moses de León is still making the transition from philosopher to kabbalist, there are numerous allegories modeled on philosophical exegesis.[69] Gradually mystical symbols replace philosophical allegories.[70] Still, the author knows how to apply the philosophical method of spiritualizing the commandments to the ritual of sacrifice, which is thereby transformed into a ritual of meditation.[71]

The kabbalist worships the God of Moses yet acknowledges the God of Maimonides. Divinity is not only Father in heaven but also Prime Mover. The Zohar strives to unite the two. It plays with the divine names *Sibbeta de-Sibbatin*, "The Cause of Causes," and *Saba de-Sabin*, "The Old Man of Old Men."[72]

On the theoretical level the issue was faith; on the practical level it was religious observance. Laxity in observance was prevalent, due to the inroads of rationalism and heresy as well as to more mundane factors: laziness and ignorance. The moralistic literature of the times lists a number of *mizvot* (commandments) that were neglected, for example, *tefillin* (phylacteries), *mezuzah* (the sign on the doorpost), *sukkah* (the booth constructed on the Festival of *Sukkot*), the ritual washing of hands, and sexual morality. The Zohar emphasizes the importance of all of these.[73]

The Zohar rarely discusses mystical experience, but it is eager to point out the mystical significance of Torah and *mizvot*. Studying and living Torah are the surest ways to direct encounter with God. "Happy are those who engage in Torah, for everyone who engages in Torah, it is as if he were joined to the Blessed Holy One" (Zohar 3:9b). "When

INTRODUCTION

a human being observes the commands of Torah, *Shekhinah* [the Divine Presence] walks with him constantly and never departs from him" (1:230a).

The author speaks with the passion of a mystical moralist. If one invites the poor into his *sukkah*, seven biblical heroes abide there with him. If one arrives early at the synagogue, *Shekhinah* joins Herself to him. Every day lived in accordance with Torah is woven into the soul's garment of splendor.[74] "Through an action below, an action above is aroused" (Zohar 3:31b). Even the inner dynamics of Divinity depend upon the human realm. The union of the divine couple, *Tif'eret* and *Shekhinah*, is effected by righteous action and destroyed by sin.[75]

Torah is not merely law; it is cosmic law, a blueprint of creation.[76] The Zohar illuminates the cosmic aspect of Torah. It strengthens tradition and at the same time transforms it. The literal sense is sanctified, but readers are urged to "look under the garment of Torah."[77]

The idea of searching for a deeper layer of meaning is not original to Kabbalah. It was adopted from Jewish philosophers who had taken it from Islamic tradition; earlier roots lie in Christian sources and Philo.[78] The Zohar employs this method for its own mystical and mythical exegesis.

Biblical and rabbinic Judaism had fought to suppress and eliminate divine mythology. Medieval Jewish philosophy tried to complete the task by explaining away all anthropomorphisms, thus purifying the conception of God. The Zohar, responding to a profound human need, resurrects myth and transforms the Torah into a mythical text. The first verse of Genesis is interpreted as a description of the emanation of the cosmic seed and the divine womb.[79] Theosophy replaces theology. The inner life of God is the hidden meaning of Torah, the true tradition: Kabbalah.

5

To promote this mythical, mystical tradition and establish its authenticity, the Zohar employs a number of devices. It reports teachings from the Academy of Heaven and from the mouth of the prophet Elijah.[80] It concludes other teachings with: "This has been said," "This has been established," "As the Comrades have established." At times these refer to actual talmudic or midrashic sources; at times to parallels in the Zohar.[81] An entire imaginary library provides proof texts whenever necessary. Its fantastic catalog includes the Book of Adam, the Book of Enoch, the Book of Wisdom of King Solomon (perhaps intended to be confused with the Apocryphal work of the same name), the Book of Rav Hamnuna Sava, the Book of Rav Yeiva Sava, the Book of Rav Yeisa Sava.[82] The Zohar cites "our Mishnah" or "the mystery of our Mishnah" when the actual source is another Zohar passage or medieval Kabbalah.[83]

A transformation of tradition could not succeed without ancient authorization. Moses de León secured this by recording the teachings in the names of the second-century sage Rabbi Shim'on son of Yohai and his wide-ranging circle. The figure of Rabbi Shim'on provided ideal sanction. Miraculous stories about him appear already in talmudic times. Opposed to the Romans, he was sentenced to death; so he and his son hid in a cave for twelve years. The eighth-century apocalyptic work *Nistarot shel Rabbi Shim'on ben Yohai* ("The Mysteries of Rabbi Shim'on") records heavenly secrets revealed to him in the cave.[84] Crowned by these traditions, Rabbi Shim'on assumed the role of Holy Light in the Zohar.[85]

The pseudepigraphic format was not something new. A whole ancient literature of pseudepigrapha is extant, and in medieval times the practice continued. An early kabbalistic text, the *Bahir*, was attributed to a rabbi of the first century, Nehunya son of ha-Kanah. Moses de León also composed several short pseudepigraphic pieces.[86]

Rabbi Shim'on and his circle enabled Moses to transmit radical teachings as ancient wisdom. At the end of one mythical passage Rabbi Shim'on alludes to this by exclaiming: "Torah has been restored to her ancientry!"[87] On the material plane the ancient format commanded a high price, as indicated in the diary of Isaac of Acre.[88]

Moses de León felt that the teachings he espoused were both new and ancient.[89] In one of his Hebrew books he writes: "Only recently has this spring of mystery begun to flow through the land."[90] God delights in new words of Torah and has commanded everyone to expand Torah daily.[91] On the other hand, Kabbalah stretches back to Moses at Mt. Sinai and ultimately to Adam.[92] Adam is the source of Kabbalah because the essential teaching conveys our original nature: the unbounded awareness of Adam. This nature is the most ancient tradition. It has been lost; that is the tragedy of Adam's Sin. The mystic yearns to recover the tradition, to regain cosmic consciousness, to see from one end of the world to the other.[93]

As a kabbalist, Moses de León was communicating this ancient wisdom. His style could be biblical or mythological, rabbinic or medieval; the essence was eternal. As one link in the chain of Kabbalah, he was transmitting something beyond himself and felt free to cite the sages who inhabited his imagination.

The pseudepigraphic and fictional design proved irresistible to centuries of readers. It also had a powerful effect on Moses de León as he composed the Zohar. This becomes clear through a comparison with his acknowledged Hebrew works, written later. As Jellinek and Scholem have demonstrated, the Hebrew writings depend heavily on the Zohar. However, some of the Zohar's most profound and radical teachings are not found in these books, for example, the detailed descriptions of the long-suffering and impatient aspects of God.[94] These secrets are so overwhelming that three of the Comrades die while hearing them. Apparently Moses felt free to set them down only in the name of Rabbi Shim'on.

The style of the Zohar is far superior to that of the Hebrew writings. In his acknowledged works Moses still displays originality and creativity, but the poet is subservient to the systematic theosophist. In the Zohar these roles coalesce, and the reader finds himself wandering through an enchanted forest, a mysticism of the imagination. Flights of lyrical freedom break through to the realm of the Divine, unlocking for the kabbalist, or any sensitive seeker, the deepest secrets of being. Nothing is dry or doctrinaire; everything breathes, sparkles, and flows. Images, colors, and streaming sermons fill the space between page and reader. The Zohar overwhelms the senses, threatening one's puny, linear understanding with hints of the beyond within.

The pseudepigraphic venture has succeeded. By surrendering his identity to Rabbi Shim'on and company, by adopting a talmudic alter ego, Moses de León has been liberated. Relieved of the burden of self-consciousness, he is free to plumb the depths of his soul and soar to timeless dimensions. Released from the constraints of acknowledged authorship, he can record his own ecstasy and pathos. The personality of Rabbi Shim'on makes him immune from criticism and enables him to publish all secrets. He expounds mythology and mysticism; revels in anthropomorphic and erotic imagery. The Zohar alludes to these liberating effects:

> [Rabbi Abba said:] "If the Holy Light [Rabbi Shim'on] had not revealed it, I could not reveal it" (Zohar 1:217a).
> [Rabbi Yose said:] "We should reflect upon this, though if the Master were not present, I would not speak" (2:144a).
> Rabbi Judah said, "The generation in which Rabbi Shim'on is present is completely worthy and devoted, completely sin-fearing. *Shekhinah* dwells among them. This is not so in other generations. Therefore words are expressed openly and not concealed. In other generations this is not so; secret words from above cannot be revealed, and those who know are afraid." (3:79a)

The literary trick has worked its magic on the author as well as his audience.

Something profound has come over Moses de León or through him. Parts of the Zohar may have been composed by automatic writing, a technique that is well attested in the history of mystical litera-ture.[95] Joseph Abulafia, an acquaintance of Moses, possessed "the writing name" (*shem ha-kotev*), a holy name that focused meditation and placed one in a trance in which automatic writings were produced. The following report appears in a kabbalistic manuscript:

> This name was given to me by the sage Rabbi Joseph ha-Levi son of Todros ha-Levi, may his memory be a blessing. He told me in *kabbalah* [i.e., handing down a secret tradition] that it was the writing name and that with it he would write whatev-

er came to his hand. He wrote a booklet in my presence and gave it to me, saying that he had written [it] by the power of this [name].[96]

Joseph son of Todros ha-Levi Abulafia was a friend and benefactor of Moses de León. Several of Moses' Hebrew writings are dedicated to him. He was also one of the first to receive booklets of the Zohar from Moses, as Isaac of Acre indicates in his diary. What Isaac also reports is that one current opinion was "that Rabbi Shim'on son of Yohai never composed this book [the Zohar], but rather, this Rabbi Moses knew the writing name, and by its power he wrote these wondrous things. In order to obtain a high price in silver and gold, he hangs his words on high tamarisks, saying: 'I am copying these words for you from the book composed by Rabbi Shim'on son of Yohai and his son, Rabbi El'azar, and his Comrades.' "[97]

Later, still searching for the true origin of the Zohar, Isaac approached Joseph Abulafia. Joseph tried to convince him that automatic writing played no part in the book's composition, but his proof is suspect:

He [Joseph] said to me: "Know and believe that *Sefer ha-Zohar* [The Book of Zohar] written by Rabbi Shim'on son of Yohai was in the possession of Rabbi Moses: from it he copied and gave to whomever he pleased. Now look at the great test with which I tested Rabbi Moses to see whether he was copying from an ancient book or by the power of the writing name. The test was this: Many days after he had written out for me numerous booklets of the Zohar, I hid one of them. I told him that I had lost it and begged him to copy it for me again. He said to me, 'Show me the end of the preceding booklet and the beginning of the following one, and I will copy it completely for you like the first one which you lost.' I did so. A few days later, he gave me a copy of the booklet. I compared it with the earlier one and saw that there was no difference at all between them, nothing added or deleted, no change in content or style, 'the same language and the same words' (Genesis 11:1), as if one had been copied from the other. Could there be a greater test than this or a more difficult trial?"[98]

INTRODUCTION

As Isaac is soon told by some skeptical residents of Toledo, this is no proof. Moses could have composed the original under the influence of the writing name and then made copies whenever he wished. Joseph was either amazingly naive or deliberately covering up for his friend.

Automatic writing would have contributed to the Zohar's freedom of style and to its peculiar Aramaic. Foreign and invented languages are known to appear in automatic writings. Several peculiarities are shared by the Zohar and such works: neologisms, reversed sequences of letters, and strange conglomerations of words in otherwise clear sentences.[99] If automatic writing contributed to the composition of the Zohar, so did conscious pseudepigraphy, fiction, and editing.[100] At times Moses de León is an inspired scribe recording the wisdom of Kabbalah as it courses through him, a vessel channeling the kabbalistic collective unconscious. The fact that the Zohar is suffused with thirteenth-century Kabbalah does not invalidate such a hypothesis; automatic writing may correspond to the agent's normal mental content.[101] Similarly, the Zohar's Aramaic derives from literary sources studied by Moses de León. Neologisms appear, but also medieval Hebraisms, Spanish syntactical constructions, and mistakes in grammar and vocabulary. The language is idiosyncratic.[102]

Certain passages in the Zohar are anonymous and appear as utterances of a heavenly voice.[103] Usually, though, the teachings are attributed to Rabbi Shim'on and his Comrades. Moses may have imagined that he was transmitting their words. But Moses is not only a medium; he is an author. He constructs discussions among his characters and weaves dramatic narratives; he employs humor and parody; he alludes to other Zohar passages; he responds polemically to Spanish Christians and Jewish rationalists. The Zohar's style of commentary embraces the precision of textual analysis and the abandon of contemplative fantasy. Its creativity is motivated both consciously and unconsciously.

All creativity links the conscious and the unconscious, the personal and the transpersonal. From a mystical perspective, creativity flowers when the human mind draws on its divine source. According to Moses Cordovero, that is why the kabbalists are called Reapers of the Field:

> The Reapers of the Field are the Comrades, masters of this wisdom, because *Malkhut* [*Shekhinah*] is called the Apple Field, and She grows sprouts of secrets and new flowerings of

Torah. Those who constantly create new interpretations of Torah are harvesting Her.[104]

The kabbalist knows that he is not the source of his teaching. His name is not essential. When a donkey driver on the road reveals mystical secrets to two of the Comrades, they dismount and kiss him and say: "All this wisdom was in your hand, and you were driving our donkeys?! Who are you?" He responds, "Do not ask who I am. Rather, let us walk on and engage in Torah. Let each of us speak words of wisdom to light up the way."[105]

Anonymity is raised to a virtue. "The best of all is he who is neither specified nor revealed, all of whose words are hidden" (Zohar 3:183a). "Every word hidden from the eye gives rise to sublime benefit."[106] Hiddenness is the key to the Zohar's success. Moses de León will not reveal his own identity, but occasionally he appears to drop a hint. "In this zohar [splendor] dwells the one who dwells. It provides a name for the one who is concealed and totally unknown." "Moses . . . this zohar of his is concealed and not revealed."[107] Both passages convey theosophical secrets and can be explained accordingly, but they may also allude to Moses' best-guarded secret, his own role and identity.

Identities are often hidden in the Zohar. A talmudic sage is disguised as a donkey driver; a nameless little boy turns out to be a wonder child and stuns the rabbis with his wisdom. Rabbi Judah says to Rabbi Isaac, "It seems that this child is not a human being!" No one can be dismissed too easily because "sometimes in those empty fools, you discover bells of gold!"[108]

The anonymous author plays with the names and identities of his characters. Shim'on son of Yose, mentioned in the Talmud, becomes Yose son of Shim'on.[109] Pinhas son of Ya'ir, Rabbi Shim'on's son-in-law, is transformed into his father-in-law.[110] A fantastic fictional framework is created in which rabbis who lived centuries apart walk together through the hills of the Galilee, discovering and sharing secrets of Torah. Anachronism is not a concern; playfulness is part of the design. "A little bit of foolishness reveals the sublime glory of wisdom better than any other way in the world" (Zohar 3:47b).

The Zohar is a mystical novel based on the Torah. Its characters include Rabbi Shim'on and his Comrades, biblical figures, and the sefirot, the various aspects of God's personality. It is sometimes difficult to distinguish between these last two sets of characters. Abraham embodies the *sefirah* of *Hesed*, Divine Love; Isaac represents *Din*, Judgment: Jacob harmonizes the two aspects and symbolizes *Rahamim*, Compassion. The stories in Genesis about these three Patriarchs are interpreted in the Zohar as accounts of their mystical journeys, their temptations and tests, and their attainment of divine qualities. Moses is the most perfect human being; he is arrayed in all ten *sefirot.*[111] The Zohar on Exodus presents his spiritual biography and his mythical romance with *Shekhinah*, the feminine Divine Presence. After the Revelation at Sinai there are relatively few narrative sections in the Torah; from here on, the Zohar weaves several exegetical tales involving Rabbi Shim'on and his circle and the amazing characters they encounter.

Through all these mystical episodes, the Zohar never loses sight of its goal: the creation of a mystical commentary on the Torah. God is hidden in the Torah; hidden and revealed there, because Torah is God's Name. This kabbalistic idea means that Torah expresses not only divine will but divine being.[112] The mystic who studies Torah is meditating on the Name of God. He sees through the text into the texture of divine life.

Through commentary, midrash, and mystical hermeneutics, the Zohar introduces the reader to this hidden dimension of Torah, confronts him with it. The literal text is the starting point, but the Zohar is dissatisfied with superficial meaning. At times, its tone seems no less irreverent than that of the rationalists: " 'In the seventh month, on the seventeenth day of the month, the ark [Noah's ark] came to rest on the mountains of Ararat' (Genesis 8:4). . . . What do we care if it rested here or there? It had to rest somewhere!"[113] If the Torah consisted only of mundane stories, "we could compose a Torah right now with ordinary words, and better than all of them!. . . . Ah, but all the words of Torah are sublime words, sublime secrets."[114]

The Zohar may abandon the literal sense of a verse or, conversely, employ the technique of mystical literalness, reading hyperliterally.[115] The goal is to penetrate, to unlock the secret content of the word, to elicit its divine essence. It is impossible to capture and formulate this flowing essence. As Maimonides stated in the Introduction to his *Guide of the Perplexed*, ultimate secrets cannot be taught, only indicated:

> Know that whenever one of the perfect wishes to mention, either orally or in writing, something that he understands of these secrets, according to the degree of his perfection, he is

unable to explain with complete clarity and coherence even the portion that he has apprehended, as he could do with the other sciences whose teaching is generally recognized. Rather, there will befall him when teaching another that which he had undergone when learning himself. I mean to say that the subject matter will appear, flash, and then be hidden again, as though this were the nature of this subject matter.[116]

Such is the nature of Torah, according to the Zohar: "Torah removes a word from her sheath, is seen for a moment, then quickly hides away.... She does so only for those who know her intimately."[117] The Zohar does the same. It hides more than it reveals; only the careful, devoted reader can learn from it. It is a common experience to read several lines of Zohar, or an entire passage, and then wonder what the message was. Cascading imagery overwhelms coherent teaching. But that is the nature of the subject matter: "... the whole spectrum of colors flashing, disappearing. Those rays of color do not wait to be seen; they merge into the fusion of *zohar*."[118]

The Zohar yearns to reveal the divine light permeating Torah, but since that dimension of meaning is beyond words, words are employed as symbols. Torah becomes a treasure house of symbols, pointing to that which cannot be expressed. Imagination guides the Zohar's reading of Torah and is essential to the reading of Zohar. God can only be "known and grasped to the degree that one opens the gates of imagination."[119]

6

The imagery and symbolism are rich and fluid, but they follow a pattern, the pattern of the *sefirot*. The Zohar rarely describes the entire sefirotic system. It even avoids the term *sefirot* and instead speaks of lights, levels, links, roots, garments of the King, crowns of the King, and dozens of other images for the individual *sefirot*. The reader must interpret the symbolism and identify the corresponding *sefirah*.[120]

As noted above, the term *sefirot* originally meant "numbers" or numerical potencies, but in medieval Kabbalah the *sefirot* became stages of God's being, aspects of divine personality. Their pattern and rhythm inform all the worlds of creation. Prior to the emanation of the *sefirot*, God is unmanifest, referred to as *Ein Sof*, Infinite. God as Infinity cannot be described or comprehended. A fourteenth-century kabbalist writes: "*Ein Sof* . . . is not hinted at in the Torah, the Prophets, the Writings, or the words of our Rabbis, may their memory be a blessing; but the Masters of Service [the kabbalists] have received a little hint of It."[121]

Critics charged that the theory of *Ein Sof* and the *sefirot* was dualistic, that by positing and describing ten aspects of Divinity, Kabbalah verged on polytheism.[122] The kabbalists insisted that *Ein Sof* and the *sefirot* formed a unity "like a flame joined to a coal."[123] "It is they, and they are It" (Zohar 3:70a). "They are Its name, and It is they" (3:11b). From the human perspective, the *sefirot* appear to have a multiple and independent existence. Ultimately, though, all of them are one; the true reality is the Infinite.[124] Nevertheless, the mythological character of the system cannot be denied; it is a prominent feature of the Zohar.

The *sefirot* are often pictured in the form of Primordial Adam or as a cosmic tree growing downward from its roots above. As the kabbalists were quick to point out, these images should not be taken literally; they are organic symbols of a spiritual reality beyond normal comprehension. At the start of one of his most anthropomorphic descriptions, Rabbi Shim'on cites a verse from Deuteronomy: "Cursed be the one who makes a carved or molten image, the work of the hands of an artisan, and sets it up in secret."[125] Sefirotic imagery is intended to convey something of the beyond; worshiping its literalness prevents profound communication.

According to Genesis 1:27, the human being is created in the image of God. The *sefirot* are the divine original of that image. As Primordial Adam, they are the mythical paragon of the human being, our archetypal nature. The human race has lost this nature, but if one were to purify himself, he would reconnect with the *sefirot* and become a vessel for them.[126] This is what the Patriarchs attained and, to a greater degree, Moses. The *sefirot* generate the ultimate confusion of identities: human and divine. Such sublime confusion catalyzes the process of enlightenment.

From above to below, the *sefirot* enact the drama of emanation, the transition from *Ein Sof* to creation. From below to above, they are a ladder of ascent back to the One.

Keter (Crown) is the first *sefirah*, coeternal with *Ein Sof*. It represents that aspect of the Infinite that turns toward manifestation and is therefore called *Razon*, Will. It is also known as *Ayin*, Nothingness, "having more being than any other being in the world, but since it is simple and all other simple things are complex compared with its simplicity, in comparison it is called Nothing."[127] No differentiation or individuality exists in *Keter*, no "thingness." From this *sefirah* all emanation flows. First the primordial point of *Hokhmah* (Wisdom) shines forth. Though it is the second *sefirah*, *Hokhmah* is called Beginning because *Keter* is eternal and has no beginning.

The point expands into a circle, the *sefirah* of *Binah* (Understanding). *Binah* is the womb, the Divine Mother. She receives the seed, the point of *Hokhmah*, and conceives the seven lower *sefirot*. Created being too has its source in Her; She is called "the totality of all individuation."[128] She is also "the world that is coming," constantly coming and flowing.[129]

The three highest *sefirot* represent the head of the divine body and are more hidden than the offspring of *Binah*. She gives birth first to *Hesed* (Love) and *Din* (Judgment). This pair of *sefirot* is also called *Gedullah* (Greatness) and *Gevurah* (Power). They are the right and left arms of God, two sides of divine personality: free-flowing love and strict judgment, grace and limitation. Both are necessary for the world to function. Ideally a balance is achieved, symbolized by the central *sefirah*, *Tif'eret* (Beauty), also called *Rahamim* (Compassion). However, if Judgment is not softened by Love, *Din* lashes out and threatens to

THE TEN SEFIROT

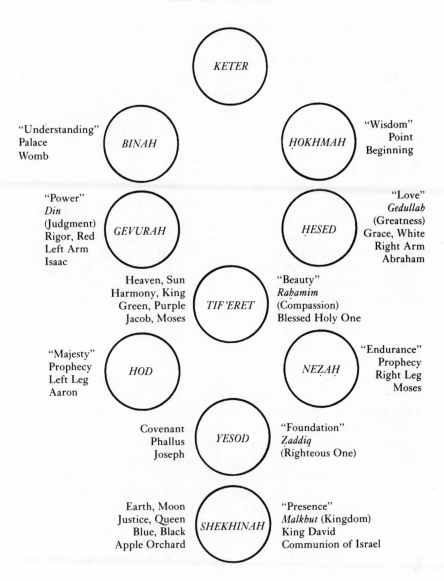

KETER

"Understanding"
Palace
Womb

BINAH

"Wisdom"
Point
Beginning

ḤOKHMAH

"Power"
Din
(Judgment)
Rigor, Red
Left Arm
Isaac

GEVURAH

"Love"
Gedullah
(Greatness)
Grace, White
Right Arm
Abraham

ḤESED

Heaven, Sun
Harmony, King
Green, Purple
Jacob, Moses

TIF'ERET

"Beauty"
Raḥamim
(Compassion)
Blessed Holy One

"Majesty"
Prophecy
Left Leg
Aaron

HOD

"Endurance"
Prophecy
Right Leg
Moses

NEẒAḤ

Covenant
Phallus
Joseph

YESOD

"Foundation"
Zaddiq
(Righteous One)

Earth, Moon
Justice, Queen
Blue, Black
Apple Orchard

SHEKHINAH

"Presence"
Malkhut (Kingdom)
King David
Communion of Israel

destroy life. This is the origin of evil, called *Sitra Aḥra*, the Other Side. From a more radical perspective, evil originates in divine thought, which eliminates waste before emanating the good. The demonic is rooted in the divine.[130]

Tif'eret is the trunk of the sefirotic body. He is called Heaven, Sun, King, and the Blessed Holy One, the standard rabbinic name for God. He is the son of *Hokhmah* and *Binah*.

The next two *sefirot* are *Nezaḥ* (Endurance) and *Hod* (Majesty). They form the right and left legs of the body and are the source of prophecy. *Yesod* (foundation) is the ninth *sefirah* and represents the phallus, the procreative life force of the universe. He is also called *Zaddiq* (Righteous One), and Proverbs 10:25 is applied to Him: "The righteous one is the foundation of the world.[131] *Yesod* is the *axis mundi*, the cosmic pillar. The light and power of the preceding *sefirot* are channeled through Him to the last *sefirah*, *Malkhut*.

Malkhut (Kingdom) is also called *Shekhinah* (Divine Presence). The term *Shekhinah* appears frequently in earlier rabbinic literature, where it signifies God's Presence and Immanence. In Kabbalah it takes on new-ancient mythological meaning. *Shekhinah* is the daughter of *Binah*, the bride of *Tif'eret*. The joining of *Tif'eret* and *Shekhinah* becomes the focus of religious life. Human righteous action stimulates *Yesod*, the Righteous One, and brings about the union of the divine couple (Zohar 3:110b). Human marriage symbolizes divine marriage. Sabbath Eve is the weekly celebration of the *hieros gamos*, the sacred wedding. This is the ideal time for mystics to make love.[132]

The tenth *sefirah* appears under many other names: Earth, Moon, *Matronita*, Mirror, Rose, Throne of Glory, Justice, Garden of Eden, Holy Apple Orchard. She reflects all aspects of Divinity and sustains all the worlds below, though "She has nothing at all of Her own."[133]

Shekhinah is also *Keneset Yisra'el*, the mystical Community of Israel. All of Israel are Her limbs (Zohar 3:231b). She symbolizes the people's intimate connection with God and accompanies them in exile.[134] She prevents the masculine aspect of God from punishing Her children, though at other times She Herself administers punishment.[135] *Shekhinah* is personally threatened by human sin because it taints Her and ruins Her union with *Tif'eret*: "When the powerful serpent up above is aroused by the sins of the world, it joins with the Feminine [*Shekhinah*] and injects venom into Her.[136] The Male [*Tif'eret*] separates from Her because She has been defiled" (3:79a).

The union of *Tif'eret* and *Shekhinah* gives birth to the human soul,[137] and the mystical journey begins with the awareness of this spiritual fact of life. Can a human being experience *Shekhinah* directly? The Talmud had posed this question rhetorically: "Is it possible for a human being to walk behind *Shekhinah*?" "Is it possible to cleave to *Shekhinah*?" No. Rather, one should engage in good deeds and thus imitate God.[138] Kabbalah is more daring. In the words of Joseph Gikatilla, a friend and colleague of Moses de León, "As to what the Rabbis have said: 'Is it possible for a human being to cleave to *Shekhinah*?,' it certainly is possible!"[139]

Shekhinah is the opening to the Divine: "One who enters must enter through this gate" (Zohar 1:7b). Once inside, the *sefirot* are no longer an abstract theological system; they become a map of consciousness. The mystic climbs and probes, discovering dimensions of being. Spiritual and psychological wholeness is achieved by meditating on the qualities of each *sefirah*, by imitating and integrating the attributes of God. The path is not easy. Divine will can be harsh: Abraham was commanded to sacrifice Isaac in order to balance love with rigor.[140] From the Other Side, demonic forces threaten and seduce. Contemplatively and psychologically, evil must be encountered, not evaded. By knowing and withstanding the dark underside of wisdom, Abraham was refined.[141]

Near the top of the sefirotic ladder, meditation reaches *Binah*. She is called *Teshuvah*, Return. The ego returns to the womb of being. *Binah* cannot be held in thought. She is called Who. Who is that? An intuitive flash illuminating and disappearing, as sunbeams play on the surface of water.[142]

In the depths of *Binah* lies *Hokhmah*, Wisdom. The mystic is nourished from this sphere.[143] It is so profound and primal that it cannot be known consciously, only absorbed. Isaac the Blind, one of the earliest kabbalists (ca. 1160–1235), says: "No creature can contemplate [the wondrous paths of Wisdom] except one who sucks from It. This is meditation through sucking, not through knowing."[144]

Beyond *Hokhmah* is the Nothingness of *Keter*, the Annihilation of Thought.[145] In this ultimate *sefirah* human consciousness expands, dissolves into Infinity.

The Zohar is rarely explicit about the ascent. In Kabbalah meditation often takes place during ritual prayer; so the Zohar correlates blessings and individual words of the liturgy with specific *sefirot*. The goal is to unify the various aspects of God through focused awareness and visualization. Successful prayer draws forth the flow of divine blessing.[146] The ecstasy of sefirotic contemplation, however, seems reserved mostly for souls who have departed this world or for the high priest on the Day of Atonement.[147] Souls of the living who succeed in prayer delight in palaces below *Shekhinah*. If especially devout, they may be raised to the level of *Yesod* or attain a sefirotic vision,[148] but the highest *sefirot* are considered unapproachable. In fact the Zohar forbids contemplation of *Binah* and what lies beyond Her. Deuteronomy 22:7 is cited as the proof text: "Let the mother go; the children you may take."[149] The Divine Mother is a cosmic question; Her children, the seven lower *sefirot*, would seem more attainable. However, even concerning these rungs of meditation, the Zohar offers little direct guidance. The Patriarchs and other biblical heroes who mastered individual *sefirot* serve as archetypes, but to the uninitiated, they are awesome. Sefirotic imagery abounds, but the reader must decipher the allusions, be open to the power of the symbol, and join the search.

Zohar is an adventure, a challenge to the normal workings of consciousness. It dares you to examine your usual ways of making sense, your assumptions about tradition, God, and self. Textual analysis is essential, but you must engage Zohar and cultivate a taste for its multiple layers of meaning. It is tempting and safe to reduce the symbols to a familiar scheme: psychological, historical, literary, or religious. But do not forfeit wonder.

What is the Concealment of the Book?[150]

Rabbi Shim'on said
"Five chapters in a great palace; they fill the whole world."

Rabbi Judah said
"If so, they are the best of all."

Rabbi Shim'on said
"So it is, for one who has entered and emerged.[151]
For one who has not entered and emerged, it is not so.

A parable.
There was a man who lived in the mountains.
He knew nothing about those who lived in the city.

INTRODUCTION

He sowed wheat and ate the kernels raw.
One day he entered the city.
They brought him good bread.
He said, 'What is this for?'
They said, 'Bread, to eat!'
He ate, and it tasted very good.
He said, 'What is it made of?' They said, 'Wheat.'
Later they brought him cakes kneaded in oil.
He tasted them and said, 'And what are these made of?'
They said, 'Wheat.'
Finally they brought him royal pastry made with honey and oil.
He said, 'And what are these made of?' They said, 'Wheat.'
He said, 'I am the master of all of these,
for I eat the essence of all of these: wheat!'[152]

Because of that view, he knew nothing of the delights of the world;
they were lost to him.
So it is with one who grasps the principle
and does not know all those delectable delights
deriving, diverging from that principle."

zohar
The Book of Enlightenment

HOW TO LOOK AT TORAH

Rabbi Shim'on said
"Woe to the human being who says
that Torah presents mere stories and ordinary words!
If so, we could compose a Torah right now with ordinary words
and better than all of them!
To present matters of the world?
Even rulers of the world possess words more sublime.
If so, let us follow them and make a Torah out of them!
Ah, but all the words of Torah are sublime words, sublime secrets!

Come and see:
The world above and the world below are perfectly balanced:
Israel below, the angels above.
Of the angels it is written:
'He makes His angels spirits'
(Psalms 104:4).
But when they descend, they put on the garment of this world.
If they did not put on a garment befitting this world
they could not endure in this world
and the world could not endure them.

If this is so with the angels, how much more so with Torah
who created them and all the worlds
and for whose sake they all exist!
In descending to this world,
if she did not put on the garments of this world
the world could not endure.

So this story of Torah is the garment of Torah.
Whoever thinks that the garment is the real Torah
and not something else—
may his spirit deflate!
He will have no portion in the world that is coming.

ZOHAR

That is why David said:
'Open my eyes
so I can see wonders out of Your Torah!'
(Psalms 119:18),
what is under the garment of Torah!

Come and see:
There is a garment visible to all.
When those fools see someone in a good-looking garment
they look no further.
But the essence of the garment is the body;
the essence of the body is the soul!

So it is with Torah.
She has a body:
the commandments of Torah,
called 'the embodiment of Torah.'

This body is clothed in garments:
the stories of this world.
Fools of the world look only at that garment, the story of Torah;
they know nothing more.
They do not look at what is under that garment.
Those who know more do not look at the garment
but rather at the body under that garment.
The wise ones, servants of the King on high,
those who stood at Mt. Sinai,
look only at the soul, root of all, real Torah!
In the time to come
they are destined to look at the soul of the soul of Torah!

Come and see:
So it is above.
There is garment and body and soul and soul of soul.
The heavens and their host are the garment.
The Communion of Israel is the body
who receives the soul, the Beauty of Israel.
So She is the body of the soul.
The soul we have mentioned is the Beauty of Israel
who is real Torah.

ZOHAR

The soul of the soul is the Holy Ancient One.
All is connected, this one to that one.

Woe to the wicked
who say that Torah is merely a story!
They look at this garment and no further.
Happy are the righteous
who look at Torah properly!

As wine must sit in a jar,
so Torah must sit in this garment.
So look only at what is under the garment!
So all those words and all those stories—
they are garments!"

ZOHAR ON GENESIS

THE CREATION OF *ELOHIM*

In the Beginning

When the King conceived ordaining
He engraved engravings in the luster on high.
A blinding spark flashed
within the Concealed of the Concealed
from the mystery of the Infinite,
a cluster of vapor in formlessness,
set in a ring,
not white, not black, not red, not green,
no color at all.
When a band spanned, it yielded radiant colors.
Deep within the spark gushed a flow
imbuing colors below,
concealed within the concealed of the mystery of the Infinite.
The flow broke through and did not break through its aura.
It was not known at all
until, under the impact of breaking through,
one high and hidden point shone.
Beyond that point, nothing is known.
So it is called Beginning,
the first command of all.

"The enlightened will shine like the *zohar* of the sky,
and those who make the masses righteous
will shine like the stars forever and ever"
(Daniel 12:3).

Zohar, Concealed of the Concealed, struck its aura.
The aura touched and did not touch this point.
Then this Beginning emanated
and made itself a palace for its glory and its praise.
There it sowed the seed of holiness

49

to give birth
for the benefit of the universe.
The secret is:
"Her stock is a holy seed"
(Isaiah 6:13).

Zohar, sowing a seed for its glory
like the seed of fine purple silk.
The silkworm wraps itself within and makes itself a palace.
This palace is its praise and a benefit to all.

With the Beginning
the Concealed One who is not known created the palace.
This palace is called *Elohim.*
The secret is:
"With Beginning, ——————— created *Elohim*"
(Genesis 1:1).

THE HIDDEN LIGHT

God said, "Let there be light!" And there was light.
                                    (Genesis 1:3)

This is the light that the Blessed Holy One created at first.
It is the light of the eye.
It is the light that the Blessed Holy One showed the first Adam;
with it he saw from one end of the world to the other.
It is the light that the Blessed Holy One showed David;
he sang its praise:
"How great is Your good that You have concealed for those who fear
    You!"
(Psalms 31:20).
It is the light that the Blessed Holy One showed Moses;
with it he saw from Gilead to Dan.
But when the Blessed Holy One saw
that three wicked generations would arise:
    the generation of Enosh, the generation of the Flood,
    and the generation of the Tower of Babel,
He hid the light away so they would not make use of it.
The Blessed Holy One gave it to Moses
and he used it for the three unused months of his gestation,
as it is said:
"She concealed him for three months"
(Exodus 2:2).
When three months had passed, he was brought before Pharaoh
and the Blessed Holy One took it away from him
until he stood on Mt. Sinai to receive the Torah.
Then He gave him back that light;
he wielded it his whole life long
and the children of Israel could not come near him
until he put a veil over his face,
as it is said:
"They were afraid to come near him"

ZOHAR

(Exodus 34:30).
He wrapped himself in it as in a *tallit*,
as it is written:
"He wraps Himself in light as in a garment"
(Psalms 104:2).

" 'Let there be light!' And there was light."
Every subject of the phrase "And there was"
exists in this world and in the world that is coming.

Rabbi Isaac said,
"The light created by the Blessed Holy One in the act of Creation
flared from one end of the world to the other
and was hidden away.
Why was it hidden away?
So the wicked of the world would not enjoy it
and the worlds would not enjoy it because of them.
It is stored away for the righteous,
for the Righteous One!
As it is written:
'Light is sown for the righteous one,
joy for the upright in heart'
(Psalms 97:11).
Then the worlds will be fragrant, and all will be one.
But until the day when the world that is coming arrives,
it is stored and hidden away. . . ."

Rabbi Judah said
"If it were completely hidden
the world would not exist for even a moment!
Rather, it is hidden and sown like a seed
that gives birth to seeds and fruit.
Thereby the world is sustained.
Every single day, a ray of that light shines into the world
and keeps everything alive,
for with that ray the Blessed Holy One feeds the world.
And everywhere that Torah is studied at night
one thread-thin ray appears from that hidden light
and flows down upon those absorbed in her,
as it is written:

ZOHAR

'By day *YHVH* will enjoin His love;
in the night His song is with me'
(Psalms 42:9),
as we have already established. . . .

Since the first day, it has never been fully revealed,
but it plays a vital role in the world,
renewing every day the act of Creation!"

ADAM'S SIN

YHVH *Elohim expelled him from the Garden of Eden . . .*
He drove out et *Adam.*

(Genesis 3:23–24)

Rabbi El'azar said
"We do not know who divorced whom,
if the Blessed Holy One divorced Adam
or not.
But the word is transposed:
'He drove out *et.*'
Et, precisely!
And who drove out *Et?*
'Adam'
Adam drove out *Et!*
Therefore it is written:
'*YHVH Elohim* expelled him from the Garden of Eden.'
Why did He expel him?
Because Adam drove out *Et,*
as we have said."

MALE AND FEMALE

This is the book of the generations of Adam.
On the day that God created Adam,
in the likeness of God He created him;
male and female He created them.
He blessed them and called their name Adam
on the day they were created.

(Genesis 5:1–2)

Rabbi Shim'on said
"High mysteries are revealed in these two verses.
'Male and female He created them'
to make known the Glory on high,
the mystery of faith.
Out of this mystery, Adam was created.

Come and see:
With the mystery by which heaven and earth were created
Adam was created.
Of them it is written:
'These are the generations of heaven and earth'
(Genesis 2:4).
Of Adam it is written:
'This is the book of the generations of Adam.'
Of them it is written:
'when they were created.'
Of Adam it is written:
'on the day they were created.'

'Male and female He created them.'
From here we learn:
Any image that does not embrace male and female
is not a high and true image.
We have established this in the mystery of our Mishnah.

ZOHAR

Come and see:
The Blessed Holy One does not place His abode
in any place where male and female are not found together.
Blessings are found only in a place where male and female are found,
as it is written:
'He blessed them and called their name Adam
on the day they were created.'
It is not written:
'He blessed him and called his name Adam.'
A human being is only called Adam
when male and female are as one."

AFTER THE FLOOD

Rabi opened
" '*YHVH* smelled the pleasing aroma and said
"Never again will I doom the world because of humankind" '
(Genesis 8:21)

When Noah came out of the ark
he opened his eyes and saw the whole world completely destroyed.
He began crying for the world and said
'Master of the world!
If You destroyed Your world because of human sin or human fools,
then why did You create them?
One or the other You should do:
either do not create the human being
or do not destroy the world!'
He offered up offerings and began to pray before Him
and the aroma ascended before the Blessed Holy One and was
      sweet."

Rabi continued
"A triple aroma ascended to God:
the aroma of Noah's offering, the aroma of his prayer,
and the aroma of his actions.
No aroma in the whole world was as pleasing to Him.
Therefore He commanded:
'Be observant and present to Me in due season My pleasing aroma'
(Numbers 28:2).
This means:
'Be observant:
Present to Me the aroma that Noah presented to Me:
the aroma of offering and prayer and right action. ' "

ZOHAR

Our Rabbis have taught:
How did the Blessed Holy One respond when Noah came out of the
    ark
and saw the whole world destroyed and began to cry over the
    holocaust?
Noah said, "Master of the world, You are called Compassionate!
You should have shown compassion for Your creatures!"
The Blessed Holy One answered him, "Foolish shepherd!
Now you say this, but not when I spoke to you tenderly, saying
'Make yourself an ark of gopher wood . . .
As for Me, I am about to bring the Flood . . . to destroy all flesh . . .
[Go into the ark, you and all your household]
for you alone have I found righteous before Me in this generation'
(Genesis 6:14, 17; 7:1).
I lingered with you and spoke to you at length
so that you would ask for mercy for the world!
But as soon as you heard that you would be safe in the ark,
the evil of the world did not touch your heart.
You built the ark and saved yourself.
Now that the world has been destroyed
you open your mouth to utter questions and pleas?"

Seeing this, Noah presented offerings and sacrifices,
as it is written:
"Taking of every clean animal and of every clean bird,
he offered up offerings on the altar"
(Genesis 8:20).

Rabbi Yohanan said
"Come and see the difference
between Noah and the righteous heroes of Israel!
Noah did not shield his generation
and did not pray for them like Abraham.
For as soon as the Blessed Holy One said to Abraham
'The outcry of Sodom and Gomorrah is so great,'
immediately, 'Abraham came forward and said
"Will You sweep away the innocent along with the guilty?" '
(Genesis 18:20, 23).
He countered the Blessed Holy One with more and more words
until finally he implored Him to forgive the entire generation

ZOHAR

if just ten innocent people could be found.
Abraham thought there were ten in the city,
counting Lot and his wife and his sons and daughters;
that is why he entreated no more.

Moses also shielded his entire generation.
As soon as the Blessed Holy One said
'Israel has sinned,
"quickly they have turned from the way," '
what is written?
'Moses implored'
(Exodus 32:8, 11).
What does 'implored' mean?
It means that he prayed until he was overtaken by trembling."

Our Rabbis have said:
"Moses did not leave the Blessed Holy One
until he pledged his life for them
both in this world and the world that is coming,
as it is written:
'And now if You would only forgive their sin!
If not, erase me from the book that You have written'
(Exodus 32:32)."

Rabbi Yose said
"[Moses' bravery is demonstrated] from this verse:
'He would have destroyed them
had not Moses, His chosen, confronted Him in the breach'
(Psalms 106:23)."

So all the righteous heroes shielded their generations
and did not allow the attribute of Judgment to have power over
    them.
And Noah?
The Blessed Holy One lingered with him and spoke many words to
    him;
perhaps, he would ask for mercy for his generation.
But he did not care and did not ask for mercy.
He just built the ark
and the whole world was destroyed.

ABRAM, THE SOUL-BREATH

YHVH *said to Abram*
"Go forth from your land, your place of birth, your father's house
to the land that I will show you.
I will make you a great nation, and I will bless you;
I will make your name great, and you will be a blessing.
I will bless those who bless you;
he who curses you I will curse;
all the families of the earth will bless themselves by you."

Abram went forth as YHVH *had directed him*
and Lot went with him.

(Genesis 12:1–4)

Rabbi Jacob son of Idi said
"All soul-breaths of the righteous
have been carved from the bedrock of the Throne of Glory
to guide the body like a father guiding his son.
For without the soul-breath, the body could not conduct itself,
would not be aware of the Will,
could not actualize the Will of its Creator.
As Rabbi Abbahu has said:
'The soul-breath directs and trains the human being
and initiates him into every straight path.'

When the Blessed Holy One sends her from the place of holiness
He blesses her with seven blessings,
as it is written:
'*YHVH said to Avram,*'
this is the soul-breath
who is *av*, 'a father,' to teach the body
and *ram*, 'high' above him
for she has come from a high and lofty place.
What does He say to her?

60

ZOHAR

' "Go forth from your land, your place of birth,"
your dwelling, your place of bliss. ' "

"And from your father's house"
Rabbi Jacob said, "This is the mirror that shines.
'To the land that I will show you'
means to such and such a body, a holy body, an upright body.
And even so, 'I will bless those who bless you,'
those who treat you correctly and virtuously,
those who bless Me for you, saying
'As long as the soul breathes within me
I acclaim in Your presence: *YHVH* is my God.'

'He who curses you I will curse,'
those who curse you by acting perversely.

'Abram went forth as *YHVH* had directed him.'
Blessed with these seven blessings,
Abram, the soul-breath, went forth,
father to the body and high from the place of the highest.
'As *YHVH* had directed him'
to enter the body that she had been commanded to guide and train."

Rabbi Jacob continued
"Look what is written about her once she has entered the body:
'And Lot went with him.'
This is the Deviser of Evil,
destined to enter along with the soul-breath
once a human is born.
How do we know that the Deviser of Evil is called by this name?
It is said:
'The devisings of the human mind are evil from youth'
(Genesis 8:21).
This is Lot, who was cursed.
This corresponds to what Rabbi Isaac has said:
'The serpent who seduced Eve was the Deviser of Evil.'
We know that he was cursed, as it is said:
'Cursed are you above all animals'
(Genesis 3:14).
Therefore, he is called Lot, Cursed.

ZOHAR

When the soul-breath enters the body,
immediately, 'Lot went with him.'
For he is destined to enter with him,
to mislead the human being and challenge the soul-breath."

ABRAM'S DESCENT INTO EGYPT

And Abram went down to Egypt.
(Genesis 12:10)

Rabbi Shim'on said
"Come and see:
Everything has secret wisdom.
This verse hints at wisdom and the levels down below,
to the depths of which Abraham descended.
He knew them but did not become attached.
He returned to face his Lord,
was not seduced by them like Adam,
was not seduced by them like Noah.

When Adam reached that level,
he was seduced by the serpent
and dragged Death into the world.

When Noah descended to that level,
what is written?
'He drank of the wine and became drunk
and uncovered himself within his tent'
(Genesis 9:21).
The spelling implies 'her tent.'

But what is written of Abraham?
'Abram went up from Egypt'
(Genesis 13:1).
He went up and did not come down.
He returned to his domain,
the high rung he had grasped before.

This story appears in the Torah to reveal wisdom.
Abraham fulfilled himself,

ZOHAR

was not seduced,
rose to his full stature,
returned to his domain:
'into the Negev'
(Genesis 13:1),
the South,
the high sphere he was linked to before.
Before, it was written:
'Abram journeyed by stages toward the Negev'
(Genesis 12:9).
Now, 'into the Negev,'
the domain he adhered to before.

Come and see the secret of the word:
If Abram had not gone down into Egypt
and been refined there first,
he could not have partaken of the Blessed Holy One.
Similarly with his children,
when the Blessed Holy One wanted to make them unique,
a perfect people,
and to draw them near to Him:
If they had not gone down to Egypt
and been refined there first,
they would not have become His special ones.

So too the Holy Land:
If she had not been given first to Canaan to control,
she would not have become the portion, the share
of the Blessed Holy One.

It is all one mystery."

OPENINGS

He [Abraham] was sitting in the opening of the tent. . . .
Sarah heard from the opening of the tent.
(Genesis 18:1, 10)

Rabbi Judah opened
" 'Her husband is known in the gates
when he sits among the elders of the land'
(Proverbs 31:23).

Come and see:
The Blessed Holy One has ascended in glory.
He is hidden, concealed, far beyond.
There is no one in the world, nor has there ever been,
who can understand His wisdom or withstand Him.
He is hidden, concealed, transcendent, beyond, beyond.

The beings up above and the creatures down below—
none of them can comprehend.
All they can say is:
'Blessed be the Presence of *YHVH* in His place'
(Ezekiel 3:12).
The ones below proclaim that He is above:
'His Presence is above the heavens'
(Psalms 113:4);
the ones above proclaim that He is below:
'Your Presence is over all the earth'
(Psalms 57:12).
Finally all of them, above and below, declare:
'Blessed be the Presence of *YHVH* wherever He is!'
For He is unknowable.
No one has ever been able to identify Him.

How, then, can you say:
'Her husband is known in the gates'?
Her husband is the Blessed Holy One!

Indeed, He is known in the gates.
He is known and grasped
to the degree that one opens the gates of imagination!
The capacity to connect with the spirit of wisdom,
to imagine in one's heart-mind—
this is how God becomes known.

Therefore 'Her husband is known in the gates,'
through the gates of imagination.
But that He be known as He really is?
No one has ever been able to attain such knowledge of Him."

Rabbi Shim'on said
" 'Her husband is known in the gates.'
Who are these gates?
The ones addressed in the Psalm:
'O gates, lift up your heads!
Be lifted up, openings of eternity,
so the King of Glory may come!'
(Psalms 24:7).
Through these gates, these spheres on high,
the Blessed Holy One becomes known.
Were it not so, no one could commune with Him.

Come and see:
Neshamah of a human being is unknowable
except through limbs of the body,
subordinates of *neshamah* who carry out what she designs.
Thus she is known and unknown.

The Blessed Holy One too is known and unknown.
For He is *Neshamah* of *neshamah*, Pneuma of pneuma,
completely hidden away;
but through these gates, openings for *neshamah*,
the Blessed Holy One becomes known.

ZOHAR

Come and see:
There is opening within opening,
level beyond level.
Through these the Glory of God becomes known.

'The opening of the tent' is the opening of Righteousness,
as the Psalmist says:
'Open for me the gates of righteousness . . .'
(Psalms 118:19).
This is the first opening to enter.
Through this opening, all other high openings come into view.
One who attains the clarity of this opening
discovers all the other openings,
for all of them abide here.

Now that Israel is in exile, this opening is unknown;
all the openings have abandoned Her.
It is impossible to know, impossible to grasp.
But when Israel comes forth from exile,
all the soaring spheres will touch down upon this opening,
one by one.
Then human beings will perceive wondrous, precious wisdom
never known by them before,
as it is written:
'The spirit of *YHVH* shall alight upon him:
a spirit of wisdom and insight,
a spirit of design and power,
a spirit of knowledge and awe of *YHVH*'
(Isaiah 11:2).
All these are destined to alight upon the opening below,
the Opening of the Tent.
All these are destined to alight upon King Messiah
so that he may judge the world,
as it is written:
'He shall judge the poor with righteousness . . .'
(Isaiah 11:4).

Therefore when Abraham received the good news,
this sphere delivered it, as has been said,
for it is written:

ZOHAR

'Then one said, "I will return to you when life is due"'
(Genesis 18:10).
'One said'
Who it was is not spelled out.
It was the Opening of the Tent!

Now the same verse says:
'Sarah heard.'
She heard this sphere speaking with her husband;
someone she had never heard before.
And so it is written:
'Sarah heard the Opening of the Tent'
who was delivering the good news:
'I will return to you when life is due
and your wife Sarah will have a son.' "

AN OFFERING TO GOD

Rabbi Shim'on opened and said
"Anyone who rejoices on the festivals
and does not give the Blessed Holy One His portion,
that stingy one with the evil eye,
Satan, Archenemy,
appears and accuses him,
removes him from the world.
Oh, how much trouble and suffering he brings upon him!

What is the portion of the Blessed Holy One?
To gladden the poor as best as one can.
For on these days
the Blessed Holy One comes to observe His broken vessels.
He enters from above
and if He sees that they have nothing to celebrate
He cries over them.
Then he ascends to destroy the world!

The members of the Academy of Heaven appear before Him and
    declare:
'Master of the world!
You are called Compassionate and Gracious.
May Your Compassion be aroused for Your children!'
He answers them:
'Does not everyone know that I based the world solely on love?
"I have said, 'The world is built by love' "
(Psalms 89:3).
It is love that sustains the world!'

The angels on high then declare:
'Master of the world!
Look at so-and-so who is eating and drinking his fill.
He could share something with the poor

but he gives them nothing at all!'
Then the Accuser steps forward, claims authority
and sets out in pursuit of that human being.

Who in the world was greater than Abraham?
He was kindhearted to all creatures.
One day he prepared a feast,
as it is written:
'The child grew up and was weaned,
and Abraham held a great feast on the day that Isaac was weaned'
(Genesis 21:8).
To this feast Abraham invited all the great people of his time.

Now we have learned that the Accuser comes to every joyous meal
to see if the host has already provided for the poor
or invited the poor into his home.
If so, the Accuser departs and does not enter.
If not, he enters and witnesses this chaos of joy
without poor, without gifts for the poor.
Then he rises above and accuses the host.

When Abraham welcomed all those great people
the Accuser descended and stood at the door
disguised as a poor man.
But no one noticed him.
Abraham was serving the kings and celebrities.
Sarah was nursing all their children,
because no one believed that she had given birth;
they said, 'It is a foundling from off the street!'
So Sarah took their children who had come along
and nursed them in front of everyone,
as it is written:
'Who would have said to Abraham that Sarah would suckle
    children?'
(Genesis 21:7),
'Children,' in the plural!

Meanwhile, the Accuser was still at the door.
Sarah said, 'God has made me a laughingstock!'
(Genesis 21:6).

ZOHAR

At once, the Accuser rose to face the Blessed Holy One.
He said, 'Master of the world!
You call Abraham "My friend"?
(Isaiah 41:8).
He held a feast and gave nothing to me and nothing to the poor;
not even a single dove did he present to You!
Furthermore, Sarah says that You made fun of her!'
The Blessed Holy One responded
'Who in the world is like Abraham?'

But he held his ground until he ruined the whole celebration
and the Blessed Holy One commanded that Isaac be brought as an
     offering
and it was decreed that Sarah would die in anguish over her son's
     ordeal.

All that suffering he brought about because he gave nothing to the
     poor!"

THE BINDING OF ABRAHAM AND ISAAC

And it came to pass after these devarim *that* Elohim *tested
    Abraham.
He said to him, "Abraham!"
and he answered, "Here I am."
He said, "Take your son, your favored one, whom you love, Isaac
and go to the land of Moriah
and offer him up as an offering . . ."*

(Genesis 22:1–2)

Rabbi Shim'on said
"We have learned
that the expression 'And it came to pass in the days of'
denotes sorrow,
while the expression 'And it came to pass'
even without 'in the days of'
is still tinged with sorrow.

'And it came to pass after,'
after the lowest of all the higher spheres.
Which is that? *Devarim.*
As Moses said: 'I am not a man of *devarim*'
(Exodus 4:10).
And who came after this sphere?
'*Elohim* tested Abraham.'
The Deviser of Evil came to accuse him
in the presence of the Blessed Holy One.

Here we must reflect:
'*Elohim* tested Abraham.'
The verse should read: 'tested Isaac,'
for Isaac was already thirty-seven years old
and his father was no longer responsible for him.
If Isaac had said, 'I refuse,'

his father would not have been punished.
Why, then, is it written: '*Elohim* tested Abraham,' and not 'Isaac'?

No, it had to be Abraham!
He had to be crowned with Rigor.
For until now, Abraham had no rigor at all.
Now Water was crowned with Fire.
Abraham was not complete until now
when he was invested with the power to execute Judgment,
to ordain it in its domain.
His whole life long, he had not been whole until now
when Water was crowned with Fire, and Fire with Water.

That is why '*Elohim* tested Abraham,' not Isaac.
He summoned Abraham to be crowned with Rigor.
When he had done so, Fire entered Water,
each completing the other.
One was judged and one executed judgment,
each crowning the other.

That is why the Deviser of Evil appeared to accuse Abraham.
For until he had executed judgment by binding Isaac
he could not attain perfection.
The Deviser of Evil always appears behind things and words;
he comes to challenge.

Come and see the secret of the word:
Even though we have said
that Abraham, not Isaac, is designated in the verse,
Isaac is secretly implied,
for it is written:
'*Elohim* tested *et* Abraham.'
Not 'Abraham,' but '*et* Abraham.'
It is precisely this *et* that refers to Isaac.
For until now, Isaac was dwelling in the sphere of low power.
As soon as he was bound on the altar,
initiated into Judgment by Abraham,
he was arrayed in his own sphere alongside Abraham.
Fire was crowned with Water; both rose higher.
Thus the battle was joined: Water versus Fire.

ZOHAR

Who has ever seen a compassionate father turn cruel?
It was only to reveal the polarity: Water versus Fire,
each one arrayed in its own sphere,
until Jacob appeared and everything harmonized:
the triad of Patriarchs,
the symmetry of above and below."

JACOB'S JOURNEY

Jacob left Be'er Sheva and set out for Ḥaran.
(Genesis 28:10)

Inside the hidden nexus,
from within the sealed secret,
a *zohar* flashed,
shining as a mirror,
embracing two colors blended together.
Once these two absorbed each other, all colors appeared:
purple, the whole spectrum of colors, flashing, disappearing.
Those rays of color do not wait to be seen;
they merge into the fusion of *zohar.*

In this *zohar* dwells the one who dwells.
It provides a name for the one who is concealed and totally
    unknown.
It is called the Voice of Jacob.
Complete faith in the one who is concealed and totally unknown
    belongs here.
Here dwells *YHVH,*
perfection of all sides, above and below.
Here Jacob is found,
perfection of the Patriarchs, linked to all sides.
This *zohar* is called by the singled-out name:
"Jacob, whom I have chosen"
(Isaiah 41:8)
Two names he is called: Jacob and Israel.
At first, Jacob; later, Israel.

The secret of this secret:
First he attained the End of Thought,
the Elucidation of the Written Torah.

ZOHAR

She is the Oral Torah, called *Be'er*,
as it is said:
"Moses began *be'er*, to explain, the Torah"
(Deuteronomy 1:5).
She is a *be'er*, a well and an explanation
of the one who is called *Sheva*, Seven,
as it is written:
"It took him *sheva*, seven, years to build it"
(1 Kings 6:38).
Sheva is the Mighty Voice,
while the End of Thought is *Be'er Sheva*.

Jacob had entered this gateway to faith.
Adhering to that faith, he had to be tested
in the same place his fathers had been tested,
entering in peace and emerging in peace.

   Adam entered but was not careful.
   Seduced by her, he sinned with that whore of a woman,
   the primordial serpent.

   Noah entered but was not careful.
   Seduced by her, he sinned as well,
   as it is written:
   "He drank of the wine and became drunk
   and uncovered himself within his tent"
   (Genesis 9:21).

   Abraham entered and emerged,
   as it is written:
   "And Abram went down to Egypt . . .
   And Abram came up from Egypt"
   (Genesis 12:10; 13:1).

   Isaac entered and emerged,
   as it is written:
   "Isaac went to Abimelech, king of the Philistines, in Gerar . . .
   From there he went up to Be'er Sheva"
   (Genesis 26:1, 23).

ZOHAR

Jacob, having entered into faith,
had to continue and probe the other side.
For one who is saved from there is a loved one,
a chosen one of the Blessed Holy One.
What is written?
"Jacob left Be'er Sheva"
the secret of the mystery of faith,
"and set out for Haran"
the side of the woman of whoredom, the adulteress.

The secret of secrets:
Out of the scorching noon of Isaac,
out of the dregs of wine,
a fungus emerged, a cluster,
male and female together,
red as a rose,
expanding in many directions and paths.
The male is called Sama'el,
his female always included within him.
Just as it is on the side of holiness,
so it is on the other side:
male and female embracing one another.
The female of Sama'el is called Serpent,
Woman of Whoredom,
End of All Flesh, End of Days.
Two evil spirits joined together:
the spirit of the male is subtle;
the spirit of the female is diffused in many ways and paths
but joined to the spirit of the male.

She bedecks herself with all kinds of jewelry
like an abhorrent prostitute posing on the corner to seduce men.
The fool who approaches her—
she grabs him and kisses him,
pours him wine from the dregs, from the venom of vipers.
As soon as he drinks, he strays after her.
Seeing him stray from the path of truth,
she strips herself of all her finery that she dangled before that fool,
her adornments for seducing men:
her hair all arranged, red as a rose,

77

her face white and red,
six trinkets dangling from her ears,
her bed covered with fabric from Egypt,
on her neck all the jewels of the East,
her mouth poised, a delicate opening,
what lovely trappings!
The tongue pointed like a sword,
her words smooth like oil,
her lips beautiful, red as a rose,
sweet with all the sweetness of the world.
She is dressed in purple,
adorned with forty adornments minus one.

This fool follows her, drinks from the cup of wine,
fornicates with her, deviates after her.
What does she do?
She leaves him sleeping in bed.
She ascends, denounces him, obtains permission, and descends.
That fool wakes up and plans to play with her as before.
But she removes her decorations
and turns into a powerful warrior confronting him.
Arrayed in armor of flashing fire,
his awesome terror vibrates the victim's body and soul.
He is full of fearsome eyes;
in his hand a sharp-edged sword drips bitter drops.
He kills that fool and flings him into hell.

Jacob descended to her,
went straight to her abode,
as it is said:
"and he set out for Haran."
He saw all the trappings of her house
and was saved from her.
Her mate, Sama'el, was offended
and swooped down to wage war
but could not overcome him,
as it is written:
"And a man wrestled with him . . ."
(Genesis 32:25).

ZOHAR

Now he was saved and perfected,
raised to a perfect sphere and called Israel.
He attained a high rung, total perfection!
He became the central pillar, of whom it is written:
"The center bar in the middle of the planks shall run from end to
    end"
(Exodus 26:28).

JOSEPH'S DREAM

Joseph dreamed a dream and told it to his brothers,
and they hated him even more.

(Genesis 37:5)

Rabbi Ḥiyya opened and said
" 'He said, "Hear my words:
If there be a prophet among you,
I, *YHVH*, make Myself known to him in a vision,
I speak with him in a dream" '
(Numbers 12:6).

Come and see how many levels within levels the Blessed Holy One
     has made,
arranged one on top of the other, step by step,
this one higher than that one,
these absorbing those, as they should,
these on the right, those on the left,
each one assigned its domain,
all as it should be.

Come and see:
All the prophets of the world were nurtured from a single aspect
through two well-known levels.
Those levels appeared in the mirror that does not shine,
as it is written:
'I make Myself known to him in a vision, *mar'ah.*'
What is this *mar'ah?*
It has been explained: a mirror in which all colors appear.
This is the mirror that does not shine.

'I speak with him in a dream.'
This is one-sixtieth of prophecy, as they have established.
It is the sixth level from the level of prophecy,

the level of Gabriel, appointed over dreams.
This has already been said.

Come and see:
Every proper dream comes from this level;
so you cannot have a dream without false imaginings intermingling,
as we have established.
Therefore parts are true and parts are false.
You cannot have a dream that does not reflect both this side and
      that.

Since everything is contained in a dream, as we have said,
all dreams of the world follow the interpretation of the mouth.
They have established this based on the verse:
'As he interpreted for us, so it came to pass'
(Genesis 41:13).
Why?
Because a dream includes illusion and truth,
and the word rules over all.
So a dream needs a good interpretation."

Rabbi Judah said
"Because every dream is from that lower level,
and Speech commands that level;
that is why every dream follows the interpretation."

He opened and said
" 'In a dream, a vision of the night,
when slumber falls on humans
as they sleep upon their bed,
He uncovers human ears,
terrifies them with warning'
(Job 33:15–16).

Come and see:
When a person climbs into bed,
first he must enthrone and accept the Kingdom of Heaven,
then say a verse of mercy,
as the Comrades have established.
For when a person sleeps in his bed,

ZOHAR

his soul leaves him and soars up above,
each one on its own path.
She ascends in this way, as has been said.
What is written?
'In a dream, a vision of the night,'
when people are lying in their beds asleep,
the soul leaves them,
as it is written:
'as they sleep upon their bed, He uncovers human ears.'
Then the Blessed Holy One reveals to the soul,
through that level presiding over dreams,
things that are destined to come about in the world
or things corresponding to the mind's reflections,
so that the dreamer will respond to the warning.

For nothing is revealed
while the person is still under the spell of the body,
as we have said.
Rather, an angel tells the soul,
and the soul, the person,
and that dream is from beyond,
when souls leave bodies and ascend,
each on its own path.

There are levels upon levels within the mystery of a dream,
all within the mystery of wisdom.
Now come and see:
Dream is one level,
vision is one level,
prophecy is one level.
All are levels within levels,
one above the other.

'Joseph dreamed a dream and told it to his brothers . . .
and they hated him even more because of his dreams'
(Genesis 37:5, 8).
From here we learn
that a person should only tell his dream to one who loves him.
Otherwise the listener interferes,
and if that dream is transformed, he is the cause.

ZOHAR

Come and see:
Joseph told the dream to his brothers,
and they made the dream disappear;
for twenty-two years it was delayed."

Rabbi Yose said, "How do we know this?
Because it is written: 'They hated him even more.'
This implies that they provoked accusations against him.
What is written?
'He said to them, "Please hear this dream that I have dreamed" '
(Genesis 37:6).
He begged them to listen;
then he revealed the dream to them.
If they had transformed its meaning,
it would have come true according to their words.
But they responded:
'Will you reign over us?
Will you rule over us?'
(Genesis 37:8).
Suddenly they had revealed the interpretation of the dream
and sealed their own fate!
That is why 'they hated him even more.' "

SEDUCTION ABOVE AND BELOW

And it came to pass after these things
that his master's wife cast her eyes upon Joseph
and said, "Lie with me!"
And he refused. . . .
Though she urged Joseph day after day, he did not yield to her,
to lie beside her, to be with her.

(Genesis 39:7–8, 10)

"Though she urged him day after day"
Rabbi El'azar opened and said
" 'To guard you from the evil woman,
the smooth-tongued alien'
(Proverbs 6:24).

Happy are the righteous
who know the paths of the Blessed Holy One,
who learn how to follow them
by striving for Torah day and night!
For everyone who engages Torah days and nights
occupies two worlds: the higher world and the lower world.
He obtains this world
even if he engages in Torah with selfish motives;
he obtains that world
if he engages in Torah for the Name within her.

Come and see what is written:
'Long life she offers with her right hand,
with her left hand riches and honor'
(Proverbs 3:16).
One who walks on the right side of Torah
is extended long life in the world that is coming.
There he acquires the splendor of Torah,
a precious crown of supreme power,

84

for the crown of Torah is in that world.
'With her left hand riches and honor'
in this world.
Even if he hasn't studied Torah for the Name within her
he still obtains in this world riches and honor.

Now when Rabbi Ḥiyya came from Babylonia to the land of Israel
he read from the Torah until his face shone like the sun,
and when everyone studying Torah stood before him
he would say:
'This one engages Torah for the Name within her;
that one does not.'
He would pray for the first one that he always be like that
and obtain the world that is coming.
He would pray for the other that he discover
how to study Torah for the Name within her
and obtain eternal life.

One day he saw a student toiling over Torah whose face turned pale.
He said, 'This one is conceiving sinful thoughts!'
He held him and looked into his eyes
and emanated words of Torah to him until he became calm.
From that day on, he resolved not to pursue those evil imaginings
and to strive to study Torah for the Name within her."

Rabbi Yose said
"When a person sees that evil imaginings are assailing him
he should occupy himself with Torah
and they will pass away."

Rabbi El'azar said
"When that evil side approaches to seduce a human being
he should pull it toward Torah
and it will leave him.
Come and see what we have learned:
When that evil side confronts the Blessed Holy One,
accusing the world of evil doings,
the Blessed Holy One feels compassion for the world
and offers a device to human beings to save themselves from him,
to neutralize his power over them and their actions.

ZOHAR

What is the device?
Engaging in Torah!
This saves them from him.
How do we know?
Because it is written:
'A *mizvah* is a lamp; Torah is light;
rules of discipline lead to life'
(Proverbs 6:23).
What is written in the following verse?
'To guard you from the evil woman,
the smooth-tongued alien.'
This is the unclean side, the Other Side,
who constantly confronts the Blessed Holy One
to press charges based on human sin,
who constantly confronts human beings
to pervert and mislead them below.
He constantly presents himself above
to report the sins of humans and accuse them of their doings
so that they be delivered into his power
as was done to Job.
At the same time, he looms over humans below
to mislead them and remind them of their sins,
everything they have done.

Especially when the Blessed Holy One stands in judgment over them
he rises to indict them and enumerate their sins.
The Blessed Holy One, however, felt compassion for Israel
and gave them a device to save themselves from him.
What?
A *shofar* on *Rosh ha-Shanah*,
and on *Yom Kippur* a scapegoat to give to him
so that he leave them alone
and occupy himself with that portion of his.
This has been established.

Come and see what is written:
'Her feet lead down to death,
her steps grasp the netherworld'
(Proverbs 5:5).
But of the mystery of faith, it is written:

86

ZOHAR

(Isaiah 30:22),
Excrement!
One who turns away from Torah is punished in excrement!
Sinners of the world who do not believe in the Blessed Holy One
are punished in excrement!

What is written?
'One such day, he came into the house to do his work.
There was no man of the household there inside'
(Genesis 39:11).
'One such day,'
a day when the Deviser of Evil is at large in the world,
coming to lead humans astray.
When is that day?
The same day a person acknowledges his sins
and begins to turn himself around,
or when he engages Torah and resolves to obey her commands.
At that very moment, he descends to lead humans astray.

'He came into the house to do his work,'
to engage Torah and obey her commands,
for that is the work a person should do in this world.
Now since a person's real work in this world
is the work of the Blessed Holy One,
he must be as strong as a lion on every side
so that the Other Side will not overpower him
or be able to seduce him.

What is written?
'There was no man,'
no man to stand up against the Deviser of Evil
and wage war with him as one should.

How does the Deviser of Evil operate?
Once he sees that no man stands in his way, ready to fight him,
immediately 'she grabbed him by his coat and said, "Lie with me!" '
(Genesis 39:12).
She grabbed him by his coat
because when the Deviser of Evil takes control of a person
he dresses him up in beautiful clothes

and curls his hair
and says, 'Lie with me! Join me!'
One who is pure steels himself and wages war.
What is written?
'But he left his coat in her hand and fled outdoors.'
One should abandon him, harden oneself against him,
flee from him to be safe from him.
Then he cannot take control."

Rabbi Isaac said
"The righteous are destined to see the Deviser of Evil
in the shape of a huge mountain.
Astounded, they will say:
'How were we able to overturn that huge mountain?'
The wicked are destined to see the Deviser of Evil
as thin as a thread of hair.
Astounded, they will say:
'How could we fail to overcome a thread of hair so thin?'
These will cry and those will cry.
The Blessed Holy One will sweep the Deviser of Evil off the earth
and slaughter him before their eyes,
and his power will be no more.
Seeing this, the righteous will rejoice,
as it is said:
'Surely the righteous will praise Your Name;
the upright will dwell in Your Presence' "
(Psalms 140:14).

JACOB'S GARMENT OF DAYS

The days of Israel drew near to die.
He summoned his son Joseph and said to him,
"If I have found favor in your eyes, place your hand under my
   thigh;
act toward me out of true love: please do not bury me in Egypt.
I will lie down with my fathers;
then take me out of Egypt and bury me in their burial place."
                                          (Genesis 47:29–30)

Rabbi Judah opened and said
" 'Listen, you deaf ones!
You blind ones, look up and see!'
(Isaiah 42:18).
'Listen, you deaf ones!'
you human beings who do not hear Torah speaking,
who do not open your ears to let in the commands of your Master.
'You blind ones'
who do not examine your own foundations,
who do not seek to know why you are alive!
Every single day a herald comes forth and proclaims
but no one hears his message!

It has been taught:
When a human being is created,
on the day he comes into the world,
simultaneously, all the days of his life are arranged above.
One by one, they come flying down into the world
to alert that human being, day by day.
If, when a day comes to alert him,
he sins on that day before his Master,
then that day climbs up in shame,
bears witness, and stands alone outside.

ZOHAR

It has been taught:
After standing alone
it sits and waits for that human to turn back to his Master,
to restore the day.
If he succeeds, that day returns to its place;
if not, that day comes down to join forces with the outlaw spirit.
It molds itself into an exact image of that human
and moves into his house to torment him.
Sometimes his stay is for the good
if one purifies himself.
If not, it is a horrible visitation.
Either way, such days are lacking, missing from the total.
Woe to the human being
who has decreased his days in the presence of the Holy King,
who has failed to reserve days up above—
days that could adorn him in that world,
days that could usher him in to the presence of the Holy King!

Come and see:
When those days draw near to the Holy King,
if the person leaving the world is pure
he ascends and enters into those days
and they become a radiant garment for his soul!
But only his days of virtue, not his days of fault.
Woe to him who has decreased his days up above!
For when he comes to be clothed in his days,
the days that he ruined are missing
and he is clothed in a tattered garment.
It is worse if there are many such days;
then he will have nothing to wear in that world!
Woe to him! Woe to his soul!
He is punished in hell for those days,
days upon days,
two days for every wasted day!
For when he left this world, he found no days to wear,
he had no garment for cover.

Happy are the righteous!
Their days are all stored up with the Holy King,
woven into radiant garments to be worn in the world that is coming.

ZOHAR

We have learned in the mystery of our Mishnah:
Why is it written:
'And they knew that they were naked'
(Genesis 3:7)?
Adam and Eve knew the naked truth:
the radiant garment woven from their days had faded away.
Not one single day was left to wear,
as it is written:
'Your eyes saw my unformed limbs;
in Your book they were all recorded.
The days that were fashioned—
not one of them is left'
(Psalms 139:16).
Exactly!
Not one of those fashioned days was left to be worn.
And so it remained
until Adam made the effort to turn back to God and mend his ways.
The Blessed Holy One accepted him
and made him different garments but not from his days,
as it is written:
'*YHVH Elohim* made garments of skin for Adam and his wife
and He clothed them'
(Genesis 3:21).

Come and see:
Abraham, who was pure, what is written of him?
'He came into days'
(Genesis 24:1).
When he left this world
he entered into his very own days and put them on to wear.
Nothing was missing from that radiant garment:
'He came into days.'

But what is written of Job?
'He said, "Naked I came from my mother's womb
and naked shall I return there"'
(Job 1:21).
No garment was left for him to wear.

ZOHAR

It has been taught:
Happy are the righteous
for their days are pure and extend to the world that is coming.
When they leave this world, all their days are sewn together,
made into radiant garments for them to wear.
Arrayed in that garment,
they are admitted to the world that is coming
to enjoy its pleasures.
Clothed in that garment,
they are destined to come back to life.
All who have a garment will be resurrected,
as it is written:
'They will rise as in a garment'
(Job 38:14).

Woe to the wicked of the world
whose days are faulty and full of holes!
There is not enough to cover them when they leave the world.

It has been taught:
All the righteous
who are privileged to wear a radiant garment of their days
are crowned in that world with crowns worn by the Patriarchs
from the stream that flows and gushes into the Garden of Eden,
as it is written:
'*YHVH* will guide you always
and satisfy your soul with sparkling flashes'
(Isaiah 58:11).
But the wicked of the world,
unfit to wear a garment of days,
of them it is written:
'He shall be like a bush in the desert,
unaware of the coming of good,
inhabiting scorched wilderness'
(Jeremiah 17:6)."

Rabbi Isaac said
"Happy is the destiny of Jacob!
He had such faith that he could say:

ZOHAR

'I will lie down with my fathers.'
He attained their level, nothing less!
He surpassed them, dressed in his days and in theirs!"

ZOHAR ON EXODUS

THE BIRTH OF MOSES

A man of the house of Levi
went and married a daughter of Levi.
The woman conceived and bore a son;
she saw how good he was, and she hid him for three months.
(Exodus 2:1–2)

"A man" is Gabriel,
as it is said:
"The man Gabriel whom I had seen in a vision . . ."
(Daniel 9:21).

"The House of Levi" means the Communion of Israel
who emanates from the left side.

"Married a daughter of Levi" refers to the soul-breath,
for we have learned:
When the body of a righteous hero is born in this world
the Blessed Holy One summons Gabriel
who carries the soul-breath from the Garden
and brings her down to his body, born into this world.
Gabriel is appointed guardian of the soul-breath . . .

"A man" is Amram.
"Married a daughter of Levi" refers to Yocheved.
A daughter of the Voice, a divine echo,
descended and told him to unite with her,
for the time was ripe for Israel to be delivered
by the son they would engender.
The Blessed Holy One assisted Amram,
for we have learned:
Shekhinah was present on their bed
and their desire joined with Her.
Therefore *Shekhinah* never left the son they engendered,
confirming what is written:

ZOHAR

"Make yourselves holy and you will be holy"
(Leviticus 11:44).
A human being who makes himself holy below
is made holy above by the Blessed Holy One.
Their desire focused on joining *Shekhinah;*
so *Shekhinah* joined in the very act they were engaged in.

Rabbi Isaac said
"Happy are the righteous!
Their desire is focused on joining the Blessed Holy One constantly.
Just as they cleave to Him constantly,
so He cleaves to them, never leaving them.
Woe to the wicked!
Their desire and attachment is far removed from Him.
Not only do they alienate themselves from Him;
they cleave to the Other Side!

Come and see:
Amram adhered to the Blessed Holy One
and Moses came forth from him.
Moses!
The Blessed Holy One never departed from him.
Shekhinah joined with him constantly.
Happy is his share!"

"The woman conceived and bore a son;
she saw how good he was . . ."
What does this mean: "how good he was"?
Rabbi Ḥiyya said
"It means that he was born circumcised,
for the secret of the covenant is called "good"
as it is written:
'Say of the righteous one that he is good'
(Isaiah 3:10)."

Rabbi Yose said
"She saw the radiance of *Shekhinah* shining in him,
for when he was born the whole house was filled with light!
This verse reads: 'She saw how good he was';
another verse reads: 'God saw how good the light was'

100

(Genesis 1:4).
That is how good he was:
he was everything!"

"She hid him for three months."
What is the point of saying "three months"?
Rabbi Judah said
"It hints at a secret:
Moses' enlightenment was not recognized until 'three months,'
as it is written:
'On the third new moon
after the Children of Israel had gone forth from the land of Egypt,
on that very day, they entered the wilderness of Sinai'
(Exodus 19:1).
Only then was Torah transmitted through him;
Shekhinah revealed Herself and rested upon him
before the eyes of all,
as it is written:
'Moses went up to *Elohim*, and *YHVH* called to him'
(Exodus 19:3)."

MOSES AND THE BLAZING BUSH

Moses was tending the flock of Jethro, his father-in-law,
the priest of Midian.
He led the flock far into the wilderness
and came to Horev, the mountain of Elohim.
The Angel of YHVH appeared to him in a flame of fire out of a
*   bush.*
He gazed: the bush is blazing in fire
yet the bush is not consumed!

(Exodus 3:1–2)

"The Angel of *YHVH* appeared to him in a flame of fire."
To Moses in a flame of fire, unlike other prophets.
Why?
Rabbi Judah said
"Moses was not like other prophets.
We have learned:
One who comes close to fire is burned.
Yet Moses came close to fire and was not burned,
as it is written:
'Moses approached the dense cloud where *Elohim* was'
(Exodus 20:18).
So here:
'The Angel of *YHVH* appeared to him in a flame of fire out of a
    bush.' "

Rabbi Abba said
"We should explore the nature of Moses in the light of wisdom.
Why is it written:
'She named him Moses, saying
"It means: I drew him out of the water" '?
(Exodus 2:10).
One who has been drawn out of water has no fear of fire.
And it has been taught in the name of Rabbi Judah:
'From the place Moses was hewn, no other human was hewn.' "

ZOHAR

Rabbi Yoḥanan said
"Moses was arrayed in all ten spheres,
as it is written:
'He is trusted throughout My household'
(Numbers 12:7).
Not just a loyal member of My household
but entrusted with everything!
Happy is the share of a human being
given such an affirmation by his Lord!"
Rav Dimi spoke up:
"But it is written:
'Never again did there arise in Israel a prophet like Moses'
(Deuteronomy 34:10),
and Rabbi Joshua son of Levi has taken this to mean:
in Israel none arose, but among the nations of the world one did!
Who was that? Balaam."

"Indeed, you are right," said Rabbi Yoḥanan,
and he was silent.

When Rabbi Shim'on son of Yoḥai appeared
they asked him about this word.
He opened and said
"Black resin mixed with finest balsam?
God forbid!
Rather, this is the true meaning:
Among the nations of the world one did arise.
Who was that? Balaam.
Moses' actions were high; those of Balaam, low.
Moses worked wonders with the holy crown of the supernal King
    above;
Balaam worked black magic with the nethermost crowns, unholy,
    below.
Because of this
'the Israelites slew Balaam son of Be'or, the sorcerer, with the sword'
(Joshua 13:22).
If you think he was any higher, go ask his ass!"

Rabbi Yose came and kissed his hands;
he said, "Ah! The coveting in my heart has disappeared,

103

for now I see that there is high and low, right and left,
compassion and judgment, Israel and the idolaters!
Israel wields high and holy crowns;
idolaters, the nethermost crowns, unholy.
Israel is on the right; idolaters, on the left.
What a difference there is between high prophets and low prophets,
holy prophets and unholy prophets!"

Rabbi Judah said
"As Moses was one of a kind among all prophets high and holy,
so Balaam was one of a kind among unholy prophets and sorcerers
    below.
Yet from every angle, Moses was up above and Balaam was down
    below.
So many levels separate the two!"

Rabbi Yohanan said in the name of Rabbi Isaac
"Moses was worried that Israel might perish from the harsh bondage
God forbid!
as it is written:
'He went out to his kinsfolk and saw their burden'
(Exodus 2:11).
Therefore
'The Angel of *YHVH* appeared to him in a flame of fire . . .
He gazed: the bush is blazing in fire,'
showing that Israel is enslaved,
but 'the bush is not consumed!' "

Happy are Israel!
The Blessed Holy One has separated them from all nations
and called them His children,
as it is written:
"You are children of *YHVH* your God!"
(Deuteronomy 14:1).

MOSES AND HIS FATHER-IN-LAW

Moses returned to YHVH.
He said, "Adonai, why did You wrong this people?
Why did You ever send me?
Since I came to Pharaoh to speak in Your name
it has gotten worse for this people;
You have certainly not delivered Your people!". . . .
Elohim *spoke to Moses;*
He said to him, "I am YHVH!"

(*Exodus 5:22–23; 6:2*)

Rabbi Yose said
"Moses!
If he had not been master of the house, husband of *Elohim*,
he would have been punished for what he said.
But since he was, he was not punished.
It is like a man who falls into an agrument with his wife
and speaks harshly to her.
She starts to get upset
but as the words begin to fly, the king appears and takes up the
    word.
She turns silent and says nothing more.
The king says to him, 'Do you not know that I am King?
It is as if you spoke these words against me!'

Here too, as if it were possible:
'Moses returned to *YHVH*.
He said, "*Adonai*, why did You wrong this people?"'
At once '*Elohim* spoke to Moses'
She started to get upset.
At once the king took up the word:
'He said to him, "I am *YHVH!*"'
'Do you not know that I am King?
You have spoken these words against Me!'

ZOHAR

'I appeared to Abraham, to Isaac, and to Jacob through *El Shaddai*'
(Exodus 6:3).
Why is this name different from the ones above?
It is like a king who had a daughter not yet married.
He also had a dear friend.
When the king wanted to speak with his friend
he would send his daughter to speak with him.
Through his daughter, the king would speak with his friend.
The time came for his daughter to be married.
On the day of her wedding, the king said
'Call my daughter, Mistress Matronita!'
He said to her,
'Until now I spoke through you to whomever I spoke with.
From now on I will talk to your husband
and he will transmit the message to whomever it should be given.'

One day her husband spoke harshly to her in the presence of the
    king.
Before she could answer back, the king took up the word and said
'Am I not King?
Until now no one has spoken with me except through my daughter.
I have given you my daughter and spoken with you openly!
Such things I have done for no one else!'

Similarly, God said to Moses:
' "I appeared to Abraham, to Isaac, and to Jacob through *El Shaddai*,"
when She was in My house, not yet married.
They did not speak with Me face to face
as I have spoken with you!
How dare you open with words such as these,
spoken to My daughter in My presence!
"I appeared to Abraham, to Isaac, and to Jacob through *El Shaddai*,
but by My name *YHVH*, I was not known to them";
I did not speak with them on the same level I have spoken with
    you!' "

COLORS AND ENLIGHTENMENT

One day Rabbi Shim'on was sitting.
Rabbi El'azar, his son, and Rabbi Abba were with him.
Rabbi El'azar said
"The verse written here:
I have appeared to Abraham, to Isaac, and to Jacob . . .
Why *appeared?*
The word should be *spoken.*"

He answered
"El'azar, my son, it is a high mystery!
Come and see:
Certain colors can be seen;
certain colors cannot.
These and those are the high mystery of faith.
But human beings do not know; they do not reflect.

The colors that can be seen—
no one was pure enough to see them
until the Patriarchs came and mastered them.
Therefore the word *appeared,*
for they saw the colors which are revealed.
Which are revealed?
Colors of *El Shaddai,* colors in a cosmic prism.
These can be seen.

But the colors above, hidden and invisible—
no human has mastered them except for Moses.
Therefore the verse concludes:
'But by My name *YHVH,* I was not known to them.'
I was not revealed to them in high colors.
Do you think that the Patriarchs were not aware of those colors at
    all?
They were aware, through those that are revealed.

ZOHAR

It is written:
'The enlightened will shine like the *zohar* of the sky,
and those who make the masses righteous
will shine like the stars forever and ever'
(Daniel 12:3).

'The enlightened will shine'
Who is enlightened?
The wise one who contemplates by himself, from himself,
words that human beings cannot mouth.

'Will shine like the *zohar* of the sky'
Which sky?
The sky of Moses
which stands in the center;
this *zohar* of his is concealed and not revealed.
It stands above the sky that does not shine,
in which colors can be seen.
There those colors can be seen,
but they do not glow with the brilliance of the hidden colors.

Come and see:
There are four lights.
Three are concealed and one is revealed.
A shining light.
A glowing light;
   it shines like the clear brilliance of heaven.
A purple light that absorbs all lights.
A light that does not shine
   but gazes toward the others and draws them in.
   Those lights are seen in her as in a crystal facing the sun.
The first three are concealed,
overseeing this one, which is revealed.

The secret is: the eye.
Come and see:
Three colors appear in the eye,
but none of them glow,
for they are overshadowed by a light that does not shine.
These are images of the colors that are hidden, which oversee them.

ZOHAR

These were shown to the Patriarchs,
so they would know those hidden ones that glow
through these that do not glow.
The ones that glow and the ones that are hidden
were revealed to Moses in that sky of his.
These oversee those colors that are seen in the eye.

The secret is: close your eye and roll your eyeball.
Those colors that shine and glow will be revealed.
Permission to see is granted only with eyes concealed,
for they are high and concealed,
overseeing those colors that can be seen but do not glow.

And so we read:
'Moses attained the mirror that shines,'
which oversees the one that does not shine.
The rest of humanity, that mirror that does not shine.
The Patriarchs saw, through these colors that are revealed,
those hidden ones, which oversee the ones that do not shine.
Therefore it is written:
'I appeared to Abraham, to Isaac, and to Jacob through *El Shaddai*,'
through the colors that can be seen.
'But by My name *YHVH*, I was not known to them.'
These are high colors, hidden and glowing.
Moses was so pure that he gazed into them!

The secret is: the eye, closed and open.
Closed, it sees the mirror that shines.
Opened, it sees the mirror that does not shine.
So, 'I appeared' in the mirror that does not shine,
which is open and revealed.
This is described as seeing.
But the mirror that shines, which is concealed—
this is described as knowing,
as it is written:
'I was not known.' "

Rabbi El'azar and Rabbi Abba came and kissed his hands.
Rabbi Abba cried, and said
"Woe when you disappear from the world!

ZOHAR

The world will be an orphan without you!
Who will be able to illumine the words of Torah?"

PHARAOH, ISRAEL, AND GOD

YHVH hardened the heart of Pharaoh, king of Egypt,
and he pursued the Children of Israel.
As the Children of Israel were departing boldly,
the Egyptians pursued them and overtook them encamped by the
    sea—
all the chariot horses of Pharaoh, his horsemen, and his warriors—
near Pi ha-Hirot, before Ba'al Zefon.
Pharaoh drew near.
The Children of Israel lifted their eyes—
and there was Egypt advancing upon them!
They were very frightened;
the Children of Israel cried out to YHVH.

                                (Exodus 14:8–10)

"Pharaoh drew near."
Rabbi Yose said
"It has been said that he brought Israel
to the point of turning back to God.
'Pharaoh drew [them] near!'

It is written:
'*YHVH!* In distress they sought You,
pouring out a whispered prayer . . .'
(Isaiah 26:16).
'In distress they sought You'
Israel does not seek the Blessed Holy One when they are
    comfortable;
only when they are in trouble.
Then all of them remember Him and seek Him.

'Pouring out a whispered prayer'
They all pray their prayers and pleadings.
They pour out prayers to Him.

ZOHAR

When?
'When Your chastisement falls upon them.'
The moment the Blessed Holy One hands them over to His scourge,
He stands over them compassionately.
Their voice of prayer pleases Him;
so the enemies of Israel are called to account.
He is filled with compassion for His people,
as we have established.

A parable: the dove and the hawk.
[A dove escaped from the hawk and took refuge in the cleft of a rock.
There she found a serpent nesting.
She tried to enter but could not because the serpent was there.
Could she go back?
She could not because the hawk was poised for attack.
What did she do?
She began to cry and clap her wings
so the owner of the dovecote would hear her and come to save her.]

So, Israel drew near to the sea.
They saw the sea raging, its waves surging.
They were frightened.
They lifted their eyes and saw Pharaoh and his army
with shooting stones and catapults.
'They were very frightened.'
What did they do?
'The Children of Israel cried out.'
Who brought it about that Israel drew near to their Father above?
Pharaoh!
This is what is written:
'Pharaoh drew [them] near.'
This has already been said."

MANNA AND WISDOM

YHVH *said to Moses*
"I am about to rain down for you bread from heaven!"...
Moses said to Aaron
"Say to the whole assemblage of the Children of Israel:
'Approach YHVH, *for He has heard your grumbling.'"*
As Aaron spoke to the whole assemblage of the Children of Israel,
they turned to face the desert,
for there, the Presence of YHVH *had appeared in the cloud....*
That evening, the quail rose and covered the camp.
In the morning, there was a fall of dew around the camp.
The fall of dew rose,
and there, on the face of the desert,
a fine coating, as fine as frost on the ground.
The Children of Israel saw.
They said to one another, "What is it?"
for they did not know what it was.
Moses said to them
"It is the bread that YHVH *has given you to eat."*

(Exodus 16:4, 9–10, 13–15)

Come and see:
Every single day, dew trickles down
from the Holy Ancient One to the Impatient One,
and the Orchard of Holy Apple Trees is blessed.
Some of the dew flows to those below;
holy angels are nourished by it,
each according to his diet,
as it is written:
"A human ate angel bread"
(Psalms 78:25).
Israel ate of that food in the desert.

Rabbi Shim'on said
"Some people are nourished by it even now!

ZOHAR

Who are they?
The Comrades, who engage Torah day and night.
Do you think they are nourished by that very food?
No, by something like that very food;
two balancing one.

Come and see:
When Israel entered and joined themselves to the Holy King
by uncovering the holy marking,
they were pure enough to eat another kind of bread,
higher than at first.
At first, when Israel went out of Egypt,
they went into the bread called *Mazzah*.
Now they were purer;
they went in to eat higher bread from a high sphere,
as it is written:
'I am about to rain down for you bread from heaven,'
literally: from Heaven!
It was then that Israel discovered the taste of this sphere.

Comrades engaging Torah are nourished from an even higher sphere.
Which is that?
That which is written:
'Wisdom gives life to those who have it'
(Ecclesiastes 7:12),
a very high sphere."

Rabbi El'azar said to him
"If so, why are they weaker than other human beings?
Other human beings are stronger and more powerful;
the Comrades should be the stronger ones."

He said to him, "A good question!
Come and see:
All human food comes from above.
The food that comes from heaven and earth is for the whole world.
It is food for all; it is coarse and dense.
The food that comes from higher above is finer food,
coming from the sphere where Judgment is found.
This is the food that Israel ate when they went out of Egypt.

ZOHAR

The food found by Israel that time in the desert,
from the higher sphere called Heaven—
it is an even finer food,
entering deepest of all into the soul,
detached from the body,
called "angel bread."

The highest food of all is the food of the Comrades,
those who engage Torah.
For they eat food of the spirit and the soul-breath;
they eat no food for the body at all.
Rather, from a high sphere, precious beyond all: Wisdom.

That is why a Comrade's body is weaker than a normal body:
they do not eat food for the body at all.
They eat food for the spirit and the soul-breath
from someplace far beyond, most precious of all.
So their food is finest of the fine, finest of all.
Happy is their portion!
As it is written:
'Wisdom gives life to those who have it.'
Happy is the body that can nourish itself on food of the soul!"

Rabbi El'azar said to him, "Certainly that is true.
But how can such food be found now?"

He answered, "Certainly a good question!
Come and see:
This is the clarity of the word. . . .
The food of the Comrades engaging Torah is most precious of all.
This food flows from Wisdom on high.
Why from this sphere?
Because Torah derives from Wisdom on high,
and those who engage Torah enter the source of her roots;
so their food flows down from that high and holy sphere."

Rabbi El'azar came and kissed his hands.
He said, "Happy is my portion! I understand these words!
Happy is the portion of the righteous!
Engaging Torah day and night

entitles them to this world and the world that is coming,
as it is written:
'That is your life and the expanse of your days.' "

IS THERE ANYONE LIKE MOSES?

On the third new moon
after the Children of Israel had gone forth from the land of Egypt,
on that very day, they entered the desert of Sinai.
They journeyed from Rephidim and entered the desert of Sinai
and camped in the desert.
Israel camped there facing the mountain
and Moses went up to Elohim . . .

(Exodus 19:1–3)

Happy is Moses!
He attained the Presence!
Torah herself is his witness:
"Moses went up to *Elohim*."

Rabbi Judah taught:
"Come and see the difference between Moses and the rest of the
    world.
For the rest of the world
'going up' means greater wealth, prestige, and power.
But when Moses went up, what is written?
'Moses went up to *Elohim*.'
Happy is he!"

Rabbi Yose said
"This is the origin of the saying of the Comrades:
'One who comes to purify himself—they help him.'
For it is written: 'Moses went up to *Elohim*.'
What is written next? '*YHVH* called to him.'
One who desires to draw himself near—they draw him near."

"*YHVH* called to him from the mountain, saying:
'Thus shall you say to the house of Jacob . . .' "

ZOHAR

Rabbi Isaac opened
" 'Happy is the one You choose and bring near;
he will dwell in Your courts'
(Psalms 65:5).
Happy is the human being whom the Blessed Holy One is drawn to,
whom He draws near to dwell in the palace!
Whomever He desires for His work is marked with markings of the
    beyond
to show that he has been chosen by the high and holy King
to dwell in His dwelling.
Whoever displays that sign passes through all gates of the beyond.
No one can stop him!"

Rabbi Judah said
"Happy is Moses! This verse was written for him:
'Happy is the one You choose and bring near.'
Of him it is written:
'Moses drew near to the thick darkness;
Moses alone shall draw near *YHVH;* they shall not draw near.' "

ALL OF ISRAEL SAW THE LETTERS

Anokhi

A secret of secrets for those who know wisdom:
The moment these letters came forth,
secretly circling as one,
a spark flashed out to engrave.
A flowing measure extended ten cubits on this side,
and out shot comets inside comets, seventy-one.
Sparks burst into flashes, up high and down below,
then quieted down and rose up high, beyond, beyond.
The flow measured out ten cubits on the other side,
and comets shot out in colors like before.
And so on every side.

The spark expanded, whirling round and round.
Sparks burst into flashes and rose high above.
The heavens blazed with all their powers;
everything flashed and sparkled as one.
Then the spark turned from the side of the South
and outlined a curve from there to the East
and from the East to the North
until it had circled back to the South, as before.
Then the spark swirled, disappearing;
comets and flashes dimmed.

Now they came forth, these carved, flaming letters
flashing like gold when it dazzles.
Like a craftsman smelting silver and gold:
when he takes them out of the blazing fire
all is bright and pure;
so the letters came forth, pure and bright
from the flowing measure of the spark.
Therefore it is written:

119

ZOHAR

"The word of *YHVH* is refined"
(Psalms 18:31),
as silver and gold are refined.
When these letters came forth, they were all refined,
carved precisely, sparkling, flashing.
All of Israel saw the letters
flying through space in every direction,
engraving themselves on the tablets of stone.

THE OLD MAN AND THE BEAUTIFUL MAIDEN

Rabbi Ḥiyya and Rabbi Yose met one night at the Tower of Tyre.
They stayed there as guests, delighting in each other.
Rabbi Yose said, "I am so glad to see the face of *Shekhinah*.
For just now, the whole way here, I was pestered by an old man,
a donkey driver, who kept asking me riddles the whole way:

'What is a serpent that flies in the air and wanders alone,
while an ant lies peacefully between its teeth?
Beginning in union, it ends in separation.

What is an eagle that nests in a tree that never was?
Its young who have been plundered,
who are not created creatures,
lie somewhere uncreated.
When they go up, they come down; coming down, they go up.
Two who are one, and one who is three.

What is a beautiful maiden who has no eyes
and a body concealed and revealed?
She comes out in the morning and is hidden all day.
She adorns herself with adornments that are not.'

All this he asked on the way; I was annoyed.
Now I can relax!
If we had been together, we would have engaged in words of Torah
instead of strange words of chaos."

Rabbi Ḥiyya said, "That old man, the donkey driver,
do you know anything about him?"

He answered, "I know that there is nothing in his words.
If he knew anything, he should have opened with Torah;
then the way would not have been empty!"

ZOHAR

Rabbi Ḥiyya said, "That donkey driver, is he here?
For sometimes in those empty fools, you discover bells of gold!"

He said to him, "Here he is! Fixing up his donkey with food."

They called to him; he came before them.
He said to them, "Now two are three, and three are like one!"

Rabbi Yose said
"Didn't I tell you that all his words are empty nonsense?"

He sat before them and said
"Rabbis, I turned into a donkey driver only a short time ago.
Before, I wasn't one.
But I have a small son, and I put him in school;
I want him to engage Torah.
When I find one of the rabbis traveling on the road
I guide his donkey from behind.
Today I thought that I would hear new words of Torah.
But I haven't heard anything!"

Rabbi Yose said, "Of all the words I heard you say,
there was one that really amazed me.
Either you said it out of folly, or they are empty words."

The Old Man said, "And which one is that?"

He said, "The one about the beautiful maiden."

The Old Man opened and said
" 'YHVH is on my side; I have no fear.
What can any human do to me?
YHVH is by my side, helping me. . . .
It is good to take refuge in YHVH. . .'
(Psalms 118:6–8).

How good and pleasant and precious and high are words of Torah!
But how can I say them in front of rabbis
from whose mouths, until now, I haven't heard a single word?
But I should say them

because there is no shame at all in saying words of Torah
in front of everyone!"

The Old Man covered himself. . . .
The Old Man opened and said
" 'Moses went inside the cloud and ascended the mountain . . .'
(Exodus 24:18).
What is this cloud?
The one of which it is written: 'I have placed My bow in the cloud'
(Genesis 9:13).
We have learned that the Rainbow took off Her garments
and gave them to Moses.
Wearing that garment, Moses went up the mountain;
from inside it he saw what he saw,
delighting in the All, up to that place."

The Comrades approached and threw themselves down
in front of the Old Man.
They cried, and said, "If we have come into the world
only to hear these words from your mouth,
it is enough for us!"

The Old Man said
"Friends, Comrades, not for this alone did I begin the word.
An old man like me doesn't rattle with just a single word.
Human beings are so confused in their minds!
They do not see the way of truth in Torah.
Torah calls out to them every day, in love,
but they do not want to turn their heads.
Even though I have said that Torah removes a word from her sheath,
is seen for a moment, then quickly hides away—
that is certainly true—
but when she reveals herself from her sheath
and hides herself right away,
she does so only for those who know her intimately.

A parable.
To what can this be compared?
To a lovely princess,
beautiful in every way and hidden deep within her palace.

ZOHAR

She has one lover, unknown to anyone; he is hidden too.
Out of his love for her, this lover passes by her gate constantly,
lifting his eyes to every side.
She knows that her lover is hovering about her gate constantly.
What does she do?
She opens a little window in her hidden palace
and reveals her face to her lover,
then swiftly withdraws, concealing herself.
No one near the lover sees or reflects,
only the lover,
and his heart and his soul and everything within him
flow out to her.
And he knows that out of love for him
she revealed herself for that one moment
to awaken love in him.

So it is with a word of Torah:
She reveals herself to no one but her lover.
Torah knows that he who is wise of heart
hovers about her gate every day.
What does she do?
She reveals her face to him from the palace
and beckons him with a hint,
then swiftly withdraws to her hiding place.
No one who is there knows or reflects;
he alone does,
and his heart and his soul and everything within him
flows out to her.
That is why Torah reveals and conceals herself.
With love she approaches her lover
to arouse love with him.

Come and see!
This is the way of Torah:
At first, when she begins to reveal herself to a human
she beckons him with a hint.
If he knows, good;
if not, she sends him a message, calling him a fool.
Torah says to her messenger:
'Tell that fool to come closer, so I can talk with him!'

ZOHAR

as it is written:
'Who is the fool without a heart?
Have him turn in here!'
(Proverbs 9:4).
He approaches.
She begins to speak with him from behind a curtain she has drawn,
words he can follow, until he reflects a little at a time.
This is *derasha*.
Then she converses with him through a veil,
words riddled with allegory.
This is *haggadah*.

Once he has grown accustomed to her,
she reveals herself face to face
and tells him all her hidden secrets,
all the hidden ways,
since primordial days secreted in her heart.

Now he is a perfect human being,
husband of Torah, master of the house.
All her secrets she has revealed to him,
withholding nothing, concealing nothing.

She says to him, 'Do you see that word,
that hint with which I beckoned you at first?
So many secrets there! This one and that one!'

Now he sees that nothing should be added to those words
and nothing taken away.
Now the *peshat* of the verse, just like it is!
Not even a single letter should be added or deleted.

Human beings must become aware!
They must pursue Torah to become her lovers! . . ."

He was silent for a moment.
The Comrades were amazed;
they did not know if it was day or night,
if they were really there or not. . . .

ZOHAR

"Enough, Comrades!
From now on, you know that the Evil Side has no power over you.
I, Yeiva Sava, have stood before you
to awaken your awareness of these words."

They rose like one who is awakened from his sleep
and threw themselves down in front of him,
unable to utter a word.
After a while they began to cry.
Rabbi Ḥiyya opened and said
" 'Set me as a seal upon your heart,
as a seal upon your arm'
(Song of Songs 8:6). . . .
Love and sparks from the flame of our heart will escort you!
May it be the Will
that our image be engraved in your heart
as your image is engraved in ours!"

He kissed them and blessed them, and they left.

When they rejoined Rabbi Shim'on
and told him everything that happened,
he was delighted and amazed.
He said, "You are so fortunate to have attained all this!
Here you were with a heavenly lion,
a powerful hero compared with whom many heroes are nothing,
and you did not know how to recognize him right away!
I am amazed that you escaped his punishment!
The Blessed Holy One must have wanted to save you!"

He called out these verses for them:

"The path of the righteous is like the light of dawn,
growing brighter and brighter until the day is full.
When you walk, your stride will be free;
if you run, you will not stumble.

Your people, all of them righteous, will inherit the land forever;
a sprout of My planting, the work of My hands, making Me
     glorious!"

THE GIFT OF DWELLING

YHVH *spoke to Moses, saying:*
"Speak to the Children of Israel and have them take Me a gift.
From everyone whose heart moves him take My gift.
This is the gift that you shall take from them:
  gold, silver and copper;
  blue, purple and crimson yarn, fine linen and goats' hair;
  rams' skins dyed red, dolphin skins, and acacia wood;
  oil for lighting, spices for the oil of anointing
  and for aromatic incense;
  lapis lazuli and precious setting stones
  for the efod *and the breastpiece.*
Have them make Me a holy place, and I will dwell in their
  midst."

(Exodus 25:1–8)

Rabbi Shim'on, Rabbi El'azar, Rabbi Abba, and Rabbi Yose
were sitting one day beneath some trees
on the plain by the Sea of Ginnosar.
Rabbi Shim'on said
"The shade spread over us by these trees is so pleasant!
We must crown this place with words of Torah!"

Rabbi Shim'on opened and said
" 'King Solomon made himself a palanquin
out of the cedars of Lebanon'
(Song of Songs 3:9).
We have already established the meaning of this verse;
but the palanquin is the Palace below
which is like the Palace on high.
The Blessed Holy One calls it Garden of Eden,
for He planted it for His pleasure
and His yearning
to delight in the souls of the righteous

who are all enrolled within.
These are souls who have no body in this world.
They all ascend; there they are crowned.
They have places from which to gaze,
to enjoy the joy on high, called Delight of *YHVH*.
There they are filled by precious flows of rivers of pure balsam. . . .

One who attains the Palanquin is entitled to everything.
He is worthy of sitting in the comfort of the shade of the Blessed
    Holy One,
as it is said:
'I delight to sit in His shade'
(Song of Songs 2:3).
Now that we are sitting in this shade of comfort,
we should be aware that we are sitting in the shade of the Blessed
    Holy One
within the Palanquin!
We should crown this place with crowns so high
that the trees of the Palanquin will be swayed
to cover us with another shade. . . .

Happy is the Holy People!
Their Master searches for them, calls to them
to bring them close to Him.
So the Holy People must join together and enter the synagogue.
Whoever arrives earliest joins himself to *Shekhinah* in a single bond!
Come and see:
The first one present in the synagogue, happy is his portion!
He stands on the level of *Zaddiq*, together with *Shekhinah*.
This is the secret meaning of:
'Those who seek Me early will find Me'
(Proverbs 8:17).
This one ascends very high!

Now you might say, 'But we have learned:
"When the Blessed Holy One comes to synagogue
and does not find ten people there,
He instantly turns angry!"
How can you say that one who comes early
joins himself to *Shekhinah* and stands on the level of *Zaddiq?*'

ZOHAR

A parable.
There was a king
who ordered all the inhabitants of the city to appear in his presence
on a certain day, at a certain place.
While the people were preparing themselves,
one came early to that place.
Meanwhile, the king came and found the person who had arrived
      early.
He said, 'You! Where are all my subjects?'
He answered, 'My Lord, I have come early,
but they are coming behind me, according to the command of the
      king.'
The king was pleased
and sat down with him and conversed with him;
he became the king's beloved.
Meanwhile, all the people arrived.
The king was appeased and sent them in peace.
But if they had not arrived,
if one had not come early to represent them,
to tell the king that all of them were on the way,
the king would have instantly turned very angry.

Here too, since one comes early and is present in the synagogue
and *Shekhinah* comes and finds him,
it is considered as if all of them were present
because this one is waiting for them.
At once *Shekhinah* joins Herself to him;
they sit in one coupling.
She comes to know him well and seats him on the level of *Zaddiq*.
But if no one comes early,
if no one is present,
what is written?
'Why have I come? There is no man!'
(Isaiah 50:2).
The verse does not read: 'There are not ten.'
It reads: 'There is no man!'
to join himself to Me,
to be with Me,
      as it is said: 'the man of *Elohim*,'
to be on the level of *Zaddiq.* . . ."

129

ZOHAR

Rabbi Shim'on rose, and the Comrades too.
They rose and walked on.
Rabbi El'azar said to Rabbi Shim'on, his father,
"Father, until now we have been sitting
in the shade of the Tree of Life, in the Garden of Eden!
From now on, since we are walking,
we must follow the paths that guard this Tree.". . .

Rabbi Abba opened and said
" 'Have them take Me a gift. From everyone . . .'
When the Blessed Holy One showed Moses the work of the
    Dwelling,
it was difficult for him; he was unable to understand it.
This has been established.
Now *we* have to raise a difficulty:
If this gift was given by the Blessed Holy One to Moses alone,
how could he give Her to another?
How could he say that the Children of Israel should take this gift?
Ah, but of course He gave Her to Moses, not to anyone else!

A parable.
There was a king among his people,
but the queen was not with the king.
As long as the queen was not with the king,
the people did not feel secure;
they could not dwell safely.
As soon as the queen came,
all the people rejoiced and dwelt safely.

So, at first, even though the Blessed Holy One
performed miracles and signs through Moses,
the people did not feel secure.
As soon as the Blessed Holy One said
'Have them take My gift: I place My Dwelling in your midst!'
everyone felt secure and rejoiced in the rite of the Blessed Holy One,
as it is written:
'On the day that Moses consummated setting up the Dwelling'
(Numbers 7:1),
for the Bride of Moses came down to earth!". . .

ZOHAR

Rabbi Shim'on cried, and said
"Now I know for sure
that the High Holy Spirit is vibrating within you.
Happy is this generation!
A generation like this will not arise until King Messiah appears!
Torah has been restored to her ancientry!
Happy are the righteous
in this world and the world that is coming!"

THE SECRET OF SABBATH

The Secret of Sabbath:
She is Sabbath!
United in the secret of One
to draw down upon Her the secret of One.

The prayer for the entrance of Sabbath:
The holy Throne of Glory is united in the secret of One,
prepared for the High Holy King to rest upon Her.
When Sabbath enters She is alone,
separated from the Other Side,
all judgments removed from Her.
Basking in the oneness of holy light,
She is crowned over and over to face the Holy King.
All powers of wrath and masters of judgment flee from Her.
There is no power in all the worlds aside from Her.
Her face shines with a light from beyond;
She is crowned below by the holy people,
and all of them are crowned with new souls.
Then the beginning of prayer
to bless Her with joy and beaming faces:
Barekhu ET YHVH ha-Mevorakh,
"Bless *ET YHVH*, the Blessed One,"
ET YHVH, blessing Her first.

THE GOLDEN CALF

*When the people saw that Moses took so long coming down from the
    mountain,*
they gathered against Aaron and said to him,
"Rise, make us Elohim *who will go before us,*
for this man Moses, who brought us out from the land of Egypt—
we do not know what happened to him!"
Aaron said to them, "Tear off the gold rings
that are in the ears of your wives, your sons, and your daughters,
and bring them to me."
So all the people tore off the gold rings that were in their ears
and brought them to Aaron.
This he took from their hands and cast in a mold
and made it into a molten calf.
They exclaimed, "This is your God, O Israel,
who brought you out from the land of Egypt!"
When Aaron saw this, he built an altar before it
and proclaimed: "Tomorrow is a feast for YHVH!"
The next day, they rose early
and offered up offerings and brought peace offerings;
they sat down to eat and drink, then got up to play.

YHVH *spoke to Moses, "Go down,*
for your people, whom you brought out from the land of Egypt,
have corrupted themselves!
Quickly they turned from the way I enjoined upon them.
They made themselves a molten calf,
bowed down to it and sacrificed to it,
saying: 'This is your God, O Israel,
who brought you out from the land of Egypt!' "

YHVH *said to Moses,*
"I have seen this people: it is a stiffnecked people.
Now leave Me alone!

133

ZOHAR

My anger will blaze against them and I will consume them,
and I will make you into a great nation!"
And Moses sweetened the face of YHVH, *his God.*
He said, "Why, YHVH, *should Your anger blaze against Your people,*
whom You brought forth from the land of Egypt
with great power and a mighty hand?
Why should Egypt say, 'With evil intent He brought them forth:
to kill them off in the mountains,
to annihilate them from the face of the earth'?
Turn from Your blazing anger!
Repent of this wrong against Your people!
Remember Abraham, Isaac, and Israel, Your servants,
how You swore to them by Your Self and said to them:
'I will multiply your seed like the stars of heaven;
I will give to your seed this whole land of which I spoke,
to possess forever.' "

And YHVH *repented of the wrong*
that He had threatened to bring upon His people.

(Exodus 32:1–14)

Rabbi Yose and Rabbi Ḥiyya were walking on the road.
While they were walking, night fell;
they sat down.
While they were sitting, morning began to shine;
they rose and walked on.
Rabbi Ḥiyya said, "See the face of the East, how it shines!
Now all the children of the East, who dwell in the mountains of
    light,
are bowing down to this light,
which shines on behalf of the sun before it comes forth,
and they are worshiping it.
Of course once the sun comes forth,
there are many who worship the sun;
but these are those who worship this light,
calling this light, 'God of the shining pearl,'
and their oath is by 'Allah of the shining pearl.'

Now you might say: 'This worship is in vain!'
But since ancient, primordial days

they have discovered wisdom through it.
When the sun begins to shine, before coming forth,
the deputy in charge of the sun comes forth,
with holy letters of the high holy Name engraved on his forehead.
With the power of those letters, he opens all the windows of heaven,
knocking them open, then moving on.
That deputy enters the shining splendor surrounding the sun,
and there he stays
until the sun comes forth and spreads over the world.
That deputy is in charge of gold and rubies,
and they worship his image there.
With points and signs inherited from the ancients, from ancient days,
they come to know the points of the sun
and find the location of gold and gems!"

Rabbi Yose said
"How long will all these rites persist in the world?
Surely falsehood has no feet on which to stand!"

Rabbi Ḥiyya opened and said
" 'The lip of truth will be established forever,
but the tongue of falsehood only till I wink my eye'
(Proverbs 12:19).
Come and see:
If all the inhabitants of the world worshiped falsehood,
it would be so.
But this light and shining splendor is certainly true;
the stars in the loft of the sky are true.
If out of their stupidity and lack of awareness
they call them 'God,'
the Blessed Holy One does not want to destroy His own creations!
Even in the time that is coming
the stars and the lights of the world will not be destroyed.
But who will be destroyed?
Those who worship them!
This is the meaning of the verse:
'The lip of truth will be established forever.'
This means Israel, who are the lip of truth:
'YHVH is our God; YHVH is one.'
All is truth, the secret of truth;

they conclude: '*YHVH*, your God, is truth.'
This is: 'The lip of truth will be established forever.'

'Only till I wink my eye'
The verse should read: 'only for a moment.'
Why does it read: 'till I wink my eye'?
To indicate how long they will last in the world:
till the time comes when I will have rest from My harsh servitude.
When I can relax and take a wink,
the tongue of falsehood will be destroyed—
those who call 'God' him who is not God.
But Israel, who are the lip of truth,
of them it is written:
'This people I formed for Myself;
they shall declare My praise'
(Isaiah 43:21).

I remember one time I was walking with Rabbi El'azar.
He met a *hegemona*, who said to him
'Are you familiar with the Torah of the Jews?'
Rabbi El'azar answered, 'Yes, I am.'
He said, 'Do you not claim that your faith is true and your Torah,
         true,
and that our faith is a lie, and our Torah, a lie?
Yet it is written: "The lip of truth will be established forever,
but the tongue of falsehood only till I wink my eye."
We have reigned since ancient times;
the kingdom has never departed from us, generation after generation:
"established forever," just like it says!
But you had a kingdom only a little while
and it was taken right away.
The verse is thus fulfilled:
"but the tongue of falsehood only till I wink my eye"!'

Rabbi El'azar said, 'I see that you are wise in Torah.
May your spirit deflate!
If the verse read: "The lip of truth You have established forever,"
it would be as you have said.
But it is written: "will be established."
The lip of truth is destined to be established,

though now it is not.
Now the lip of falsehood stands,
while the lip of truth lies in the dust.
But in the time when truth stands erect
and springs forth from the midst of the earth,
then "the lip of truth will be established forever. . . ." ' "

The *hegemon* said, 'You are right!
Happy are the people who possess the Torah of truth!'
Later I heard that he converted."

They walked on and came to a field and prayed their prayers.
Having prayed their prayers, they said
"From here on, let us join with *Shekhinah*,
engaging in Torah as we walk.". . .

Rabbi Yose said
"There has never been a father so compassionate to his children
as the Blessed Holy One.
This is demonstrated in a verse:
'Not a single word has failed of all His good words . . .'
(1 Kings 8:56).
Come and see His compassion!
If the verse read: 'Not a single word has failed of all His words,'
and nothing more,
it would be better for the world to have never been created!
But since it reads: 'of all His good words,'
the bad is left behind,
for He does not want to carry out a bad word.
Even though He threatens and raises the lash,
Mother comes and grabs hold of His right arm
and the lash is suspended,
the sentence is not carried out,
because both of them share one design:
He by threatening, She by holding back His right.

If you ask: 'How do we know this?'
From a word that is revealed,
as it is written:
'Go down, for your people have corrupted themselves!'

He began to raise the lash,
and Moses, not knowing the way of the Mother, was silent.
As soon as the Blessed Holy One saw this,
He penetrated him and prodded him by saying, 'Now leave Me
    alone!'
Moses was instantly roused
and he seized the arm of the Blessed Holy One,
as it is written:
'Remember Abraham!'
This is the right arm.
So the lash did not come down.

If you ask:
'Where was Mother, who usually holds back the lash of the King?
Why did She leave it to Moses?'
I ask this question myself!
We will not know the clarity of the word
until we are in the presence of the Holy Light!"

When they came into the presence of Rabbi Shim'on
he saw a sign in their faces.
He said, "Come in, my holy children!
Come in, beloved of the King!
Come in, my beloved ones!
Come in, you who love one another!"

As Rabbi Abba has said:
"All those Comrades who do not love one another
pass away from the world before their time.
All the Comrades in the days of Rabbi Shim'on
shared a vital, spiritual love.
That is why Torah was revealed in the generation of Rabbi
    Shim'on."

As Rabbi Shim'on used to say:
"All Comrades who do not love one another
divert [themselves] from the straight path.
Moreover, they produce a defect in her!
For Torah embodies love, friendship, and truth:
Abraham loves Isaac; Isaac, Abraham;

they embrace one another.
Jacob is held by both of them in brotherhood and love.
They offer to one another their spirit, their breath of life!
Comrades must be just like that and not produce a defect!"

Once he saw the sign in their faces and said what he said,
they said to him
"Indeed a spirit of prophecy rests upon the Holy Light,
and so we should have known!"

Rabbi Shim'on cried, and said
"A word of those words whispered to me
from the head of the Academy of the Garden of Eden!
Never spoken openly!
This word is a secret,
but I will tell you, my beloved children,
my children, beloved of my soul.
What can I do?
They said it to me in a whisper, but I will say it openly!
And when the time comes that we see face to face,
all faces will be in agreement.

My children,
the sin committed by the mixed multitude, the outsiders,
the sin in which the holy people joined,
was a sin against Mother,
as it is written:
'Rise, make us *Elohim!*'
the real *Elohim*, the Glory of Israel,
the one who hovers over them like a mother over her children.
This is the secret of what is written:
'They exchanged their Glory for the image of a bull'
(Psalms 106:20).
This means the Glory of Israel, their Mother;
and therefore it is written:
'Glory has gone into exile'
(1 Samuel 4:22),
for they drew *Shekhinah* into exile along with them.
So 'they exchanged their Glory.'
For what? 'For the image of a bull.'

Here is the secret of the word:
Come and see!
Below, within the dregs of wine, the evil dregs,
there emerges an agitator, an accuser, the primordial demon.
He is disguised in the form of a man when he approaches the holy
    place.
As soon as he moves on from there, eager to come down below,
he must clothe himself in a garment to victimize the world.
Then he swoops down with his chariots.
The first garment that he seizes is 'the image of a bull,'
the form of a bull. . . .

That is why Mother was not there;
it would not have been right for Her to be there.
But since Father knew the compassion of Mother and Her loving
    ways,
He said to Moses—

  Oh, my beloved children,
  the design of them both is always for this!
  This is what they whispered to me in a whispering,
  for it is not meant to be revealed,
  so that the son will not know and see that the lash is poised
  and be always afraid.
  But both of them share this design, one design. . . .

So, my beloved children,
since they desired *Elohim*
and the work was constructed on the verge of *Elohim*,
Holy *Elohim*,
  Mother, who always grasps the arm of the King
  and suspends the lash,
was not there.
Moses had to take Her place.
As soon as the Blessed Holy One penetrated him, he saw clearly.
Three times he penetrated him!
O Moses, Faithful Shepherd!
How mighty is your strength, how great is your power.
Three times He penetrated you!
As it is written:

ZOHAR

'Now leave Me alone!'
that is one.
'My anger will blaze against them and I will consume them,'
that is two.
'And I will make you into a great nation!'
that is three.
The wisdom of Moses was in these three points.
He grasped His right arm in response to: 'Leave Me alone!'
He grasped His left arm in response to:
'My anger will blaze against them and I will consume them.'
He embraced the body of the King in response to:
'I will make you into a great nation!'
Having embraced the body, both arms on this side and that,
He could not move to any side at all!
This was the wisdom of Moses:
he knew the various points of the King,
where to be firm on each one.
He acted in wisdom!"

Rabbi El'azar and the Comrades came and kissed his hands.
Rabbi Abba was there, and he said
"If we have come into the world only to hear this,
it is enough for us!"
Then he cried, and said
"Woe unto us, Rabbi, when you depart from the world!
Who will illumine and reveal the lights of Torah?
This word was hidden in darkness until now.
Suddenly it has emerged and shines up to the loft of the sky
and is engraved on the throne of the King.
The Blessed Holy One is rejoicing now in this word.
Joy is added to joy in the presence of the Holy King!
Who will awaken words of wisdom in this world as you do?"

ZOHAR ON LEVITICUS, NUMBERS, AND DEUTERONOMY

QORBAN AND *OLAH*,
DRAWING NEAR AND ASCENDING

He called to Moses.
YHVH spoke to him from the Tent of Meeting, saying:
"Speak to the Children of Israel and say to them:
When any of you brings qorban *to YHVH . . ."*

(Leviticus 1:1–2)

Rabbi Hizkiyah was in the presence of Rabbi Shim'on.
He said to him
"That which is called *qorban*—
it should be called *qeiruv*, drawing near,
or *qereivut*, nearness.
Why *qorban*?"

Rabbi Shim'on replied
"This is well-known to the Comrades!
Qorban, their drawing near,
the drawing near of those holy crowns,
drawing near to one another, connecting with each other,
until all turn into one, complete oneness,
to perfect the Holy Name,
as it is written: '*qorban* to *YHVH.*'
The drawing near of those holy crowns is to *YHVH*
so that the Holy Name be perfected and united,
so that compassion fill all the worlds
and the Holy Name be crowned with its crowns
and everything be sweetened.

All this is intended to arouse Compassion,
not to arouse Judgment.
Therefore 'to *YHVH*,'
not 'to *Elohim.*'
'To *YHVH*'

ZOHAR

We must arouse Compassion!
Not 'to *Elohim*'
We need Compassion, not Judgment!"

Rabbi Ḥizkiyah said
"I am so happy that I asked and gained these words!
This is the clarity of the word!"

ZOHAR

YHVH *spoke to Moses, saying:*
"Enjoin Aaron and his sons, saying:
This is the torah *of the* olah ..."
                    (Leviticus 6:1–2)

Rabbi El'azar asked Rabbi Shim'on, his father,
"The bond of *olah*, bound to the Holy of Holies,
lighting up the joining of desire
of priests, Levites, and Israel up above—
how high does it ascend?"

He replied
"We have already established this: to Infinity.
For all binding and union and wholeness
are secreted in the secrecy
that cannot be grasped and cannot be known,
that includes the desire of all desires.

Infinity does not abide being known,
does not produce end or beginning.
Primordial Nothingness brought forth Beginning and End.
Who is Beginning?
The highest point, beginning of all,
the concealed one abiding in thought.
And It produces End, 'the end of the matter.'
But there, no end.
No desires, no lights, no sparks in that Infinity.
All these lights and sparks are dependent on It
but cannot comprehend.
The only one who knows, yet without knowing,
is the highest desire, concealed of all concealed, Nothingness.
And when the highest point and the world that is coming ascend,
they know only the aroma,
as one inhaling an aroma is sweetened."

147

GUESTS IN THE *SUKKAH*

YHVH *spoke to Moses, saying:*
"Speak to the Children of Israel, saying:
On the fifteenth day of this seventh month
the Festival of Sukkot, *seven days for* YHVH. . . .
When you have gathered in the yield of the land
celebrate the Festival of YHVH *seven days:*
a complete rest on the first day
and a complete rest on the eighth day.
On the first day take fruit of lovely trees,
branches of palm trees, boughs of leafy trees
and willows of the brook.
Rejoice in the presence of YHVH *your God seven days.*
Celebrate it, a festival to YHVH, *seven days a year.*
An eternal decree throughout the generations:
celebrate it in the seventh month.
Seven days dwell in sukkot;
every citizen in Israel shall dwell in sukkot,
so that your generations may know
that I lodged the Children of Israel in sukkot
when I brought them out of the land of Egypt,
I, YHVH *your God."*
(Leviticus 23:33–34, 39–43)

Rabbi El'azar opened
" 'Thus says *YHVH:*
"I remember the devotion of your youth,
your love as a bride
how you followed Me in the wilderness, in a land unsown" '
(Jeremiah 2:2).

This verse refers to the Communion of Israel
when She was walking in the wilderness along with Israel.
'I remember the devotion'
This is the cloud of Aaron

ZOHAR

which floated along with five others,
all bound to You, shining on You.
'Your love as a bride'
They decorated, crowned, and arrayed You
like a bride bedecked with jewels.
Why all this?
Because 'You followed Me in the wilderness, in a land unsown.'

Come and see:
When one sits in this dwelling, the shade of faith,
Shekhinah spreads Her wings over him from above,
Abraham and five other righteous heroes come to dwell with him!"

Rabbi Abba said
"Abraham, five righteous heroes, and King David dwell with him!
As it is written:
'Seven Days dwell in *sukkot.*'
'Seven days' it says, not 'For seven days.'
Similarly it is written:
'Six Days *YHVH* made heaven . . .'
(Exodus 31:17).
Day after day, one should rejoice with a radiant face
along with these guests who abide with him."

And Rabbi Abba said
"It is written: 'Seven days dwell in *sukkot*';
then, 'shall dwell in *sukkot.*'
First, 'dwell'; then, 'shall dwell.'
The first is for the guests;
the second, for human beings.

The first is for the guests:
as Rav Hamnuna Sava, upon entering the *sukkah,*
used to stand in joy inside the opening and say:
'Let us invite the guests!'
He would set the table, stand erect, recite a blessing
and then say:
'Seven Days, dwell in *sukkot!*
Sit down, sublime guests, have a seat!
Sit down, guests of faith, have a seat!'

149

ZOHAR

Raising his hands in joy, he would say:
'Happy is our portion!
Happy is the portion of Israel!
As it is written:
"The portion of *YHVH* is His people"'
(Deuteronomy 32:9).
Then he would sit down.

The second, for human beings:
One who has a portion among the holy people and in the holy land
sits in the shade of faith to welcome the guests,
to rejoice in this world and the world that is coming.
Nevertheless, he must make the poor happy.
Why?
Because the portion of those guests whom he has invited
belongs to the poor.
One who sits in this shade of faith
and invites these sublime guests, guests of faith,
and does not give them their portion—
all of them rise to leave, saying:
'Do not eat the food of a stingy person ...'
(Proverbs 23:6).
It turns out that the table he set is his own, not divine.
Of him it is written:
'I will spread dung upon your faces,
the dung of your festal offerings'
(Malachi 2:3),
'your festal offerings,' not Mine!
Woe to that human being
when these guests of faith rise to leave his table!"

And Rabbi Abba said
"All the days of his life, Abraham used to stand at the crossroads
to invite guests and set a table for them.
Now that he is invited
along with all those righteous heroes and King David too,
and they are not given their portion,
Abraham rises from the table and calls out:
'Move away from the tents of these wicked people!'
(Numbers 16:26).

ZOHAR

All of them get up to leave.
Isaac says, 'The belly of the wicked will feel want'
(Proverbs 13:25).
Jacob says, 'After eating your morsel, you will vomit it up!'
(Proverbs 23:8).
All the other righteous heroes say
'All tables are covered with vomit and filth;
there is no place!'
(Isaiah 28:8)...."

Rabbi El'azar said
"Torah does not demand of a person more than he can do,
as it is written:
'Each according to what he can give ...'
(Deuteronomy 16:17).
But a person should not say:
'First, I will fill myself with food and drink;
what is left I will give to the poor.'
No, the prime portion belongs to the guests.
If he makes the guests happy and full,
the Blessed Holy One rejoices with him!
Abraham calls out: 'Then you will delight in *YHVH*!'
(Isaiah 58:14).
Isaac calls out: 'No weapon formed against you will succeed!'
(Isaiah 54:17)."

Rabbi Shim'on interrupted,
"This verse is said by King David,
because all weapons of the King and battles of the King
have been handed over to David.
What Isaac says is: 'His seed will be powerful on earth! ...
Wealth and riches in his house! ...'
(Psalms 112:2–3).
Jacob says, 'Then your light will burst through like the dawn! ...'
(Isaiah 58:8).
The other righteous heroes say
'*YHVH* will guide you always and satisfy ...'
(Isaiah 58:11).
King David says, 'No weapon formed against you will succeed!'
For he has been appointed over all weapons of the world.

ZOHAR

Happy is the portion of the human being who attains all this!
Happy is the portion of the righteous
in this world and the world that is coming!
Of them it is written:
'Your people, all of them are righteous! . . .' "

GOD, ISRAEL, AND *SHEKHINAH*

"If you follow My decrees
and observe My commands and carry them out . . .
I will place My mishkan *in your midst*
and My soul will not abhor you.
I will move about in your midst:
I will be your God, and you will be My people. . . .

But if you spurn My decrees,
and if your soul abhors My judgments,
so that you do not carry out My commands,
so that you break My covenant . . .
I will set My face against you:
you will be routed by your enemies
and your foes will dominate you.
You will flee though none pursues.
And if, for all that, you do not obey Me,
I will discipline you more, seven for your sins . . .
I will discipline you Myself, seven for your sins . . .
and I will scatter you among the nations. . . .

Yet even at this point,
when they are in the land of their enemies,
I will not spurn them or abhor them so as to destroy them,
breaking My covenant with them,
for I am YHVH, their God."

                                              (Leviticus 26, passim)

"I will place My *mishkan* in your midst . . ."
My *mishkan* is *Shekhinah*,
My *mishkan* is My *mashkon*,
My dwelling is My pledge,
who has been seized on account of Israel's sins.

153

ZOHAR

"I will place My *mishkan*"
My *mashkon*, literally Mine!
A parable:
One person loved another, and said
"My love for you is so high I want to live with you!"
The other said, "How can I be sure that you will stay with me?"
So he took all his most precious belongings
and brought them to the other, saying
"Here is a pledge to you that I will never part from you."

So, the Blessed Holy One desired to dwell with Israel.
What did He do?
He took His most precious possession
and brought it down to them, saying
"Israel, now you have My pledge; so I will never part from you."

Even though the Blessed Holy One has removed Himself from us,
He has left a pledge in our hands,
and we guard that treasure of His.
If He wants His pledge, let Him come and dwell among us!

So "I will place My *mishkan* in your midst"
means "I will deposit a *mashkon* in your hands
to ensure that I will dwell with you."
Even though Israel is now in exile,
the pledge of the Blessed Holy One is with them,
and they have never forsaken it.

"And My soul will not abhor you."
A parable:
One person loved his friend and wanted to live together.
What did he do?
He took his bed and brought it to his friend's house.
He said, "My bed is now in your house,
so I will not go far from you or your bed or your things."

So, the Blessed Holy One said
"I will place My Dwelling in your midst
and My soul will not abhor you.

154

Here, My Bed is in your house!
Since My Bed is with you, you know I will not leave you:
My soul will not abhor you."

"I will move about in your midst: I will be your God."
Since My Dwelling is with you,
you can be certain that I will go with you,
as it is written:
"For *YHVH* your God moves about in your camp
to deliver you and deliver your enemies to you:
let your camp be holy"
(Deuteronomy 23:15).

One night, Rabbi Isaac and Rabbi Judah
were staying in a village near the Sea of Tiberias.
They rose at midnight.
Rabbi Isaac said to Rabbi Judah, "Let us converse in words of Torah,
for even though we are in this place,
we must not separate ourselves from the Tree of Life."

Rabbi Judah opened and said
" 'Moses took the Tent and pitched it outside the camp . . .'
(Exodus 33:7).
Why?
Moses said to himself,
'Since Israel has dealt falsely with the Blessed Holy One
and exchanged His Glory,
let His pledge be placed in the hands of a trustee
until we see with whom it remains.'
So he said to Joshua,
'You will be the trustee between the Blessed Holy One and Israel.
The pledge will remain in your trust
and we will see with whom it remains.'
What is written?
'And he [Moses] returned to the camp,
but his attendant, Joshua the son of Nun, a youth,
did not stir out of the Tent'
(Exodus 33:11).
Why Joshua?
Because he was to Moses as the moon is to the sun.

155

ZOHAR

He was worthy to guard the pledge;
so he 'did not stir out of the Tent.'

The Blessed Holy One said to Moses,
'Moses, this is not right!
I have given My pledge to them!
Even though they have sinned against Me,
the pledge must remain with them so that I will not leave them.
Do you want Me to depart from Israel and never return?
Return My pledge to them,
and for its sake I will not abandon them, wherever they are.'

Even though Israel has sinned against God,
they have not abandoned this pledge of His,
and the Blessed Holy One has not taken it from them.
So wherever Israel goes in exile, *Shekhinah* is with them.
Therefore it is written: 'I will place My *mishkan* in your midst.'
This has been established."

Rabbi Isaac opened and said
" 'My beloved is like a gazelle, like a young deer.
There he stands behind our wall,
gazing through the windows, peering through the holes'
(Song of Songs 2:9).

Happy are Israel!
They are privileged to hold this pledge of the Supreme King!
For even though they are in exile,
every new moon and Sabbath and festival
the Blessed Holy One comes to watch over them
and to gaze at His pledge which is with them, His treasure.
A parable:
There was a king whose queen offended him.
He expelled her from the palace.
What did she do?
She took his son, his precious beloved.
Since the king was fond of her, he let him go with her.
When the king began to yearn for the queen and her son
he climbed up on roofs, ran down stairs, scaled walls;
he peered through the holes in the walls just to see them!

ZOHAR

When he caught a glimpse of them
he started to cry from behind the wall.
Then he went away.

So, with Israel:
Even though they have left the palace of the King,
they have not abandoned that pledge.
And since the King loves them, He has left it with them.
When the Holy King begins to yearn for the Queen and for Israel
He climbs up on roofs, runs down stairs, scales walls;
He peers through the holes in the walls just to see them!
When He catches a glimpse of them, He starts to cry.
As it is written:
'My beloved is like a gazelle, like a young deer,'
jumping from wall to roof, from roof to wall.
'There he stands behind our wall'
in the synagogues and houses of study.
'Gazing through the windows,'
for indeed, a synagogue must have windows.
'Peering through the holes'
to look at them, to look after them.

Therefore Israel should rejoice on that day,
for they know this, and they say:
'This is the day *YHVH* has made—
let us rejoice and be happy!'
(Psalms 118:24)."

"But if you spurn My decrees ..."
Rabbi Yose opened
" 'My son, do not spurn the discipline of *YHVH*,
do not dread His correction'
(Proverbs 3:11).
How beloved are Israel to the Blessed Holy One!
He wants to correct them and guide them in a straight path
like a father who loves his son:
because of his love for him, there is always a rod in his hand
to guide him in a straight path
so that he will not stray to the right or the left;
as it is written:

157

ZOHAR

'*YHVH* corrects the one whom He loves;
as a father, the son he delights in'
(Proverbs 3:12).

One who is not loved by the Blessed Holy One,
one who is hated by Him—
the correction is removed from him, the rod is removed.
It is written:
'I have loved you, says *YHVH* . . .'
(Malachi 1:2).
Because of His love, there is always a rod in His hand to guide him.
'But Esau I hated'
(Malachi 1:3);
so I removed the rod from him, removed the correction,
so as not to share Myself with him.
He is far from My soul,
but as for you, 'I have loved you!'

Therefore, 'My son, do not spurn the discipline of *YHVH*,
do not dread His correction.'
What does this mean: 'do not dread'?
Do not bristle from it, like one who flees from thorns,
for those things are like thorns in the flesh.

Come and see:
When Justice is aroused with Her powers
flashing forces arise on the right and on the left.
Many shafts fly forth from them:
shafts of fire, shafts of coal, shafts of flame!
They materialize to strike at human beings.
Under them are other deputies,
sparklers charged with forty-minus-one.
They hover and swoop down, strike and dart up.
Empowered, they enter the Hollow of the Great Abyss.
Here their sparks are dyed red;
a blazing fire is fused to them.
Embers explode,
flying, falling, befalling human beings!
Just as it is written:
'I will discipline you more!'

ZOHAR

I will give something more to the Masters of Judgment
over and above their claim!
Whereas after the Flood, God said:
'I shall not doom the world any more because of humankind'
(Genesis 8:21).
What does this mean: 'any more'?
I will not give more to the Masters of Judgment
lest they destroy the world,
but only as much as the world can endure.
So 'I will discipline you more' means 'I will give them more.'
Why more?
To discipline you 'seven for your sins.'
Seven?
But if the Blessed Holy One collected His due,
the world could not endure for even a moment,
as it is written:
'If you kept account of sins, *YH YHVH*, who would survive?'
(Psalms 130:3).
How can you say: 'seven for your sins'?
Rather, what does 'seven' mean?
Seven is confronting you!
Who is She?
Release, who is seven, and called Seven,
as it is said:
'At the end of seven years enact a release'
(Deuteronomy 15:1).
Therefore 'Seven for your sins'. . . ."

Rabbi Abba said
" 'I will discipline you Myself, seven for your sins.'
I disciplined you through other deputies,
as has been established.
'Myself'
Now I will confront you!
Seven will be aroused against you!

Come and see the pure love of the Blessed Holy One for Israel.
A parable:
There was a king who had a single son who kept misbehaving.
One day he offended the king.

159

ZOHAR

The king said, 'I have punished you so many times
and you have not received.
Now look, what should I do with you?
If I banish you from the land and expel you from the kingdom,
perhaps wild beasts or wolves or robbers will attack you
and you will be no more.
What can I do?
The only solution is that I and you together leave the land!'

So, 'Myself': I and you together will leave the land!
The Blessed Holy One said as follows:
'Israel, what should I do with you?
I have already punished you, and you have not heeded Me.
I have brought fearsome warriors and flaming forces to strike at you
and you have not obeyed.
If I expel you from the land alone,
I fear that packs of wolves and bears will attack you
and you will be no more.
But what can I do with you?
The only solution is that I and you together leave the land
and both of us go into exile.
As it is written:
"I will discipline you,"
forcing you into exile;
but if you think that I will abandon you—
"Myself" too, along with you!'

'Seven for your sins'
This means Seven, who will be banished along with you.
Why? 'For your sins,'
as it is written:
'For your crimes, your Mother was sent away'
(Isaiah 50:1).
The Blessed Holy One said
'You have made Me homeless as well as yourselves,
for the Queen has left the palace along with you.
Everything is ruined, My palace and yours!
For a palace is worthless to a king unless he can enter with his
        queen.
A king is only happy when he enters the queen's palace

and finds her with her son;
they all rejoice as one.
Now neither the son nor the queen is present;
the palace is totally desolate.
What can I do?
I Myself will be with you!'

So now, even though Israel is in exile,
the Blessed Holy One is with them and has not abandoned them.
And when Israel comes out of exile
the Blessed Holy One will return with them,
as it is written:
'*YHVH* your God will return'
(Deuteronomy 30:3),
He Himself will return!
This has already been said."

Rabbi Ḥiyya and Rabbi Yose were walking on the road.
They happened upon a certain cave in a field. . . .
Rabbi Ḥiyya said
"I have heard a new word said by Rabbi El'azar:
' "I will not spurn them or abhor them so as to destroy them."
The verse should read:
"I will not strike them or kill them so as to destroy them."
But instead we find: "I will not spurn them or abhor them."
Usually, one who is hated by another
is repulsive and utterly abhorrent to him;
but here, "I will not spurn them or abhor them."
Why?
Because My soul's beloved is among them
and because of Her, all of them are beloved to Me,
as it is written:
le-khallotam,
spelled: *le-khalltam,* without the *o.*
Because of Her, "I will not spurn them or abhor them,"
because She is the love of My life.

A parable:
A man loved a woman.
She lived in the tanners' market.

If she were not there, he would never enter the place.
Since she is there, it appears to him as a market of spice-peddlers
with all the world's finest aromas in the air.

Here too:
"Yet even at this point, when they are in the land of their enemies,"
which is a tanners' market,
"I will not spurn them or abhor them."
Why?
Le-khallatam, "Because of their bride,"
for I love Her!
She is the beloved of My soul dwelling there!
It seems filled with all the finest aromas of the world
because of the bride in their midst.' "

Rabbi Yose said
"If I have come here only to hear this word, it is enough for me!"

THRESHING OUT THE SECRETS

It has been told:
Rabbi Shim'on said to the Comrades,
"How long will we sit on a one-legged stand?
It is written:
'Time to act for *YHVH!*
They have violated Your Torah!'
(Psalms 119:126).
The days are few,
the Creditor is pressing,
a herald cries out every day!
The Reapers of the Field are few
and only at the edge of the vineyard!
They do not watch or know where they are going,
as they should.

Assemble, Comrades, at the threshing house,
wearing coats of mail,
with swords and spears in your hands!
Arm yourselves with your array:
Design, Wisdom, Intellect, Knowledge, and Vision,
the power of Hands and Feet.
Enthrone and acknowledge the King
who has the power of life and death,
that words of truth may be ordained,
words followed by high holy ones,
happy to hear them and know them!"

Rabbi Shim'on sat down.
He cried, and said, "Woe if I reveal! Woe if I do not reveal!"

The Comrades were silent.
Rabbi Abba rose and said to him,
"If it pleases the Master to reveal,

it is written:
'The secret of *YHVH* is for those who fear Him'
(Psalms 25:14),
and these Comrades are God-fearing.
They have already crossed the threshold of the Dwelling.
Some have entered; some have emerged."

It has been told:
The Comrades were mustered before Rabbi Shim'on.
Present were: Rabbi El'azar, his son,
Rabbi Abba, Rabbi Judah, Rabbi Yose son of Jacob,
Rabbi Isaac, Rabbi Hizkiyah son of Rav,
Rabbi Hiyya, Rabbi Yose, Rabbi Yeisa.
Giving hands to Rabbi Shim'on, raising fingers above,
they entered the field and amidst the trees sat down.

Rabbi Shim'on rose and prayed his prayer.
He sat down among them, and said
"Let everyone place his hands on my breast."
They placed their hands, and he took them.
He opened and said
" 'Cursed be the one who makes a carved or molten image,
the work of the hands of an artisan,
and sets it up in secret!' "
(Deuteronomy 27:15).
They all responded, "Amen!"

Rabbi Shim'on opened and said
" 'Time to act for *YHVH!*'
Why is it time to act for *YHVH?*
Because 'they have violated Your Torah!'
What does this mean?
The Torah up above is nullified
if this Name is not arrayed perfectly.
The verse is addressed to the Ancient of Days.

It is written:
'O happy Israel! Who is like you?'
(Deuteronomy 33:29),
and it is written:

ZOHAR

'Who is like You among the gods, *YHVH?*'
(Exodus 15:11)."

He called Rabbi El'azar, his son, and sat him in front
and Rabbi Abba on the other side.
He said, "We are the sum of the whole!
Now the pillars stand firm!"

They were silent.
They heard a sound, and their knees knocked, one against the other.
What sound?
The sound of the Assembly on High assembling.

Rabbi Shim'on rejoiced, and said
" '*YHVH,* I heard of You; I was afraid!'
(Habakuk 3:2).
There it was right to be afraid;
for us the word depends on love,
as it is written:
'Love your neighbor as yourself,'
'Love *YHVH* your God,'
'Because *YHVH* loved you,'
'I have loved you.' . . .

It has been told:
When the desire arose in the Will of the White Head
to manifest Its Glory,
It arrayed, prepared, and generated from the Blinding Flash
one spark, radiating in 370 directions.
The spark stood still.
A pure aura emerged whirling and breathed upon the spark.
The spark congealed
and one hard skull emerged, emanating to four sides.
Surrounded by this pure aura, the spark was contained and absorbed.
Completely absorbed, you think?
No, secreted within.
That is how this skull emanated to its sides.
This aura is the secret of secrets of the Ancient of Days.
Through the breath hidden in this skull
fire emanated on one side, and air on the other,

with the pure aura standing over this side
and pure fire over the other.
What is fire doing here?
It is not fire,
but the spark surrounded by the pure aura illuminates 270 worlds,
and from its side, Judgment comes into being.
That is why this skull is called the Hard Skull.

Inside this skull lie ninety million worlds
moving with it, relying upon it.
Into this skull trickles dew from the White Head,
constantly overflowing.
From this dew shaken from Its Head
the dead are destined to come to life.
It is a dew composed of two colors:
from the aspect of the White Head
it is imbued with a white embracing all whites,
but when it settles upon the Head of the Impatient One
red appears.
Like this crystal that is white:
the color red appears within the color white.
Therefore it is written:
'Many of those who sleep in the dust of the earth will awake;
these to eternal life, those to shame and eternal horror!'
(Daniel 12:2).
'To eternal life'
because they deserve the white
that comes from the aspect of the Ancient of Days, the Patient One.
'To shame and eternal horror'
because they deserve the red of the Impatient One.
All is contained in that dew,
as it is written:
'Your dew is a dew of lights'
(Isaiah 26:19);
'lights,' two of them!
That dew that trickles
trickles every day to the Apple Orchard, colored white and red.

This skull lights up in two colors, on this side and that.
From this pure aura

one-and-a-half million worlds emanate through the skull to His face.
That is why He is called the Impatient One.
When necessary, His face expands and becomes long-suffering,
for then He is gazing into the Face of the Ancient of Ancients
and He feels compassion for the world. . . ."

It has been told:
Before they left that threshing place
Rabbi Yose son of Jacob, Rabbi Hizkiyah, and Rabbi Yeisa died.
The Comrades saw holy angels carrying them off in a canopy.
Rabbi Shim'on said a word, and they settled down.
He cried, and said, "Perhaps, God forbid,
a decree has been issued for us to be punished
because through us has been revealed
something not revealed since the day Moses stood on Mt. Sinai,
as it is written:
'He was there with *YHVH* forty days and forty nights . . .'"
(Exodus 34:28).
What am I doing here?
Were they punished because of this?"

He heard a voice:
"Happy are you, Rabbi Shim'on! Happy is your portion!
Happy are the Comrades who stand with you!
For something not revealed to all the powers above
has been revealed to you!
But come and see what is written:
'At the cost of his firstborn, he shall lay its foundations;
at the cost of his youngest, he shall set up its gates'
(Joshua 6:26).
All the more so,
for by intense desire, their souls joined the Divine
the moment they were taken.
Happy is their portion! They rose in perfection!"

It has been told:
While the words were being revealed,
those above and those below were shaken
and a voice stirred through 250 worlds,
for ancient words were being revealed below!

ZOHAR

While the souls of these ones were being sweetened with those
    words,
their souls departed by a kiss and were bound in that canopy.
The angels took them away and lifted them above.
Why these ones?
Because on a previous occasion they had entered and not emerged.
All the others had entered and emerged.

Rabbi Shim'on said
"How happy is the portion of these three!
Happy is our portion in the world that is coming, because of this!"

The voice resounded:
"You who cleave to *YHVH* your God are alive, every one of you,
    today!"
(Deuteronomy 4:4).

They rose and walked on.
Wherever they looked, aromas arose.
Rabbi Shim'on said
"This proves that the world is being blessed because of us!"
Everyone's face shone, and human beings could not look at them!

It has been told:
Ten entered; seven emerged.
Rabbi Shim'on was happy; Rabbi Abba was sad.
One day Rabbi Shim'on was sitting, and Rabbi Abba was with him.
Rabbi Shim'on said a word, and they saw these three.
Angels were carrying them gloriously,
showing them treasures and threshing houses in the sky,
bringing them to mountains of pure balsam!
Rabbi Abba's mind was eased.

It has been told:
From that day on
the Comrades did not leave the house of Rabbi Shim'on.
When Rabbi Shim'on revealed secrets, only they were present.
Rabbi Shim'on called out to them:
"The seven of us are the eyes of *YHVH*,
as it is written:

ZOHAR

'These seven are the eyes of *YHVH*'
(Zechariah 4:10).
This verse was said for us!"

Rabbi Abba said
"We are six lights shining from the seventh.
You are the seventh of all!
The six exist only because of the seventh.
All depends on the seventh!"

Rabbi Judah called him "Sabbath,
source of blessing for all six,
as it is written:
'Sabbath for *YHVH*,' 'Holy to *YHVH*.'
Just as Sabbath is holy to *YHVH*,
so Rabbi Shim'on is Sabbath, holy to *YHVH!*"

THE RABBIS ENCOUNTER A CHILD

Rabbi Isaac and Rabbi Judah were out on the road.
They reached the village of Sikhnin
and stayed there with a woman who had one little son
who went to school every day.
That day he left school and came home.
He saw these wise men.
His mother said to him, "Approach these distinguished men;
you will gain blessings from them!"
He approached them and suddenly turned back.
He said to his mother, "I don't want to go near them
because they haven't recited *Shema* today,
and I have been taught:
'Anyone who has not recited *Shema* at its proper time
is under a ban that entire day.'"

They heard this and were amazed.
Raising their hands, they blessed him.
They said, "Indeed, it is so!
Today we were engaged with a bride and groom
who did not have what they needed and were delaying their union.
There was no one to engage in helping them,
so we engaged, and we did not recite *Shema* at its proper time.
One who is busy doing a *mizvah* is exempt from another *mizvah*."
Then they said, "My son, how did you know?"

He said, "I knew by the smell of your clothes when I came near
    you."
They were amazed.
They sat down, washed their hands, and broke bread.
Rabbi Judah's hands were dirty, and he blessed before he washed.
The boy said to them, "If you are students of Rabbi Shema'yah the
    Hasid
you should not have blessed with filthy hands.
One who blesses with filthy hands should be put to death!"

ZOHAR

The child opened and said
" 'When they enter the Tent of Meeting
they shall wash with water so they will not die . . .'
(Exodus 30:20).
We learn from this verse that one who is not careful
and appears in the presence of the King with filthy hands
should be put to death.
Why?
Because the hands of a human being inhabit the height of the world.

There is one finger on the human hand: the finger that Moses raised.
It is written:
'You shall make bars of acacia wood:
five for the planks of one side of the Dwelling,
five for the planks of the other side of the Dwelling.'
And it is written:
'The center bar in the middle of the planks shall run from end to
    end'
(Exodus 26:26–28).
Now you might say that the center bar is another one,
not included in those five.
Not so! That center bar is one of those five.
Two on this side, two on that side, and one in the middle.
This is the Center Bar, Pillar of Jacob, Secret of Moses!
Corresponding to this are the five fingers on the human hand.
The center bar is in the middle, greatest and highest of all.
All the others exist through it.
Those five bars are the five hundred years
through which the Tree of Life extends.
The Holy Covenant is aroused by the five fingers of the hand.
It is a secret word that I have spoken!

That is why all the blessings of the priest depend on the fingers.
Moses' hand was spread out because of this.
If they embody all this,
doesn't it follow that they must be clean
when with them one blesses the Blessed Holy One?
For by them and their paradigm, the Holy Name is blessed!
You who are so wise, how could you be so careless?
Didn't you serve Rabbi Shema'yah the *Hasid*?

171

ZOHAR

He himself said: 'All filth and all dirt heighten the Other Side,
for the Other Side feeds on filth and dirt.'
That is why washing after a meal is compulsory, a compulsory
    offering!"

They were amazed and could not speak.
Rabbi Judah said, "My son, what is the name of your father?"
The child was silent for a moment.
He rose and went over to his mother and kissed her.
He said, "Mother, these wise men have asked me about father.
Should I tell them?"
His mother said, "My son, have you tested them?"
He said, "I've tested them and found them lacking!"
His mother whispered to him, and he returned to them.
He said, "You have asked about father.
He has departed from the world,
but whenever holy devotees are walking on the road
he appears as a donkey driver behind them.
If you are so high and holy, how could you have missed him
following you as a donkey driver?
Ah, but right from the start I saw who you were,
and now I see through you!
For father never sees a donkey and fails to goad it from behind
so he can share the yoke of Torah.
Since you weren't worthy enough for father to follow you,
I won't say who father is!"

Rabbi Judah said to Rabbi Isaac,
"It seems that this child is not a human being!"
They began to eat, and that child spoke words of Torah,
new discoveries of Torah. . . .

Rabbi Judah said, "Happy are we!
Since the day of the world, I have never heard such words!
Just as I said, this is no human being!"

He said to him, "Son, Angel of *YHVH*, His beloved!
What you said before:
'You shall make bars of acacia wood:
five for the planks of one side of the Dwelling,

172

five . . . and five at the rear to the west.'
There are many bars, but only two hands!"

He said to him, "Just as they say:
'From a person's mouth you hear who he is.'
But since you weren't paying attention, I will explain."
He opened and said
" 'One who is wise has his eyes on his head . . .'
(Ecclesiastes 2:14).
Now where are a person's eyes but on his head?
Perhaps on the trunk of his body or on his arm?
Does this distinguish one who is wise from everyone else?
Ah, but the verse means this:
We have learned:
'A person should not walk four cubits with his head uncovered.'
Why?
Because *Shekhinah* rests on his head.
Every wise person has his eyes and his words on his head,
focused on the one who is resting right there!
With his eyes there
he knows that the light kindled on his head needs oil.
For the human body is a wick, and a light is kindled above,
and King Solomon cried out: 'Never let your head lack oil!'
(Ecclesiastes 9:8).
The light on one's head needs oil, the oil of good deeds!
That is why 'One who is wise has his eyes on his head'
and not somewhere else!
You are certainly wise, and *Shekhinah* rests on your heads.
How could you be so careless not to see what is written:
'You shall make bars . . . for the planks of one side of the Dwelling,
five for the planks of the other side of the Dwelling'?
The verse says 'one' and 'the other';
it doesn't say 'third' and 'fourth.'
'One' and 'the other' are the essence of the two sides;
so only these two are enumerated."

They came and kissed him.
Rabbi Judah cried, and said
"Rabbi Shim'on, happy are you! Happy is the generation!

ZOHAR

Because of you
even little schoolchildren are towering, invincible rocks!"

His mother came and said to them,
"Masters, please look upon my son only with a good eye!"
They said to her, "Happy are you, worthy woman!
Singled out from among all women!
The Blessed Holy One has selected your portion,
raised your banner above all women of the world!"

The child said, "I am not afraid of the evil eye,
for I am the son of a great and precious fish
and fish do not fear the evil eye,
as it is written:
'They shall multiply like fish in the midst of the earth'
(Genesis 48:16).
This blessing includes protection from the evil eye,
for we have learned:
'Just as fish of the sea are covered by water
and are immune to the evil eye, etc.
[so the descendants of Joseph are immune to the evil eye].'
'In the midst of the earth' indeed!
Among human beings on earth!"

They said, "Son, Angel of *YHVH!*
There is no evil eye in us;
we do not come from the side of the evil eye.
The Blessed Holy One is covering you with His wings!" ...

They kissed him as before and said, "Come, let us bless."
He said, "I will bless
because everything you've heard until now was from me.
I will fulfill the verse:
'One whose eye is generous will be blessed.'
Read it: 'will bless.'
Why?
'Because he gave of his own bread to the needy'
(Proverbs 22:9).
From the bread and food of my Torah you have eaten!"

ZOHAR

Rabbi Judah said, "Son, Beloved of the Blessed Holy One!
We have learned:
'The master of the house breaks bread, and the guest blesses.' "

He said to them,
"I am not master of the house, and you are not guests!
But I have found a verse and I will fulfill it,
for I am truly generous.
Without your asking, I have spoken until now
and you have eaten my bread and my food."

He took the cup of blessing and began to bless.
His hands could not hold the cup; they were trembling.
When he reached "for the land and the food," he said
"I raise the cup of salvation and invoke the Name, *YHVH!*"
(Psalms 116:13).
The cup stood firm and settled in his right hand
and he continued blessing.
At the end he said, "May it be the Will
that life be extended to one of these
from the Tree of Life, on which all life depends!
May the Blessed Holy One be surety for him!
May he find surety below to share his surety with the Holy King!"

Having finished blessing, he closed his eyes for a moment.
Then he opened them and said
"Comrades, *Shalom* to you from the good Lord who possesses all
   Shalom!"
They were amazed, and cried, and blessed him.

They stayed that night.
In the morning they rose early and left.
When they reached Rabbi Shim'on, they told him what had
   happened.
Rabbi Shim'on was amazed.
He said, "He is the son of an invincible rock!
He deserves this and more than any human can imagine!
He is the son of Rav Hamnuna Sava!"

ZOHAR

Rabbi El'azar was excited;
he said, "I must go see that flaming light!"

Rabbi Shim'on said
"This one is not known by any name in the world,
for something sublime is inside him.
It is a secret!
The flowing light of his father shines upon him!
This secret has not spread among the Comrades."

MIRACLES

Rabbi Pinhas was going to see his daughter,
the wife of Rabbi Shim'on, who was ill.
Comrades were accompanying him, and he was riding on his donkey.
On the way he met two Arabs.
He said to them, "Since days of old has a voice arisen in this field?"
They said, "We don't know about days of old;
we know about our own days!
One day highway robbers were passing through that field.
They ran into some Jews and were just about to rob them
when from a distance, in this field,
this donkey's voice was heard braying two times;
a flame of fire shot through its voice and burned them
and those Jews were saved!"

He said to them, "O Arabs!
For telling me this, you will be saved today from other robbers
who are lying in wait for you on the way!"

Rabbi Pinhas cried, and said, "Master of the world!
You brought about this miracle for my sake
and those Jews were saved, and I did not even know!"

He opened and said
" 'To the One who performs great wonders alone,
for His love is everlasting'
(Psalms 136:4).
So much goodness the Blessed Holy One performs for human beings!
So many miracles He brings about for them every day!
And no one knows except for Him!
A person gets up in the morning, and a snake comes to kill him.
He steps on the snake's head and kills it without knowing;
only the Blessed Holy One knows,
'the One who performs great wonders alone.'

ZOHAR

A person is walking on the road,
and robbers are lying in wait to kill him.
Someone else comes along and is given as ransom
and he is saved
without knowing the goodness performed for him by the Blessed
    Holy One,
the miracle brought about by Him!
Only He knows, 'the One who performs great wonders alone.'
Alone He performs and knows, and no one else knows!"

He said to the Comrades,
"Comrades, what I was asking these Arabs, who are always in the
    fields,
was if they had heard the voice of the Comrades who engage in
    Torah.
For Rabbi Shim'on and Rabbi El'azar, his son, and the other
    Comrades
are ahead of us and do not know that we are here.
So I asked these Arabs about them,
for I know that the voice of Rabbi Shim'on
makes fields and mountains quake!
But they revealed to me something I never knew!"

As they were leaving, those Arabs came back and said
"Old man! Old man!
You asked us about days of old and not about today!
Today we saw wonder of wonders!
We saw five men sitting and one old man among them.
We saw birds gathering and spreading their wings over them.
While some flew away, others flew back;
so the shade over their heads never disappeared.
That old man raised his voice, and they obeyed!"

Rabbi Pinḥas said, "That is what I was asking about!
Arabs, Arabs, be on your way
and may the way be paved for you with everything you desire!
You have told me two things over which I rejoice."
They departed.
The Comrades said to him, "How will we know where Rabbi
    Shim'on is?"

ZOHAR

He said, "Leave it to the Master of the steps of my animal!
He will guide its steps there."
With no prodding, his donkey turned aside from the road
and walked one mile.
It brayed three times.
Rabbi Pinhas dismounted and said to the Comrades,
"Let us prepare ourselves to receive the Countenance of Days,
for the Great Face and the Small Face are about to appear!"

Rabbi Shim'on heard the braying of the donkey.
He said to the Comrades, "Let us rise,
for the voice of the donkey of the old *Hasid*
has been aroused toward us!"
Rabbi Shim'on rose and the Comrades rose. . . .
They saw Rabbi Pinhas coming and went up to him.
Rabbi Pinhas kissed Rabbi Shim'on.
He said, "I have kissed the mouth of *YHVH*,
scented with the spices of His garden!"
They delighted as one and sat down.
As soon as they sat,
all the birds providing shade flew off and scattered.
Rabbi Shim'on turned his head and shouted to them:
"Birds of heaven!
Have you no respect for your Master standing here?"
They stopped and did not go further and did not come closer.
Rabbi Pinhas said, "Tell them to go on their way,
for they are not allowed to come back."
Rabbi Shim'on said
"I know that the Blessed Holy One wants to perform a miracle for
    us!
Birds, birds, go your ways
and tell him who is in charge of you
that at first it was in his power and now it is not.
But I have reserved him for the Day of the Rock,
when a cloud rises between two mighty ones, and they do not join."
The birds scattered and flew away.

Meanwhile
three trees were spreading their branches over them in three
    directions;

179

a spring of water was gushing in front of them.
All the Comrades rejoiced;
Rabbi Pinhas and Rabbi Shim'on rejoiced.

Rabbi Pinhas said
"It was so much trouble for those birds at first!
We do not want to trouble living creatures,
for 'His compassion is upon all His works'
(Psalms 145:9)."
Rabbi Shim'on said, "I did not trouble them;
but if the Blessed Holy One is kind to us
we cannot reject His gifts!"
They sat down under that tree,
drank from the water, and enjoyed themselves.

Rabbi Pinhas opened and said
" 'A spring of gardens,
a well of living water,
flows from Lebanon'
(Song of Songs 4:15).
'A spring of gardens'
Is this the only kind of spring?
There are so many good and precious springs in the world!
Ah, but not all pleasures are the same!
There is a spring gushing forth in the wilderness, in a parched place.
It is a pleasure for one to rest there and drink.
But 'a spring of gardens,' how good and precious!
Such a spring nourishes plants and fruit;
one who draws near enjoys everything:
he enjoys the water, he enjoys the plants, he enjoys the fruit!
Such a spring is crowned with everything!
So many roses and fragrant herbs all around!
How much finer is this spring than all others,
'a well of living water'!

We have established that all this refers to the Communion of Israel.
She is 'a spring of gardens.'
Who are the gardens?
The Blessed Holy One has five gardens in which He delights
and one spring above that waters and drenches them,

secret and hidden;
they all produce abundant fruit.
There is one garden below them;
that garden is guarded round, on every flank.
Beneath this garden are other gardens, bearing fruit of every kind.
This garden turns into a spring, watering them.

'A well of living water'
When the need arises, She becomes a spring;
when the need arises, She becomes a well.
What is the difference?
There is no comparison
between water flowing by itself and water drawn for watering.

'Flows from Lebanon'
What flows?
Five sources issuing from Lebanon above become flows,
for when they turn into a spring, water flows, trickles drop by drop.
Sweet water, pursued by the soul!

So, the Blessed Holy One has brought about a miracle for us
right here with this spring!
For this spring I recite this verse."

THE WEDDING CELEBRATION

It has been told:
On the day that Rabbi Shim'on was to leave the world,
while he was arranging his affairs,
the Comrades assembled at his house.
Present were Rabbi El'azar, his son, Rabbi Abba, and the other
    Comrades.
The house was full.
Rabbi Shim'on raised his eyes and saw that the house was filled.
He cried, and said
"The other time I was ill, Rabbi Pinhas son of Ya'ir was in my
    presence.
I was already selecting my place in Paradise next to Ahiyah of Shiloh
when they extended my life until now!
When I returned, fire was whirling in front of me; it has never gone
    out.
No human has entered without permission.
Now I see that it has gone out, and the house is filled!"

While they were sitting
Rabbi Shim'on opened his eyes and saw what he saw;
fire whirled through the house.
Everyone left;
Rabbi El'azar, his son, and Rabbi Abba remained;
the other Comrades sat outside.
Rabbi Shim'on said to Rabbi El'azar, his son,
"Go out and see if Rabbi Isaac is here,
for I have been surety for him.
Tell him to arrange his affairs and sit by my side.
Happy is his portion!"

Rabbi Shim'on rose and laughed in delight.
He said, "Where are the Comrades?"
Rabbi El'azar rose and brought them in.

ZOHAR

They sat in front of him.
Rabbi Shim'on raised his hands and prayed a prayer.
He rejoiced and said
"Those Comrades who were present at the threshing house
will convene here!"
Everyone left;
Rabbi El'azar, his son, Rabbi Abba, Rabbi Judah,
Rabbi Yose, and Rabbi Ḥiyya remained.
Meanwhile, Rabbi Isaac came in.
Rabbi Shim'on said to him, "Your portion is so fine!
So much joy will be yours today!"

Rabbi Abba sat behind him and Rabbi El'azar in front.
Rabbi Shim'on said, "Now is a time of favor!
I want to enter without shame into the world that is coming.
Holy words, until now unrevealed,
I want to reveal in the presence of *Shekhinah*;
so it will not be said that I left the world deficiently.
Until now they were hidden in my heart
as a password to the world that is coming.
I will arrange you like this:
Rabbi Abba will write; Rabbi El'azar, my son, will repeat;
the other Comrades will meditate within."

Rabbi Abba rose from behind him;
Rabbi El'azar, his son, sat in front.
Rabbi Shim'on said, "Rise, my son,
for someone else will sit in that place."
Rabbi El'azar rose.
Rabbi Shim'on enwrapped himself and sat down.
He opened and said
" 'The dead cannot praise *Yah*,
nor any who go down to Dumah'
(Psalms 115:17).
'The dead cannot praise *Yah*'
the ones who are really dead!
For the Blessed Holy One is alive
and He dwells among the living, not with those called 'dead.'
The verse concludes: 'nor any who go down to Dumah.'
All those who go down to Dumah remain in hell.

It is different with those called 'living,'
for the Blessed Holy One wants them to be honored."

Rabbi Shim'on said
"It is so different now than at the threshing house.
There the Blessed Holy One and His chariots convened.
Now He is accompanied by the righteous from the Garden of Eden!
This did not happen before!
The Blessed Holy One wants the righteous to be honored
more than He wants Himself to be honored!
So it is written concerning Jeroboam.
He offered incense to idols and worshiped them;
yet the Blessed Holy One was patient.
But as soon as he stretched out his hand against Ido the prophet,
his hand dried up,
as it is written: 'His hand dried up. . . .'
(1 Kings 13:4).
Not because he worshiped idols,
but because he threatened Ido the prophet!
Now the Blessed Holy One wants *us* to be honored
and all of them are coming with Him!
Here is Rav Hamnuna Sava
surrounded by seventy of the righteous adorned with crowns,
each one shining from the splendor of the luster
of the Holy Ancient One, Concealed of all Concealed!
He is coming to hear in joy these words I am about to speak."

He was about to sit down when he exclaimed:
"Look! Here is Rabbi Pinḥas son of Ya'ir!
Prepare his place!"
The Comrades trembled;
they got up and moved to the outskirts of the house.
Rabbi El'azar and Rabbi Abba remained with Rabbi Shim'on.

Rabbi Shim'on said
"In the threshing house, we were found to be:
all the Comrades speaking, I among them.
Now I alone will speak;
all are listening to my words, those above and those below.
Happy is my portion this day!"

ZOHAR

Rabbi Shim'on opened and said
" 'I am my Beloved's,
His desire is upon me'
(Song of Songs 7:11).
All the days that I have been bound to this world
I have been bound in a single bond with the Blessed Holy One.
That is why now 'His desire is upon me'!
He and His holy company have come to hear in joy concealed words
and praise for the Holy Ancient One, Concealed of all Concealed!
Separate, separated from all, yet not separate!
For all is attached to It, and It is attached to all.
It is all!
Ancient of all Ancients! Concealed of all Concealed!
Arrayed and not arrayed.
Arrayed in order to sustain all;
not arrayed, for It is not to be found.
When arrayed, It generates nine lights,
flaming from It, from Its array.
Those lights, sparkling, flashing,
radiate, emanate to all sides. . . .

Until now these words were concealed,
for I was scared to reveal;
now they have been revealed!
Yet it is revealed before the Holy Ancient One
that I have not acted for my own honor
nor for the honor of my family
but rather so I will not enter His palace in shame.
Furthermore, I see that the Blessed Holy One
and all these righteous ones approve:
I see all of them rejoicing in this, my wedding celebration!
All of them are invited, in that world, to my wedding celebration!
Happy is my portion!"

Rabbi Abba said
"When the Holy Spark, the High Spark, finished this word
he raised his hands and cried and laughed.
He wanted to reveal one word.
He said, 'I have been troubled by this word all my days
and now they are not giving me permission!'

ZOHAR

Summoning up his courage,
he sat and moved his lips and bowed three times.
No one could look at his place, certainly not at him!
He said, 'Mouth, mouth, you have attained so much!
Your spring has not dried up!
Your spring flows endlessly!
For you we read:
"A river issues from Eden"
(Genesis 2:10),
and it is written:
"Like a spring whose waters do not fail"
(Isaiah 58:11).
Now I avow:
All the days I have been alive, I have yearned to see this day!
Now my desire is crowned with success.
This day itself is crowned!
Now I want to reveal words in the presence of the Blessed Holy
        One;
all those words are adorning my head like a crown!
This day will not miss its mark like the other day,
for this whole day is mine!
I have now begun revealing words
so I will not enter shamefully into the world that is coming.
I have begun! I will speak! . . .

I have seen that all those sparks sparkle from the High Spark,
Hidden of all Hidden!
All are levels of enlightenment.
In the light of each and every level
there is revealed what is revealed.
All those lights are connected:
this light to that light, that light to this light,
one shining into the other,
inseparable, one from the other.

The light of each and every spark,
called Adornments of the King, Crowns of the King—
each one shines into, joins onto
the light within, within,
not separating without.

ZOHAR

So all rises to one level,
all is crowned with one word;
no separating one from the other.
It and Its Name is one.

The light that is revealed is called the Garment of the King.
The light within, within is a concealed light.
In that light dwells the Ineffable One, the Unrevealed.
All those sparks and all those lights
sparkle from the Holy Ancient One,
Concealed of all Concealed, the High Spark.
Upon reflecting,
all those lights emanating—
there is nothing but the High Spark,
hidden and unrevealed! . . .' "

Rabbi Abba said
"Before the Holy Spark finished saying 'life,'
his words subsided.
I was still writing, intending to write more
but I heard nothing.
I did not raise my head:
the light was overwhelming; I could not look.
Then I started trembling.
I heard a voice calling:
'Length of days and years of life . . .'
(Proverbs 3:2).
I heard another voice:
'He asked You for life . . .'
(Psalms 21:5).

All day long, the fire in the house did not go out.
No one reached him; no one could:
light and fire surrounded him!
All day long, I lay on the ground and wailed.
After the fire disappeared
I saw the Holy Spark, Holy of Holies, leaving the world,
enwrapped, lying on his right, his face smiling.

ZOHAR

Rabbi El'azar, his son, rose, took his hands and kissed them.
As for me, I licked the dust from the bottom of his feet.
The Comrades wanted to cry but could not utter a sound.
Finally they let out a cry,
but Rabbi El'azar, his son, fell three times, unable to open his mouth.
Finally he opened and said, 'Father! Father!
Three there were! Turned back into one!
Now the animals will wander off!
Birds are flying away, sinking into the bowels of the Great Sea!
All the Comrades are drinking blood!' "

Rabbi Ḥiyya rose to his feet and said
"Until now the Holy Spark has looked after us;
now is the time to engage in honoring him!"
Rabbi El'azar and Rabbi Abba rose.
They carried him in a truckle made out of a gangplank—
    Who has seen the confusion of the Comrades?—
and the whole house was fragrant.
They lifted him onto his bed;
only Rabbi El'azar and Rabbi Abba attended him.
Truculent stingers and shield-bearing warriors from Sepphoris
came and beset them.
The people of Meron ganged together and shouted,
for they feared he would not be buried there.

After the bed emerged from the house
it rose into the air; fire blazed before it.
They heard a voice:
"Come and enter!
Assemble for the wedding celebration of Rabbi Shim'on!
'He shall come to peace;
they shall rest on their couches'
(Isaiah 57:2)."

As he entered the cave, they heard a voice from inside:
"This is the man who shook the earth, who made kingdoms tremble!
Many open mouths of accusation up in heaven
subside today because of you, Rabbi Shim'on son of Yoḥai!
His Lord prides Himself on him every day!

ZOHAR

Happy is his portion above and below!
Many sublime treasures lie in store for him!
Of him it is said:
'As for you,
go to the end and take your rest;
you will rise for your reward at the end of days.' "

NOTES

FOREWORD & INTRODUCTION

Foreword

1. Literally, *zohar* means "splendor, radiance." In the Zohar the root *zhr* often appears in the context of mystical perception or an enlightened state of being; see Zohar 1:52a–b, 234a (*Tosefta*); 2:2a, 23a–b; 3:202a; cf. Daniel 12:3: "The enlightened will shine like the *zohar* of the sky," cited frequently in the Zohar; Psalms 19:12; Mitchell Dahood, *Psalms* (New York, 1965), 1:121, 124; Efraim Gottlieb, *Meḥqarim be-Sifrut ha-Qabbalah*, pp. 210–1 (hereafter cited as *Meḥqarim*).

Introduction

1. Benjamin Mintz, ed., *Shivḥei ha-Besht* (Tel Aviv, 1961), p. 61; Gershom Scholem, *Major Trends in Jewish Mysticism*, pp. 156–7 (hereafter cited as *Major Trends*).

2. Isaac's diary, *Sefer Divrei ha-Yamim*, is cited in *Sefer ha-Yuḥasin*, written by the astronomer and historian Avraham Zacuto. Zacuto himself believed in the antiquity of the Zohar despite the critical conclusions that could be drawn from the story. For an analysis of the document see Scholem, *Madda'ei ha-Yahadut* 1 (1926): 16–29; idem, *Major Trends*, pp. 190–2; Isaiah Tishby, *Mishnat ha-Zohar* 1:28–33 (Introduction), who includes a corrected text of the citation.

3. On the chanting of Zohar, cf. the remark by the eighteenth-century scholar Moses Hayyim Luzzatto (cited by Tishby, *Mishnat ha-Zohar*, 1:44 (Introduction): "Even if one does not understand, the language is suited to the soul."

4. *Sheqel ha-Qodesh*, ed. A. W. Greenup, p. 3.

5. This MS is described in the catalogue of the Guenzberg collection (no. 771), now in Moscow; see Israel Zinberg, *A History of Jewish Literature*, trans. Bernard Martin, 3:41; Scholem, *Major Trends*, p. 194.

6. On the early stages of Kabbalah see Scholem, *Ursprung und Anfänge der Kabbala* (hereafter cited as *Ursprung*); idem, *Kabbalah*, pp. 8–57.

7. The Hebrew text appears in Scholem, *Major Trends*, pp. 397–8, n. 154. On the role played by Kabbalah in the Maimonidean controversy see idem, *Ursprung*, pp. 357–66; Daniel J. Silver, *Maimonidean Criticism and the Maimonidean Controversy*, pp. 182–98 (hereafter cited as *Maimonidean Criticism*).

8. *Or Zaru'a*, ed. Alexander Altmann, *Qovez al Yad*, n.s. 9 (1980): 249. On the last lines see 1 Samuel 14:29; Isaiah 2:5. On the concept of "Know yourself"

NOTES

see Altmann, *Studies in Religious Philosophy and Mysticism*, pp. 1–40 (hereafter cited as *Studies*).

9. See Scholem, *Major Trends*, p. 183; *Kabbalah*, pp. 217, 432; cf. Zohar 3:23a. The phrase is also employed by Moses' contemporary, Moses of Burgos, who calls the kabbalists "masters of *ha-midrash ha-ne'elam*" (Scholem, *Tarbiz* 5 [1934]: 51).

10. See Scholem, *Kabbalah*, p. 217; *Major Trends*, pp. 181–6; Tishby, *Mishnat ha-Zohar*, 1:18 (Introduction).

11. See above, "Abram, the Soul-Breath." Other passages from the *Midrash ha-Ne'elam* are "After the Flood" and "Moses and the Blazing Bush." See also Zohar 1:135b, where Moses de León adopts Maimonides' allegorization of the feast awaiting the righteous in the hereafter (*Mishneh Torah, Hilkhot Teshuvah* 8:4). For examples of philosophical terminology see Tishby, *Mishnat ha-Zohar*, 1:77 (Introduction).

12. Several earlier mystical writings had been written in artificial Aramaic, e.g., *Shimmusha Rabba* and *Aggadat Rabbi Yehoshu'a ben Levi*.

13. See Scholem, *Kiryat Sefer* 6 (1929–1930): 109–18; idem, *Tarbiz* 3 (1932): 181–3; idem, *Major Trends*, pp. 187–8; Yitzhak Baer, *Toledot ha-Yehudim bi-Sefarad ha-Nozrit* (Tel Aviv, 1959), pp. 508–9. The Zohar occasionally refers to its teachings as "new ancient words" (*millin hadtin attiqin*): Zohar 1:243a; 2:183b; 3:166b, 171b; *Zohar Hadash, Rut*, 85b (*Midrash ha-Ne'elam*).

14. Selections from several of these appear in this volume: "The Old Man and the Beautiful Maiden," "Threshing Out the Secrets," "The Rabbis Encounter a Child," "The Wedding Celebration." For a full description of the various units see Scholem, *Kabbalah*, pp. 214–7. The years 1280–1286 are proposed by Scholem in *Major Trends*, p. 188. Tishby suggests a later dating (*Mishnat ha-Zohar*, 1:105–8 [Introduction]), but the evidence favors Scholem's thesis; see below, and Gottlieb, *Ha-Qabbalah be-Khitvei Rabbenu Bahya ben Asher*, p. 168 (hereafter cited as *Bahya*).

15. Scholem, *Major Trends*, p. 185.

16. See Scholem, *Kabbalah*, p. 234. For a full list of Moses' Hebrew writings see ibid., p. 433; cf. below, Bibliography.

17. At the beginning of *Sheqel ha-Qodesh*, Moses writes: "I composed this composition in the year 5052 after Creation [1291–1292] in the city of Guadalajara."

18. See Tishby, *Mishnat ha-Zohar*, 1:30–1, 35–7, 110–2 (Introduction). The additional volume was later called *Zohar Hadash* ("New Zohar"), a misleading title, since the volume contains much of *Midrash ha-Ne'elam*, the oldest stratum of the Zohar.

19. Scholem, *Major Trends*, pp. 189; 394, n. 124; *Kabbalah*, pp. 236–7. For the attitude of Bahya son of Asher see Gottlieb, *Bahya*, pp. 168–71.

20. *Ra'aya Meheimna* expounds the mystical significance of the command-

NOTES

ments; *Tiqqunei Zohar* is a wide-ranging commentary on the first portion of the Torah; see Scholem, *Kabbalah,* pp. 218–19. No selections from these works are included in this volume since Moses de León is not the author.

21. See my "David ben Yehudah he-Hasid and His *Book of Mirrors,*" *HUCA* 51 (1980): 129–72; and my edition of *The Book of Mirrors: Sefer Mar'ot ha-Zove'ot by R. David ben Yehudah he-Hasid.* For further examples of Zohar imitations see Tishby, *Mishnat ha-Zohar,* 1:39–40 (Introduction).

22. Scholem, *Major Trends,* p. 407, n. 1.

23. Quoted from an unknown kabbalist by Abraham Azulai in his introduction to *Or ha-Hammah.* Cf. Zohar 3:124b (*Ra'aya Meheimna*): "Since Israel is destined to taste the Tree of Life, namely, this *Book of Zohar,* they will come forth from exile by [divine] compassion."

24. On the controversy see Tishby, *Mishnat ha-Zohar* 1:45–6, 108 (Introduction); idem, *Peraqim* 1 (1967–1968): 131–82.

25. On the phenomenon of Christian Kabbalah see Scholem, *Kabbalah,* pp. 198–201, and the bibliography on pp. 209–10.

26. On Modena and the Christian Kabbalah see Tishby, *Mishnat ha-Zohar* 1:47–50 (Introduction).

27. His book is entitled *Hoqer u-Mequbbal* ("Scholar and Kabbalist"); see Tishby, *Mishnat ha-Zohar* 1:50 (Introduction).

28. Scholem, *Sabbatai Sevi: The Mystical Messiah* (Princeton, 1973), p. 118. For a general overview of the movement see idem, *Kabbalah,* pp. 244–86.

29. See Emden, *Mitpahat Sefarim,* esp. pp. 38–40; Tishby, *Mishnat ha-Zohar* 1:52–6 (Introduction).

30. Cf. above, n. 16.

31. Adolf Jellinek, *Moses ben Schem-Tob de Leon und sein Verhältniss zum Sohar,* esp. pp. 24–36; idem, *Beiträge zur Geschichte der Kabbala* 1:41–5.

32. See above, §1; Graetz, *History of the Jews,* 4:10–24.

33. *Madda'ei ha-Yahadut* 1 (1926): 16–29.

34. Scholem, *Major Trends,* p. 198. In *Qovez al Yad,* n.s. 8 (1975): 325–84, Scholem provides examples of Moses' method of utilizing the Zohar in his Hebrew writings.

35. Scholem's research is summarized in *Major Trends,* pp. 156–204; *Kabbalah,* pp. 213–43.

36. For selections from *Las Siete Partidas* see Jacob Marcus, *The Jew in the Medieval World* (New York, 1965), pp. 34–40.

37. For a study of this period see Baer, *A History of the Jews in Christian Spain* 1:111–37, 177–305 (hereafter cited as *History*).

38. Zohar 3:220b–221b. The image of Israel as the heart derives from Judah Halevi (eleventh–twelfth centuries), *Kuzari* 2:36. For another confrontation with a gentile see above, "The Golden Calf"; also Wilhelm Bacher, "Judaeo-Christian Polemics in the Zohar," *JQR* 3 (1891): 781–4.

NOTES

39. See above, "God, Israel, and *Shekhinah.*"

40. Zohar 2:188b. Edom symbolizes medieval Christendom; see above, loc. cit.

41. Zohar 2:188b; *Zohar Hadash, Bereshit,* 8a (*Midrash ha-Ne'elam*). On the calculations for the coming of Messiah see Abba H. Silver, *A History of Messianic Speculation in Israel* (New York, 1927), pp. 90–2; Scholem, *Kabbalah,* p. 232. On the messianic aspect of R. Shim'on's personality in the Zohar see Yehuda Liebes, "*Ha-Mashiah shel ha-Zohar.*"

42. Rabbi Shim'on's teaching appears in Talmud, *Megillah* 29a. For an example of the Zohar's presentation of the theme see above, "God, Israel, and *Shekhinah.*"

43. Zohar 3:212a; 2:188b.

44. Zohar 3:197b; cf. above, n. 23. On "the tracks of the sheep" as a designation for kabbalists cf. *Zohar Hadash, Shir ha-Shirim,* 70d.

45. See Baer, *History* 1:266–9; 437, n. 24; Scholem, *Major Trends,* p. 234. The Spirituals had a stronger influence on the author of *Ra'aya Meheimna,* one of the early imitations of the Zohar; see Baer, *History,* pp. 270–7; idem, *Zion* 5 (1940): 1–44; Scholem, *Major Trends,* pp. 180; 392, n. 97.

46. On the vigil see above, "God, Israel, and *Shekhinah*"; on the four levels see Scholem, *On the Kabbalah and Its Symbolism,* pp. 50–62 (hereafter cited as *On the Kabbalah*); and above, "The Old Man and the Beautiful Maiden." For another parallel, see Liebes, "*Peraqim be-Millon Sefer ha-Zohar,*" p. 226 (hereafter cited as "*Peraqim*"); he compares the phrase *gufa de-malka* ("the body of the King") to *corpus domini.*

47. Zohar 2:37a. In one passage the Zohar indicates that Christianity and Islam approximate Israelite monotheism: ". . . two other nations who are close in [their conception of] unity to Israel" (1:13a); cf. Nahmanides on Genesis 2:3 (end); Maimonides, *Mishneh Torah, Hilkhot Melakhim* 11:4.

48. Zohar 3:206a. Following the practice of Isaac Luria (1534–1572), the famous kabbalist of Safed, these words are recited as part of the Sabbath liturgy at the designated point in the service. On the phrase "a son of divinity" (*bar elahin*) see Tishby's note, *Mishnat ha-Zohar* 2:327.

49. Zohar 3:149a; cf. 1:154b; 3:7b; above, "Moses and the Blazing Bush"; Mishnah, *Avot* 3:18; John 3:16.

50. Zohar 3:218a; cf. 1:65a; 2:269a; 3:231a; Adolf Neubauer and S. R. Driver, *The Fifty-Third Chapter of Isaiah according to the Jewish Interpreters* (New York, 1970), 1:111; 2:117–18; George Foot Moore, *Judaism* (New York, 1971), 1:546–52. Talmud, *Mo'ed Qatan* 28a, reports a teaching in the name of Rabbi Ammi (third century): "Just as the red heifer atones, so the death of the righteous atones." Cf. Zohar 2:212a, where the Messiah is described as bearing all the suffering of Israel and Isaiah 53:5 is cited; also *Zohar Hadash, Eikhah,* 91a (*Midrash ha-Ne'elam*).

51. Zohar 3:191b; cf. 2:79a–b, 147a. The *Ra'aya Meheimna* refers to Moses,

NOTES

its central figure, as the son of God (3:243a) and applies to him the phrase "Kiss the son" (3:281b) as well as certain verses from Isaiah 53 (3:280a, 282b); cf. Talmud, *Sotah* 14a.

52. Graetz, *History of the Jews* 4:23.

53. Scholem, *Major Trends*, pp. 129; 380, n. 37; cf. above, "The Old Man and the Beautiful Maiden": Now two are three, and three are like one!"

54. See above, "Male and Female"; cf. Zohar 1:230b; 2:126b.

55. Cited by Tishby, *Mishnat ha-Zohar* 2:279. One rationalistic opponent of Kabbalah stated: "The Christians believe in the Trinity; the kabbalists believe in the Decade."

56. For a discussion of the historical development of the sefirotic system see Scholem, *Ursprung; Kabbalah*, pp. 23–116.

57. See Jacob Katz, *Exclusiveness and Tolerance* (New York, 1961), p. 19.

58. See above, "Colors and Enlightenment."

59. This is clear from the context in Zohar 2:43b. Elsewhere the phrase "*YHVH*, our God, *YHVH*" is applied to different sets of three *sefirot*, though the central *sefirah*, *Tif'eret*, is always included; see Tishby, *Mishnat ha-Zohar* 2:278–9. Cf. Zohar 2:38a; 3:36a, where the middle triad is referred to as "three bonds of faith."

60. See above, "The Old Man and the Beautiful Maiden," "The Rabbis Encounter a Child," and "The Wedding Celebration."

61. Scholem, *Major Trends*, pp. 202; 397, n. 152; cf. p. 396, n. 151; Zohar 1:72b, 243a.

62. Moses of Burgos, cited by Isaac of Acre; see Scholem, *Major Trends*, pp. 24; 354, n. 22. Cf. Isaac ha-Kohen's statement: "The quality of *Malkhut* [the tenth *sefirah*] causes the supernal flow to emanate from high above all the separate levels [i.e., Intelligences] until the emanation reaches the Active Intellect" (*Mishkan ha-'Edut*, Berlin MS Or. 833, f. 40b).

63. For one example see above, "*Qorban* and *Olah*."

64. Zohar 2:176a; 3:141b; see Scholem, *Major Trends*, p. 402, n. 66.

65. See above, "Openings."

66. Silver, *Maimonidean Criticism*, p. 190.

67. *Benei meheimanuta;* Zohar 1:36b, 37b (see *Ketem Paz*, ad loc.), 43a; 2:262a; 3:12b–13a, 105a, 110b, 267a.

68. See above, "How to Look at Torah."

69. See above, n. 11.

70. On the distinction see Scholem, *Major Trends*, pp. 25–8. The prestige of mystical symbolism is indicated by the fact that at the beginning of the fourteenth century Rabbi Jacob ibn Tibbon argued that the allegorism of the rationalists was no less legitimate than the symbolism of the kabbalists; see Baer, *History* 1:296.

71. See above "*Qorban* and *Olah*." There is a subtle antirationalistic polemic involved here; see the corresponding notes.

NOTES

72. Zohar 3:288b (*Idra Zuta*); 1:72b; see Scholem, "Das Ringen zwischen dem biblischen Gott und dem Gott Plotins in der alten Kabbala," *Über einige Grundbegriffe des Judentums*, p. 50.

73. Rabbi Jonah Gerondi (1200–1263), the Spanish moralist, notes that these *mizvot* were neglected or violated; see Baer, *History* 1:250; cf. 236. For the Zohar's response see above "Jacob's Journey," "Seduction Above and Below"; Zohar 2:3b, 61a, 87b (sexual morality); "Guests in the *Sukkah*"; "The Rabbis Encounter a Child" (ritual washing); Zohar 1:13b–14a; 3:269b (*tefillin;* cf. above, n. 7); 3:265b, 266b–267a (*mezuzah*). The command "You shall not bow down to a foreign god" (Psalms 81:10) is taken to mean: "You shall not lie down with a foreign woman" (*Zohar Hadash, Noah,* 21a [*Midrash ha-Ne'elam*]).

74. See above, "Jacob's Garment of Days" and "The Gift of Dwelling." The *Ra'aya Meheimna*, written soon after the Zohar, offers a harsh criticism of Spanish Jewish society; see Baer, *Zion 5* (1940): 1–44; *History* 1:270–7; Scholem, *Major Trends*, p. 180.

75. See above, "Adam's Sin," "God, Israel, and *Shekhinah*"; Zohar 3:44b, 110b.

76. See *Bereshit Rabba* 1:1: "The Blessed Holy One looked into the Torah and created the world." Cf. Harry A. Wolfson, *Philo* (Cambridge, 1968), 1:242–5.

77. See above, "How to Look at Torah," "The Old Man and the Beautiful Maiden."

78. See Scholem, *On the Kabbalah*, pp. 50–2; Leo Strauss, *Persecution and the Art of Writing* (Glencoe, Ill., 1952). As noted above, n. 46, the Christian theory of the fourfold meaning of Scripture appears in the Zohar.

79. See above, "The Creation of *Elohim*"; Zohar 1:29b–31b. On the relation between Kabbalah and myth see Scholem, *On the Kabbalah*, pp. 87–117.

80. See above, "The Golden Calf." For Elijah's teachings see Zohar 1:1b–2a; 3:221a, 231a; *Zohar Hadash, Ki Tavo,* 59d. In 3:241b Elijah turns to Rabbi Shim'on for instruction. Elsewhere (*Zohar Hadash, Shir ha-Shirim,* 63d, 70d, 73c) Elijah encourages him to reveal the secrets, and says (ibid., 62c): "My words will be written by you." For earlier reliance on the figure of Elijah see Scholem, *On the Kabbalah*, pp. 19–21.

81. See above, "Joseph's Dream," "Pharoah, Israel, and God," "*Qorban* and *Olah*," "God, Israel, and *Shekhinah*." Cf. *Zohar Hadash, Toledot,* 27a (*Sitrei Torah*).

82. See Scholem, *Major Trends*, p. 174; *Kabbalah*, p. 223. Simon Neuhausen published a catalogue of these works entitled *Sifriyyah shel Ma'lah* ("Library of the Upper World") (Baltimore, 1937). On the Book of Enoch see Louis Ginzberg, *Legends of the Jews* 5:158, n. 60. One commentator on the Zohar tries to explain why these books appear nowhere else: "All the books mentioned in the Zohar ... have been lost in the wandering of exile due to our many sins.

NOTES

Nothing is left of them except what is mentioned in the Zohar" (Shim'on Labi, *Ketem Paz* on Zohar 1:7a).

83. See above, "Male and Female," "Jacob's Garment of Days"; Zohar 1:93a, 95b, 96a, 137a (*Midrash ha-Ne'elam*), 223b; 2:5a, 123b; 3:75b, 78a, 284b, 285a, 292b (*Idra Zuta*); *Zohar Hadash, Bereshit*, 16a (*Midrash ha-Ne'elam*). In some cases "our Mishnah" refers to genuine, ancient rabbinic sources, but these citations are usually altered or interpreted mystically; see Zohar 1:226b; *Zohar Hadash, Bereshit*, 15b–c, 18b, 20a (*Midrash ha-Ne'elam*). In one of his Hebrew works Moses de León introduces a Zohar passage with the line: "I have seen in the words of the sages of the Mishnah"; see Scholem, *Major Trends*, p. 394, n. 122. The Zohar also contains numerous kabbalistic pieces entitled *Matnitin* and *Tosefta;* see Scholem, *Kabbalah*, p. 216; Gottlieb, *Mehqarim*, pp. 163–214.

84. On the development of legends around Rabbi Shim'on see Lee Levine, "R. Simeon b. Yohai and the Purification of Tiberias: History and Tradition," *HUCA* 49 (1978): 143–85. The *Nistarot* is printed in Yehudah Ibn Shemu'el, *Midreshei Ge'ullah* (Jerusalem, 1968), pp. 161–98; cf. pp. 253–86.

85. In the earlier stratum, *Midrash ha-Ne'elam*, Moses' imagination had not yet focused sharply on Rabbi Shim'on; see above, §§1–2; Scholem, *Major Trends*, pp. 182–3.

86. Scholem, *Major Trends*, p. 200; *Kabbalah*, pp. 231–2, 432.

87. See above, "The Gift of Dwelling."

88. See Moses' wife's statement, above, §1; Tishby, *Mishnat ha-Zohar* 1:29–30 (Introduction). Scholem questions its authenticity; see *Major Trends*, p. 192; *Madda'ei ha-Yahadut* 1 (1926): 18–20. However, other, independent testimony recorded by Isaac supports her statement; see below, n. 97. Cf. Zohar 3:153b (*Ra'aya Meheimna*) and Tishby's interpretation, *Mishnat ha-Zohar* 2:393, n. 100.

89. See above, n. 13.

90. Scholem, *Major Trends*, p. 201; cf. Zohar 2:215a; 3:87b–88a.

91. See above, "The Golden Calf"; Zohar 1:12b.

92. The Book of Adam is located in the Library of the Upper World. *Ketem Paz* (on Zohar 1:55a) traces the book's transmission from Adam to Rabbi Shim'on. See also Scholem, *Major Trends*, pp. 21; 354, n. 21.

93. See above, "The Hidden Light" and "Adam's Sin"; cf. the Ba'al Shem Tov's statement, above, n. 1.

94. See Zohar 3:127b–145a (*Idra Rabba*); 3:287b–296b (*Idra Zuta*); above, "Threshing Out the Secrets," "The Wedding Celebration"; Liebes, *"Peraqim,"* pp. 2–3.

95. See R. J. Zwi Werblowsky's comments on automatic writing and speech in *Joseph Karo: Lawyer and Mystic* (Philadelphia, 1977), pp. 287–8; cf. pp. 47, 82; Philo, *De Migratione Abrahami*, §35; Scholem, *Sefunot* 11 (1973): 67–112; Lawrence Fine, "Maggidic Revelation in the Teachings of Isaac Luria," in *Mystics, Philosophers, and Politicians—Essays in Jewish Intellectual History in Honor*

NOTES

of Alexander Altmann, ed. Jehuda Reinharz, Daniel Swetchinski, and Kalman P. Bland (Durham, N.C., 1982); idem, "Recitation of Mishnah as a Vehicle for Mystical Inspiration," *REJ* (in press); Ian Stevenson, "Some Comments on Automatic Writing," *Journal of the American Society for Psychical Research* 72 (1978): 315–32.

96. Published by Jellinek in *Kerem Ḥemed* 8 (1854): 105; see Scholem, *Kabbalah,* p. 188.

97. Tishby, *Mishnat ha-Zohar* 1:29 (Introduction).

98. Ibid., p. 30.

99. See Carl Jung, *The Psychogenesis of Mental Disease, Collected Works* 3:75–7; Leslie Shepherd, ed., *Encyclopedia of Occultism and Parapsychology* (Detroit, 1978), p. 78. On the Zohar's Aramaic see Scholem, *Major Trends,* pp. 163–8; *Kabbalah,* pp. 226–9; Tishby, *Mishnat ha-Zohar,* 1:76–80; Menahem Z. Kaddari, *Diqduq ha-Lashon ha-'Aramit shel ha-Zohar;* also above, "How to Look at To-rah," "Moses and the Blazing Bush," "The Wedding Celebration," and passim in the Notes.

100. For an example of revision see Scholem in *Sefer ha-Yovel li-Khevod Levi Ginzberg,* pp. 425–46; *Kabbalah,* p. 230; cf. *Major Trends,* pp. 172; 390, n. 73.

101. *Encyclopaedia Britannica,* 15th ed., s.v. "automatic writing."

102. On the Zohar's Aramaic see the sources cited above, n. 99; cf. Werblowsky, *Joseph Karo,* pp. 262–3. Certain linguistic peculiarities of the Zohar reappear in Moses' Hebrew writings; see above, nn. 34–5; Scholem, *Major Trends,* pp. 196–7. Cf. the following description of automatic speech offered by Seth and transmitted through his medium, Ruburt: "All knowledge or information bears the stamp of the personality who holds it or passes it on. Ruburt makes his verbal knowledge available for our use, and quite automatically the two of us together cause the various words that will be spoken" (Jane Roberts, *Seth Speaks* [New York, 1974], p. 17).

103. I.e., the *Matnitin* and *Tosefta,* scattered throughout the Zohar; see Scholem, *Kabbalah,* p. 216; Gottlieb, *Meḥqarim,* pp. 163–214.

104. Cordovero, *Or ha-Ḥammah* on Zohar 3:106a; see above, "Threshing Out the Secrets."

105. Zohar 1:6a; cf. *Zohar Ḥadash, Bereshit,* 11c; *Rut,* 85b (*Midrash ha-Ne'elam*).

106. Zohar 1:5a; cf. Talmud, *Ta'anit* 8b: "Blessing is not found in anything weighed, measured, or counted, but only in that which is hidden from the eye"; cf. Zohar 2:230b.

107. See above, "Jacob's Journey," "Colors and Enlightenment."

108. See above, "The Old Man and the Beautiful Maiden," "The Rabbis Encounter a Child"; cf. Zohar 2:155b; 3:157b.

109. See Scholem, *Major Trends,* pp. 169–70; *Kabbalah,* p. 222; Tishby, *Mishnat ha-Zohar* 1:71 (Introduction); cf. *Zohar Ḥadash, Noaḥ,* 22c (*Midrash ha-Ne'elam*) with Jerusalem Talmud, *Ma'aserot* 3:8, 50d.

NOTES

110. See above, "Miracles."

111. See above, "Moses and the Blazing Bush." Moses is usually identified with *Raḥamim* (*Tif'eret*), sometimes with *Nezaḥ*.

112. See Scholem, *On the Kabbalah*, pp. 37–44.

113. Zohar 3:149b; cf. *Bahir*, §161; Zohar 1:203a. 249a; 3:170b, 188b, 266b; and above, "The Rabbis Encounter a Child."

114. "How to Look at Torah."

115. For examples of the latter technique see above, "Openings," "Jacob's Garment of Days," "Guests in the *Sukkah*."

116. Maimonides, *Guide of the Perplexed*, trans. Shlomo Pines (Chicago, 1963), p. 8.

117. See above, "The Old Man and the Beautiful Maiden."

118. See above, "Jacob's Journey."

119. See above, "Openings."

120. Consult Scholem, *Major Trends*, pp. 207–39; *Kabbalah*, pp. 88–116; Tishby, *Mishnat ha-Zohar*, 1:95–283; David Blumenthal, *Understanding Jewish Mysticism*, pp. 113–9; Adin Steinsaltz, *The Thirteen Petalled Rose*, pp. 37–47, 59–65. Joseph Gikatilla's *Sha'arei Orah* is a useful guide to the sefirotic symbolism of the Zohar.

121. *Ma'arekhet ha-'Elohut*, p. 82b. The author is unknown.

122. See Tishby, *Mishnat ha-Zohar*, 1:43 (Introduction), 104–5; cf. above, n. 55.

123. Zohar 3:70a. The expression appears in *Sefer Yezirah* 1:7; cf. 1:5.

124. See above, "The Wedding Celebration"; cf. Zohar 3:297a; and above, n. 64.

125. See above, "Threshing Out the Secrets."

126. Cf. Gikatilla, *Sha'arei Orah*, pp. 4–5.

127. David son of Abraham ha-Lavan (ca. 1300), in *Masoret ha-Berit;* see Scholem, *Kabbalah*, p. 95.

128. *Kelala de-khol perata*, Zohar 3:65b; see Scholem, *Major Trends*, p. 219.

129. See above, "*Qorban* and *Olah*."

130. On the Zohar's doctrine of evil see above, "Adam's Sin," "Abram's Descent into Egypt," "An Offering to God," "Jacob's Journey," "Seduction Above and Below," "The Golden Calf"; Scholem, *Major Trends*, pp. 235–9; *Kabbalah*, pp. 122–8; *Von der mystischen Gestalt der Gottheit*, pp. 49–82 (Hebrew translation: *Pirqei Yesod be-Havanat ha-Qabbalah u-Semaleha*, pp. 187–212 [hereafter cited as *Pirqei Yesod*]); Tishby, *Mishnat ha-Zohar* 1:285–377. On the cathartic view of evil see Zohar 2:254b–255a; 3:292b (*Idra Zuta*); Tishby, *Mishnat ha-Zohar* 1:150–1, 296; Gottlieb, *Meḥqarim*, pp. 178–82; Liebes, "*Peraqim*," p. 147; Moshe Idel, "Ha-Maḥshavah ha-ra'ah shel ha-'el," *Tarbiz* 49 (1980): 356–64.

131. This midrashic reading of the verse appears in Talmud, *Ḥagigah* 12b; cf. *Bahir*, §102.

132. See above, "Male and Female," "The Secret of Sabbath"; Zohar

NOTES

2:63b, 204b–205a; cf. Talmud, *Ketubbot* 62b. For a full discussion of the development of the concept of *Shekhinah* see Scholem, *Von der mystischen Gestalt der Gottheit*, pp. 135–91 (Hebrew translation: *Pirqei Yesod*, pp. 259–307); Tishby, *Mishnat ha-Zohar* 1:219–31; Raphael Patai, *The Hebrew Goddess*.

133. Zohar 1:181a. The phrase derives from medieval astronomers' description of the moon; see Scholem, *Qovez al Yad*, n.s. 8 (1976): 338, 381.

134. See above, "God, Israel, and *Shekhinah*."

135. See ibid. and "The Golden Calf."

136. The image appears in Talmud, *Shabbat* 146a and *Yevamot* 103b, where it is said that the serpent injected its venom into Eve.

137. Zohar 3:7a; *Zohar Hadash, Yitro*, 37b. For a discussion of the sources of the various parts of the soul see Tishby, *Mishnat ha-Zohar*, 2:20–6.

138. Talmud, *Sotah* 14a, *Ketubbot* 111b.

139. Gikatilla, *Sha'arei Orah*, p. 166. On the relationship between Gikatilla and Moses de León see Scholem, *Major Trends*, pp. 194–6; Altmann, *Qovez al Yad* 9 (1980): 217–93; and the recent studies by Asi Farber listed in the Bibliography. On the concept of *devequt*, communion with God, see Scholem, *The Messianic Idea in Judaism*, pp. 203–27.

140. See above, "The Binding of Abraham and Isaac."

141. See above, "Abram's Descent into Egypt"; cf. "Jacob's Journey." Scholem has noted (*On the Kabbalah*, pp. 99–100) that such willingness to deal with the reality of evil contributed to the appeal and influence of kabbalistic thought.

142. Moses de León employs this image in his Hebrew writings and in the Zohar; see *Sheqel ha-Qodesh*, p. 113; Zohar 1:41b; *Zohar Hadash, Yitro*, 39d; Scholem, *MGWJ* 71 (1927): 118–9; *Major Trends*, pp. 220–1.

143. See above, "Manna and Wisdom."

144. Isaac the Blind, *Commentary on Sefer Yezirah*, printed in Scholem, *Ha-Qabbalah be-Provans* (Jerusalem, 1963), Appendix, p. 1; cf. *Ursprung*, pp. 246–7.

145. See Tishby, ed., *Perush ha-'Aggadot le-Rabbi Azri'el*, pp. 40, 116; Scholem in *Sefer Bialik* (Tel Aviv, 1934), p. 160, n. 8; Moses de León, *Shushan Edut*, ed. Scholem, *Qovez al Yad*, n.s. 8 (1976): 334.

146. See Tishby, *Mishnat ha-Zohar* 2:247–306; above, "The Secret of Sabbath," "*Qorban* and *Olah*." On meditation see Scholem, *Kabbalah*, pp. 369–72; Perle Epstein, *Kabbalah: The Way of the Jewish Mystic*; Aryeh Kaplan, *Meditation and Kabbalah*.

147. See above, "The Gift of Dwelling"; Zohar 3:67a.

148. The seven palaces below *Shekhinah* are described in the *Heikhalot* (Zohar 1:38a–45b; 2:244b–262b). On *Yesod* see above, "The Gift of Dwelling." For a cryptic description of sefirotic vision see "Colors and Enlightenment"; cf. Rabbi Shim'on's revelation before his death in "The Wedding Celebration."

149. Zohar 2:93a; cf. 3:254b.

150. An inversion of "The Book of Concealment," one of the most obscure

sections of the Zohar (2:176b–179a). It contains five brief chapters and is preceded by this passage.

151. For the kabbalist who has entered the secret realm and emerged unscathed with wisdom; see above, "Threshing Out the Secrets."

152. In Talmud, *Berakhot* 64a, the phrase "master of wheat" means one who has mastered the literal traditions. Here wheat and its products (kernels, bread, cake, and royal pastry) may symbolize the four levels of meaning in Torah (literal, midrashic, allegorical, and mystical).

How to Look at Torah

Torah "Teaching," the first five books of the Bible.

ordinary words Aramaic, *millin de-hedyotei*. *Millin* has several meanings in this passage: words, things, matters. *Hedyotei* means "common, popular, ignoble." The phrase may be translated: "everyday matters." Cf. Zohar 3:149b, where the phrase refers to secular, ignoble stories of the Torah, in contrast to *millin qaddishin*, "holy words, holy matters."

better than all of them! than all the stories of Torah, or than all its ordinary words; see next note.

rulers of the world Aramaic, *qafsirei de-'alma. Qafsir* is a neologism. Elsewhere in the Zohar it appears to mean "ruler"; see 1:37a, 177a, 243a; Shim'on Labi, *Ketem Paz* on 1:37a; cf. Aramaic, *tafsera*, "royal dignitary," and Zohar 1:243b. The neologisms of the Zohar often contain the letters *t* and *q;* see Scholem, *Major Trends*, p. 166. In 3:36b the word means something else, perhaps "pieces." In his *Be'ur miqzat millot zarot she-be-Sefer ha-Zohar* ("Explanation of Some Strange Words in the Zohar") Labi comments on this phrase: "Rulers have many stories and chronicles from which they learn wisdom and ethics, such as *Meshal ha-Qadmonim* and the like." *Meshal ha-Qadmoni* ("The Fable of the Ancient") is a collection of fables and homilies written in 1281 in Guadalajara by a friend of Moses de León, the poet and kabbalist Isaac ibn Sahula. Noted for its beautiful Hebrew, this book was modeled on popular works such as *Kalila and Dimna,* a collection of moral fables supposedly compiled for the king of Persia from all the books of wisdom that could be found. Ibn Sahula wanted to show Jews that they need not rely on foreign material, that Jewish works were equally edifying and entertaining. He describes his fables as "secular things based on the purity of holiness" (*Meshal ha-Qadmoni* [Tel Aviv, 1952], p. 6). In his book Isaac quotes one passage from the *Midrash ha-Ne'elam* (the earliest stratum of the Zohar), paraphrases another, and refers to the work obliquely several times; see Scholem, *Tarbiz* 3 (1932): 181–3; Baer, *A History of the Jews in Christian Spain* 1:436–7, n. 17; idem, *Toledot ha-Yehudim bi-Sefarad ha-Nozrit,* pp. 508–9, n. 61a. Is Moses de León returning the favor and alluding here to *Meshal ha-Qadmoni,* written by his friend? The neologism hides more than it reveals. Tishby (*Mishnat ha-Zohar* 2:402) renders the phrase: "Booklets [*quntresim*] of the world," which he takes to mean secular compositions. He rejects the interpretation "rulers" and translates according to the context.

make a Torah out of them   deleting the words *ke-hai gavvna*, in accord with the reading of the Cremona edition; see Tishby, *Mishnat ha-Zohar* 2:402, 769.

all the words of Torah . . .   a basic exegetical principle of the Zohar; cf. 2:55b: "There is no word in the Torah that does not contain many secrets, many reasons, many roots, many branches"; cf. 3:79b, 174b.

are perfectly balanced   Aramaic, *be-had matqela itqelu;* the same phrase recurs in Zohar 2:176b (*Sifra di-Zeni'uta*); 3:138b (*Idra Rabba*), 290a (*Idra Zuta*). Cf. *Bereshit Rabba* 1:15: Rabbi El'azar son of Rabbi Shim'on said, ". . . Both [heaven and earth] are balanced by each other."

'He makes His angels spirits'   The verse in Psalms means: "He makes winds His messengers." Rabbi Shim'on reads the words in the literal order they appear, in order to introduce his teaching. Cf. Zohar 1:101a; 3:126b.

they put on the garment of this world   they appear as physical beings, e.g., to Abraham; see Genesis 18:1–2.

Torah, who created them and all the worlds   Torah is the instrument with which God created the universe; cf. Wolfson, *Philo* 1:243–5; *Bereshit Rabba* 1:1: "The Torah says, 'I was the instrument of the Blessed Holy One.' . . . The Blessed Holy One looked in the Torah and created the world."

for whose sake . . .   Cf. Talmud, *Pesahim* 68b: Rabbi El'azar said, "Were it not for Torah, heaven and earth would not have remained in existence."

may his spirit deflate!   Aramaic, *tippah ruheih*, "may his spirit [or "breath"] blow out"; cf. Zohar 3:149b: "Whoever says that the story of Torah is intended to show only itself, may his spirit deflate!"

the world that is coming   Aramaic, *alma de-'atei;* on the mystical significance of the phrase, see below, notes to "*Qorban* and *Olah.*"

under the garment of Torah   The search for the wonders, the mystical essence of Torah, has an erotic quality to it; cf. above, "The Old Man and the Beautiful Maiden"; Zohar 2:98b; 3:49b, 81a; *Tanhuma, Ki Tissa,* §16.

'embodiment of Torah'   Hebrew, *gufei Torah*, "bodies of Torah." In the Mishnah this term denotes the essential teachings of Torah; see Mishnah, *Hagigah* 1:8: "Judgments and the laws of sacrifices, what is pure and impure, sexual immorality . . . these are *gufei Torah*"; cf. Tosefta, *Shabbat* 2:10; Mishnah, *Avot* 3:23. Here the category is broadened to include all the commandments; cf. Zohar 2:85b.

garments: the stories   Several of the Torah's commandments are clothed in stories; see Genesis 32:24–32; Numbers 9:6–14; 15:32–36; 27:1–11. Furthermore, the narrative format of the Torah transmits moral teaching throughout, as noted by Moses Cordovero: "The entire Torah—ethics, laws, and piety—is [presented] through stories" (*Or ha-Hammah*, on this passage).

do not look at the garment but rather at the body   Such readers penetrate the narrative layer and concentrate on the commandments of Torah.

The wise ones . . .   Mystics, kabbalists.

those who stood at Mt. Sinai According to the Midrash, the souls of all those not yet born were present at Sinai; see *Shemot Rabbah* 28:4; *Tanhuma, Yitro,* §11; *Pirqei de-Rabbi Eli'ezer,* Chap. 41; cf. Zohar 1:91a. Here the Zohar implies that only the souls of mystics were actually present; perhaps only mystics are aware that they were present at Sinai.

look only at the soul, root of all, real Torah! The mystics see through the outer, physical layers of Torah, both her garment of stories and her body of commandments, into her soul. Real Torah, *oraita mammash*, is their sole object of study and contemplation. What this soul is becomes clear below. Cf. Philo's description of the Therapeutae, the contemplative Jewish sect: "The whole of the law seems to these people to resemble a living being, with the literal commandments for its body, and for its soul the invisible meaning stored away in its words" (*De vita contemplativa* 10:78, trans. David Winston, *Philo of Alexandria* [Ramsey, N.J., 1981], p. 55). Cf. Origen: "Just as a human being is said to be made up of body, soul, and spirit, so also is sacred Scripture" (*De principiis* 4:2,4, trans. Rowan Greer, *Origen* [New York, 1979], p. 182). Cf. Rumi, *Mathnawi* (trans. E. H. Whinfield [London, 1887], p. 169): "The outward sense of the Qur'ān is like Adam's body: only its exterior is visible; its soul is hidden."

the soul of the soul of Torah see below.

the Communion of Israel Hebrew, *Keneset Yisra'el,* "Community of Israel." In earlier rabbinic literature this phrase denotes the people of Israel, the Ecclesia of Israel. In the Zohar *Keneset Yisra'el* refers to *Shekhinah,* the divine counterpart of the people, that aspect of God most intimately connected with them, "She in whom the Jew has his communion" (Robert Duncan, cited in Jerome Rothenberg, *A Big Jewish Book* [New York, 1978], p. 36). Here *Shekhinah* is described as the divine body clothed by the heavens who receives the soul, a higher *sefirah.*

the soul, the Beauty of Israel The masculine aspect of God is called *Tif'eret Yisra'el,* "the Beauty of Israel" (cf. Lamentations 2:1). *Shekhinah* receives Him as the body receives the soul.

So She is the body of the soul This is not merely redundant. Talmud, *Yevamot* 62a speaks of a cosmic body that contains all souls; cf. Rashi, ad loc. Moses de León identifies this body with *Shekhinah;* see his *Sefer ha-Mishqal,* p. 93; Liebes, "*Peraqim,*" pp. 179–80, 226; cf. Zohar 2:142a, 157a. *Shekhinah* receives the soul of *Tif'eret* and thereby carries all human souls, which are engendered by the union of these two *sefirot;* see 1:13a, 197a, 209a; Tishby, *Mishnat ha-Zohar,* 2:20–6.

The soul we have mentioned . . . This refers not only to the immediately preceding lines but also to the preceding passage: "The wise ones . . . look only at the soul." The mystics gaze into the soul of Torah, which is none other than the *sefirah* of *Tif'eret.* One of the names of this *sefirah* is the Written Torah, while *Shekhinah* is called the Oral Torah. The hidden essence of Torah is God. The ultimate purpose of study is direct experience of the divine, who is real Torah; the search for meaning culminates in revelation. Cf. Zohar 2:60a, 90b; 3:9b; Scholem, *On the Kabbalah and Its Symbolism*, pp. 37–50.

The soul of the soul is the Holy Ancient One   *Attiqa Qaddisha*, the Holy Ancient One, is the primal, most ancient manifestation of *Ein Sof*, the Infinite, through *Keter*, Its Crown, beyond both *Shekhinah* and *Tif'eret*. The phrase "soul of the soul" derives from Solomon ibn Gabirol (eleventh century): "You are soul of the soul" (*Keter Malkhut*); cf. Zohar 1:45a, 79a (*Sitrei Torah*), 103b, 245a; 2:156b; *Zohar Hadash, Rut* 75a, 82c (*Midrash ha-Ne'elam*); Philo, *De Opificio Mundi*, §66; Lucretius, *De rerum natura*, trans. Cyril Bailey (Oxford, 1947) 3:275 (*anima animae*).

Woe to the wicked ...   The literalists are not merely fools; they are wicked sinners, *hayyavayya*. The Zohar is referring here to radical rationalists who read the Torah critically and question its divine origin, thus undermining its authority. Cf. above, Introduction, n. 7; Zohar 1:163a; "All those close-minded fools, when they see words of Torah, not only do they not know [the mystical meaning]; they even say that those are defective words, useless words!" Reacting to this heretical attitude, Rabbi Shim'on urges readers of Torah not to be content with the superficial garment but to penetrate to the inner meaning and divine core.

As wine must sit in a jar ...   Cf. Mishnah, *Avot* 4:27: Rabbi Meir said, "Do not look at the jar, but rather what is inside." Cf. Talmud, *Ta'anit* 7a: Rabbi Hosha'ya said, "Why have the words of Torah been compared to these three drinks: water, wine, and milk? ... Just as these three drinks keep only in the most inferior vessels, so words of Torah keep only in one who is humble."

The Creation of *Elohim*

Elohim   one of the names of God; see below.

In the Beginning   Genesis 1:1. This selection is a commentary on the first half of the verse; it appears at the beginning of the Zohar on Genesis.

the King   the Infinite, *Ein Sof*, about to begin Its manifestation.

the luster on high   the brilliance of the first *sefirah*, *Keter*, the Crown. *Keter* is coeternal with *Ein Sof*.

A blinding spark   Aramaic, *bozina de-qardinuta*. *Bozina* means "lamp," but in the Zohar also "light" and "spark." *Qardinuta* offers a good example of the author's linguistic method. In conveying mystical secrets, he fashions words that conceal more than they reveal. *Qardinuta* is based partially on a phrase in Talmud, *Pesahim* 7a: *hittei qurdanaita*, "wheat from Kurdistan." This kind of wheat is very hard (see Rashi, ad loc.), and, drawing on this association, the author employs the word here to describe the spark; cf. Scholem, *Kabbalah*, p. 228: "a very powerful light." *Qardinuta* is also intended to evoke an image of darkness, *qadrut;* cf. *Zohar Hadash, Bereshit* 2a, where *qardenuta de-sihara* means "eclipse of the moon" (Hebrew, *qadrut ha-yareah*). Some Zohar MSS read here: *bozina de-qadrinuta,* and a number of translators, though retaining *qardinuta,* render the phrase in this sense: "spark of darkness" (*Ketem Paz* and, following him, Tishby, *Mishnat ha-Zohar* 1:163); "a dark flame" (Scholem, *Zohar,* p. 27). Cf. Shemot Rabbah 2:10: "The fire up above . . . is black." On the Sufi image of "the black light" (nūr-e siyāh) see Henry Corbin, *The Man of Light in Iranian Sufism,* trans. Nancy Pearson (Boulder, 1978), pp. 99–120. The spark is overwhelming, so bright and powerful that it cannot be seen. This blinding spark is the first impulse of emanation proceeding from *Ein Sof,* the Infinite, through *Keter.* The goal of meditation is to attain this spark and participate in the flow of being; see *Zohar Hadash, Va-'Ethannan,* 57d–58a, 58c–d (*Qav ha-Middah*). On the meaning and connotations of this phrase see the wealth of material collected by Liebes, *"Peraqim,"* pp. 145–51, 161–4.

the Concealed of the Concealed the luster on high, the first and most hidden *sefirah, Keter.*

the Infinite *Ein Sof,* "there is no end." On the evolution of this term see Scholem, *Kabbalah,* pp. 88–9.

a cluster of vapor in formlessness . . . Aramaic, *qutra be-golma. Qutra* means both "knot" and "smoke" in the Zohar; see 1:30a, 33b, 94b, 161b; 2:80a, 124a; 3:45b, 51a–b, 107a, 289b, 295b (*Idra Zuta*). The ring is *Keter,* the Crown.

not white, not black . . . Abraham Galante (sixteenth century) suggests that these two colors are excluded first to remove the notion that the spark is of a physical nature, either white light or black darkness (*Or ha-Hammah,* ad loc.). The four colors are associated elsewhere with four *sefirot: Hesed, Shekhinah, Gevurah,* and *Tif'eret,* none of which appear until a later stage of emanation.

When a band spanned . . . The spark that is a vapor is also a band or cord (Aramaic, *meshiha*), referred to elsewhere in the Zohar as *qav ha-middah,* "the line of measure"; see *Zohar Hadash, Va-'Ethannan,* 56d–58d (*Qav ha-Middah*); and on the connection between *qardinuta* and measurement, Liebes, *"Peraqim,"* pp. 149, 162–3. The line maps out the paths and stages of emanation, the spectrum of divine colors.

concealed within the concealed . . . The flow of emanation has just begun. Everything is still hidden within the mystery of *Ein Sof.*

broke through and did not break through its aura It is impossible to describe the spiritual nature of the breakthrough; so the act is stated and immediately denied; see Scholem's remarks on expressions of this kind in *Major Trends,* pp. 166–7. The aura (or "ether" or "air"; Aramaic, *avira*) is *Keter;* cf. Zohar 1:16b; 3:135b (*Idra Rabba*); Altmann, *Studies in Religious Philosophy and Mysticism,* p. 174. The designation derives from *Sefer Yezirah* 2:6: "He formed substance from chaos and made that which is not into that which is. He hewed great pillars out of *avir* that cannot be grasped."

one high and hidden point . . . Beginning The flow of emanation manifests as a point of light. This is the second *sefirah: Hokhmah*, Wisdom. It is the Beginning mentioned in the first verse of Genesis; cf. *Targum Yerushalmi* and Ramban, ad loc.; *Bereshit Rabba* 1:1; Wolfson, *Philo*, 1:242–5, 266–9; Scholem, *Major Trends*, p. 391, n. 80. The point is called Beginning because it is the first ray of divine light to appear outside of *Keter*, the first aspect of God that can be known.

the first command of all The Mishnah states that God created the world with ten commands. Only nine explicit commands appear in Genesis 1, but the decade is completed by counting the phrase "In the Beginning." See Mishnah, *Avot* 5:1; Talmud, *Rosh ha-Shanah* 32a, *Megillah* 21b.

"The enlightened ..." Hebrew, *ha-maskilim*. On the following pages of the Zohar this term is applied to secret aspects of the alphabet and the *sefirot;* see 1:15b–16a. Elsewhere the Zohar employs the term to designate kabbalists, masters of meditation. The citation of this verse here, at the beginning of the Zohar on Genesis, may also refer to them. The Zohar on Exodus opens with the same verse and spells out the referent: "The enlightened are those who contemplate the secret of wisdom" (2:2a); cf. *Zohar Hadash, Va-'Ethannan*, 58c (*Qav ha-Middah*); above, "Colors and Enlightenment"; *Bahir*, §139.

"like the zohar of the sky" In the verse *zohar* means "splendor, brilliance." Here the word designates the hidden power of emanation (see below) and suggests the title of the book; cf. Zohar 3:124b, 153b (*Ra'aya Meheimna*).

"make the masses righteous" cf. Zohar 1:15b. Converting the masses into righteous human beings is one of the goals of the Zohar; cf. above, Introduction, §4.

Zohar ... this point The spark of emanation flashes again, and *Keter*, the aura, transmits the impulse to *Hokhmah*, the point of Wisdom.

a palace for its glory ... sowed the seed ... The purpose of emanation is to display the glory of the hidden God. This is achieved through a rhythm of revelation and concealment. The point expands into a circle, a palace; cf. *Bereshit Rabba* 1:1. This palace is the third *sefirah: Binah*, Understanding. She is the divine womb; the seed of holiness, another name for *Hokhmah*, is sown inside Her. *Binah* will give birth to the seven lower *sefirot*, which bring about the rest of Creation.

"Her stock is a holy seed" Isaiah refers here to one-tenth of the people of Israel, who will be saved. The Zohar cites the verse as an allusion to *Shekhinah*, the mystical Community of Israel, the tenth *sefirah*, whose origin is the seed of holiness sown in *Binah*.

The silkworm ... As the silkworm spins a cocoon out of its own substance, so *Hokhmah*, the point of Beginning, expands into the palace of *Binah*. Cf. *Bereshit Rabba* 21:5: "like the locust whose garment is of itself"; Shnei'ur Zalman of Lyady, *Sha'ar ha-Yihud ve-ha-'Emunah*, Chap. 7; and the spider simile in the Upanishads: Robert E. Hume, ed., *The Thirteen Principal Upanishads* (New York, 1971), pp. 95, 367.

209

the Concealed One who is not known the hidden source of emanation, *Ein Sof* or *Keter*.

Elohim a divine name meaning "God" or "gods." Here the name signifies *Binah*, the Divine Mother who gives birth to the seven lower *sefirot;* cf. Zohar 1:3b, 15b.

The secret is... The Zohar offers its mystical reading of the first words of Genesis. The following should be noted: (1) The Hebrew preposition *be-* means both "in" and "with." Therefore the first word of the Bible, *Be-Reshit,* may be translated: "With [the] Beginning" as well as: "In the Beginning"; cf. *Targum Yerushalmi* and Ramban, ad loc.; *Bereshit Rabbah* 1:1. (2) The subject of the verse, *Elohim,* "God," follows the verb, "created." The Zohar insists on reading the words in the exact order they appear and thereby transforms *Elohim* into the object; cf. *Megillah* 9a. This means that there is now no subject, but that is perfect because the true subject of emanation cannot be named. For the Zohar the words no longer mean: "In the Beginning God created," but rather: "With Beginning [by means of the point of Wisdom] the Ineffable Source created *Elohim* [the palace of *Binah*]."

The Hidden Light

the light ... created at first The primordial light of the first day of Creation. Elsewhere the Zohar identifies this light with the *sefirah* of *Hesed,* Love; see 1:20a; 2:137a, 166b. *Hesed* is the first *sefirah* that emanates from *Binah.*

the light of the eye A rabbinic tradition on the primordial light indicates its overwhelming brilliance; see *Bereshit Rabba* 3:6: "The light created during the six days of Creation cannot shine during the daytime because it overwhelms [literally, "dims"] the orb of the sun"; cf. Isaiah 30:26. A contrary view appears in *Shemot Rabbah* 35:1: "Its light was pleasant for the world and did not cause harm like the sun." *Bahir,* §§147, 190 state: "No creature could look at it"; cf. *Zohar Hadash, Bereshit* 15b (*Midrash ha-Ne'elam*); Philo, *De Opificio Mundi,* §§29–31. Here the Zohar draws a direct parallel between the primordial light and the light of vision. This may be an allusion to the mystical properties of the eye; see above, "Colors and Enlightenment."

the first Adam Aramaic, *Adam Qadma'ah,* "the first Adam," or "Primordial Adam." The term appears in both senses in the Zohar; see 1:37b, 91b, 139b; 2:144a, 167b, 262b, 275b; 3:43b. On the mythological and mystical implications, see below.

he saw from one end of the world to the other Cf. Talmud, *Hagigah* 12a; Rabbi El'azar said, "With the light that the Blessed Holy One created on the First Day, Adam could see from one end of the world to the other"; cf. *Bereshit Rabba* 41:3. There is a close parallel between the primordial light and the original nature of Adam; see Talmud, loc. cit.: Rabbi Judah said in the name of Rav, "Adam extended from one end of the world to the other." Like the primordial light, "the apple of Adam's heel overwhelmed [literally, "dimmed"] the orb of the sun" (*Tanḥuma, Aḥarei Mot*, §2). See Ginzberg, *Legends of the Jews* 5:112–3, n. 104 (hereafter cited as *Legends*); Altmann, "Gnostic Themes in Rabbinic Cosmology," *Essays in Honour of the Very Rev. Dr. J. H. Hertz* (London, 1942), pp. 28–32; idem, *Studies*, p. 133; Ephraim E. Urbach, *Ḥazal*, pp. 202–4; Lawrence Kushner, *Honey from the Rock*, pp. 93–120; idem, *The River of Light*, pp. 93–110. Numerous parallels exist in Gnostic, Iranian, and Buddhist traditions; see Mircea Eliade, "Spirit, Light, and Seed," *History of Religions* 11 (1971): 1–30. In Kabbalah the relationship between Adam and the light is regarded as one of the deepest secrets; see *Ketem Paz* on Zohar 1:37b: "My teacher taught me that Adam resembled the primordial light that was hidden away. Afterwards a thread-thin ray appeared to give breath [or "soul"; Hebrew, *neshamah*] to people on earth and life to those who walk thereon [see Isaiah 42:5].... Understand this, for the secret is one and of one foundation. I cannot expand on this, for thus have I been commanded."

"How great is your good ..." This verse is cited frequently in reference to the primordial light reserved for the righteous; cf. Genesis 1:4; see *Bahir*, §147; Zohar 1:47a; 2:220b; 3:88a.

Moses; ... saw When he was about to die, Moses climbed Mt. Nebo in Moab and saw the entire land of Israel from a distance; Deuteronomy 32:48–52; 34:1–5. In *Sifrei*, Deuteronomy, §338 Rabbi Joshua says that Moses was able to view the entire land because God "placed power in Moses' eyes and he saw from one end of the world to the other." The Zohar connects his vision with the power of the primordial light.

three wicked generations would arise ... He hid the light away Cf. *Shemot Rabbah* 35:1: Rabbi Judah son of Simon said, "As soon as the Blessed Holy One saw the generation of Enosh, the generation of the Flood, and the generation of the Tower of Babel, whose actions were corrupt, He hid the light away from them, as it is said: 'The light of the wicked is withheld' (Job 38:15). For whom did He hide it? For the righteous in the hereafter.... Where did He hide it? In the Garden of Eden, as it is said: 'Light is sown for the righteous' (Psalms 97:11)." Cf. Talmud, *Ḥagigah* 12a; *Bereshit Rabba* 3:6; 41:3. Concerning the generation of Enosh, Genesis 4:26 states: "Then, for the first time, the name YHVH was invoked." The Midrash takes this to mean that his was the first generation to worship idols and address them by the name *YHVH*; see *Bereshit Rabba* 23:7; cf. Maimonides, *Mishneh Torah, Hilkhot Avodah Zarah* 1:1.

the three unused months of his gestation ... Literally, "the three remaining months of his gestation." According to one midrashic tradition, Moses was born three months premature, and the phrase in Exodus 2:2, "She concealed him for three months," refers to the last three months of the normal period of pregnancy, which were the first three months of Moses' life; see *Targum Yerushalmi* and *Midrash ha-Gadol*, ad loc.; Rashi on Exodus 2:3. Talmud,

Sotah 12a, cites a tradition that when Moses was born the whole house filled with light; cf. *Shemot Rabbah* 1:24, and above, "The Birth of Moses," where rabbinic inference and allusion are spelled out mystically.

he was brought before Pharaoh ... See Exodus 2:3–10. Pharaoh's evil nature was incompatible with the holy light.

he wielded it Aramaic, *ishtammash beih*, "he used it." This verb can have theurgic connotations; see Mishnah, *Avot* 1:13; Scholem, *Jewish Gnosticism, Merkabah Mysticism, and Talmudic Tradition*, p. 54, n. 36; *Major Trends*, p. 358, n. 17; Urbach, *Hazal*, pp. 110–1.

"They were afraid to come near him" The entire verse reads: "Aaron and all the Children of Israel saw Moses, and behold, the skin of his face was radiant! They were afraid to come near him."

He wrapped himself in it as in a tallit ... *Tallit* originally meant "gown" or "cloak" and was worn by the wealthy and by distinguished rabbis and scholars. Later it came to mean "a prayer shawl." The image here derives from the Midrash; see *Midrash Tehillim* 104:4: "Rabbi Shim'on son of Yehoza-daq asked Rabbi Shemu'el son of Nahman, 'How did the Blessed Holy One create the light?' He answered, 'He wrapped Himself in a white *tallit*, and the world shone from His light.' He said this to him in a whisper. Rabbi Shim'on said, 'Is this not stated explicitly in the Bible? "He wraps Himself in light as in a garment."' Rabbi Shemu'el replied, 'As I received it in a whisper, so I told it to you in a whisper.'" Cf. *Bereshit Rabba* 3:4, and the parallels cited in Julius Theodor's edition (Jerusalem, 1965), p. 19. The image of God wrapping Himself in a garment of light appears in Greek, Iranian, and kabbalistic sources; see Robert Eisler, *Weltenmantel und Himmelszelt* (Munich, 1910), pp. 49–112; R. C. Zaehner, *Zurvan, A Zoroastrian Dilemma* (Oxford, 1955); Altmann, *Studies*, pp. 128–39; Scholem, *Jewish Gnosticism*, pp. 57–62. The Zohar employs the image frequently in describing the process of emanation; see 1:2a, 29a, 90a (*Sitrei Torah*); 2:39b, 164b. Here the image is transferred from God to Moses, and he wraps himself in the garment of light. The mythical nature of Moses unfolds in the Zohar on Exodus.

Every subject of the phrase ... Here the Zohar formulates its own exegetical principle while drawing on older rabbinic models. Cf. *Tanhuma* (ed. Buber), *Naso*, §24: Rabbi Shim'on son of Yohai said, "Wherever the phrase 'And there was' appears, it refers to something that was and ceased for many days and returned to its original state." Cf. *Bereshit Rabba* 41:3: "Rabbi Shim'on said in the name of Rabbi Yohanan, 'Wherever the phrase "And there was" appears, it serves for sorrow and for joy. If sorrow, there is none like it; if joy, there is none like it.' Rabbi Shemu'el son of Nahman came and made a distinction: 'Wherever it says, "And there was," there is sorrow; wherever it says, "And there will be," there is joy.' It was objected: 'But it is written: "God said, 'Let there be light!' And there was light."' He responded, 'There is no longer any joy, for the world was not worthy to use that light.'" Cf. Talmud,

Megillah 10b. The Zohar is alluding to the tradition that the light was hidden away for the righteous in the hereafter; see above. *Bahir*, §160, identifies the hidden light with the world that is coming, which it takes to mean: "the world that already came"; see below, end of notes to "*Qorban* and *Olah.*" The phrase "And there was light" is similarly taken to mean: "There already was light," i.e., the primordial light; see *Bahir*, §25; Zohar 1:16b, 30b, 45b; *Zohar Hadash*, *Bereshit*, la; *Yitro*, 37d; *Bereshit Rabba* 3:2, the variant readings, and Theodor's note, p. 19.

flared   Aramaic, *havah seliq nehoreih*, "its light rose"; cf. Zohar 1:45b.

and the worlds would not enjoy it because of them   The wicked have deprived the world of the primordial light.

the Righteous One! . . .   Hebrew, *zaddiq*. The appearance of this word in the verse from Psalms is proof to Rabbi Isaac that the reference is to the *sefirah* of *Yesod*, Foundation, who is called the Righteous One; cf. Proverbs 10:25; Talmud, *Hagigah* 12b; *Bahir*, §102. *Yesod* is the procreative power of God, and the primordial light is hidden there; cf. Zohar 1:1a, 45b; 2:35a, 166b–167a; *Tiqqunei Zohar*, §18, 31b; Eliade, "Spirit, Light, and Seed," p. 4. The same verse from Psalms is cited in the Midrash in reference to the hidden light; see above; *Midrash Tehillim* 27:1.

the worlds will be fragrant   Aramaic, *yitbassemun almin*; cf. similar phrases in Zohar 1:34a; 2:143a, 168a, 227a; 3:18a. The Zohar's use of the root *bsm* is influenced by Spanish *endulzar*; see Scholem, *Kabbalah*, p. 228; cf. idem, *Zohar*, p. 30: "then the worlds will be in harmony."

until the day . . .   literally, "until the day when it will be the world that is coming." The world that is coming reveals the hidden light; see above.

Rabbi Judah said . . .   The rest of this selection is from another discussion of Genesis 1:3 found in Zohar 2:148b–149a. It is no accident that the name Rabbi Judah appears here. The teaching that follows is a radical interpretation of the theme of the hidden light. Moses de León lends it an aura of tradition by transmitting it in the name of Rabbi Judah, who delivered a teaching on this theme in the Midrash; see *Bereshit Rabba* 41:3, and Theodor's note, pp. 405–6. Rabbi Judah introduces other variations on the hidden light in Zohar 1:121b (*Midrash ha-Ne'elam*); 3:88a. Zohar 2:166a–167a contains an elaborate sefirotic homily on the light. Here Rabbi Judah does not appear; instead, a young boy who is thought to be illiterate leaps over the heads of the rabbis, sits down and smiles, and begins to spout mystical secrets. Moses de León alternates between wrapping himself in the garment of tradition and startling the traditionalists.

absorbed in her   Aramaic, *de-la'an bah; la'ei* means "to work, toil, study." Torah is feminine.

as we have already established   in Talmud, *Hagigah* 12b: Resh Laqish said, "Whoever engages in Torah at night, the Blessed Holy One extends a thread-thin ray of love to him during the day, as it is said: 'By day *YHVH* will enjoin his love.' Why? Because 'in the night His song is with me.' " "His song" is the song of Torah; "His love," *ḥasdo*, suggests the *sefirah* of *Hesed*, the primordial light. With the words "as we have already established," Rabbi Judah conveys the impression that the motif of the hidden light is implied in the talmudic midrash. This midrash is often applied by the Zohar to the kabbalistic midnight study session; see, e.g., 1:82b; 2:46a; 3:22a. On the connection between Torah and the hidden light see *Bahir*, §§147–149; Zohar 1:47a; 2:167a; and the teaching of the Ba'al Shem Tov: "With the light of the six days of Creation, one could see from one end of the world to the other. Where did the Blessed Holy One hide it? He hid it in the Torah. And when it says: 'for the righteous,' this means for the righteous who will come into the world [i.e., not merely as their reward in the afterlife]. Whoever attains the light hidden in the Torah can see with it from one end of the world to the other" (*Shivḥei ha-Besht*, ed. Mintz, p. 79).

Since the first day of Creation. The reading "Since that day" is found in many editions; see the entire passage in Zohar 2:149a.

it plays a vital role Aramaic, *shimmusha qa meshammesh*, "it certainly does function"; cf. the use of the root *shmsh* above: "make use," "used," "wielded"; and Zohar 2:148b.

renewing every day the act of Creation! Cf. the morning liturgy: "Lord of wonders, the One who renews in His goodness every day continually the act of Creation." Cf. Augustine's image of the *semina seminum* implanted in the world at Creation to give rise to miracles (*De trinitate* 3:5–10). On the creative power of the primordial light see *Pirqei de-Rabbi Eli'ezer*, Chap. 3; Zohar 2:220b; *Zohar Hadash, Rut*, 85a (*Midrash ha-Ne'elam*); Menahem Recanati, *Commentary on the Torah*, p. 8c; Urbach, *Hazal, pp. 184–5*; and *Ketem Paz* on Zohar 1:47a: "For with the appearance of the light, the universe expanded. With its concealment, all existing things were created according to their species.... This is the secret of the act of Creation. One who is able to understand will understand."

Adam's Sin

YHVH Elohim two divine names. *YHVH* is the ineffable name of God; *Elohim* means "God" or "gods."

et Adam *Et* is an accusative particle introducing a determinate object. It has no independent sense and is lost in translation, though originally it may have meant "substance" or "essence." The Midrash often interprets this seemingly insignificant little word as an amplification of a biblical verse; see Talmud, *Pesaḥim* 22b. Here the word *et* and the apparent redundancy of the clause in which it occurs stimulate Rabbi El'azar to create a mystical midrash that hints at the true nature of Adam's sin.

divorced Aramaic, *aveid tirukhin*. Several *midrashim* interpret the Hebrew word *va-yegaresh*, "He drove out," in the sense of *geirushin* (Aramaic, *tirukhin*), "divorce." See *Tanna de-Vei Eliyahu*, §1: "*Va-yegaresh et ha-'adam*. This teaches that the Blessed Holy One gave him a divorce like a wife." Cf. *Ziqquqin de-Nura*, ad loc.; and *Midrash ha-Gadol* on this verse: "This teaches that he was divorced like a wife who is divorced from her husband because of something indecent [*ervat davar;* see Deuteronomy 24:1]." Cf. *Bereshit Rabba* 21:8; *Yalqut Shim'oni*, Genesis, §34. Adam's harmonious and intimate relationship with God is destroyed by sin. The Zohar adopts this midrashic view but reassigns the roles.

Et, precisely! In the Zohar *et* is a kabbalistic code name for *Shekhinah*, the last *sefirah*. Expressing the fullness of divine speech, *Shekhinah* spells out all the letters of the Hebrew alphabet, *alef* to *tav: et*. See Zohar 1:15b (and *Ketem Paz*, ad loc.), 30b. Once *Et* was driven out of the Garden, language became corrupt and remained so until the Revelation at Sinai; see *Zohar Hadash, Bereshit*, 8c (*Sitrei Otiyyot*); Zohar 1:55b–56a; and *Ketem Paz*, ad loc.

Adam drove out Et! The nature of Adam's sin is one of the most tightly guarded secrets of the Zohar. The language of Genesis 3, the Garden story, is understood as hiding the true meaning of the sin; see *Zohar Hadash, Bereshit*, 19a (*Midrash ha-Ne'elam*), where Rabbi Shim'on recounts a conversation he had with Adam while selecting his future place in Paradise: "Adam . . . was sitting next to me and speaking with me, and he asked that his sin not be revealed to the whole world beyond what the Torah had said concerning it. It is concealed in that tree in the Garden of Eden." The Tree of Knowledge of Good and Evil is a symbol of *Shekhinah*. Adam's sin was that he worshiped and partook of *Shekhinah* alone, thus splitting Her off from the higher *sefirot* and divorcing Her from Her husband, *Tif'eret*, the Tree of Life. Adam disrupted the unity of the cosmos and "severed the young trees" (*qizzez ha-neti'ot*). This last image, employed by the Talmud, to describe heresy, is applied by the Kabbalah to Adam's sin; see Talmud, *Hagigah* 14b; *Bereshit Rabba* 19:3; Zohar 1:12a–b, 35b–36a, 221a–b; 3:182a, 240a; Scholem, *Major Trends*, pp. 231–2, 236, 404–5, n. 105; *On the Kabbalah*, p. 108; *Ursprung*, p. 273; Tishby, *Mishnat ha-Zohar*, 1:221–3. On the psychological plane, the sin corresponds to the splitting off of consciousness from the unconscious; see Jung, *The Structure and Dynamics of the Psyche, Collected Works* 8:157; Erich Neumann, *The Origins and History of Consciousness* (Princeton, 1970), pp. 102–27; Julian Jaynes, *The Origin of Consciousness in the Breakdown of the Bicameral Mind* (Boston, 1976), p. 299; cf. Scholem, *Major Trends*, pp. 216, 236–7.

Here, by means of a midrashic twist, Rabbi El'azar indicates that Adam has divorced *Shekhinah*. This may mean "divorced Her from *Tif'eret*" or "divorced Her from himself." The first interpretation accords with the kabbalistic scheme outlined above; cf. Zohar 1:53a: "He caused a defect, separating the Wife from Her Husband." The second interpretation fits Rabbi El'azar's opening remark, though note the cryptic words "or not," which leave open the exact nature of the alternative. Cf. *Bereshit Rabba* 19:7: Rabbi Abba son of

Kahana said, "The essence of *Shekhinah* was in the lower worlds. As soon as Adam sinned, She withdrew to the first heaven." Moses de León's friend and fellow kabbalist, Joseph Gikatilla, expands this midrash in his *Sha'arei Orah*, p. 15: "You must realize an essential principle. Know that at the beginning of Creation, the essence of *Shekhinah* was in the lower worlds, for the arrangement of all creatures was in accord with the levels, high corresponding to high, low corresponding to low. So *Shekhinah* was in the lower worlds. Since She was below, heaven and earth were united ... perfecting one another, filling one another. The channels and wellsprings were working perfectly, conducting the flow from above to below. Thus *YHVH*, may He be blessed, filled everything from above to below....He was present equally in the upper and lower worlds. Then Adam came and sinned. The lines were ruined, the channels broken, the pools cut off; *Shekhinah* withdrew and the bond was severed."

Adam's sin has dissolved the union and driven *Shekhinah* from the Garden. But it has also dissolved the higher, sefirotic union, and *Shekhinah* finds Herself abandoned in a no man's land. Meanwhile, as a result of his sin, Adam is banished from the Garden. Wandering outside, he finds *Shekhinah*, and together they go into exile. Cf. above, "God, Israel, and *Shekhinah*"; Zohar 1:237a: "Come and see the secret of the word: Adam was caught by his very sin. He brought death upon himself and upon the whole world. He caused that Tree with which he sinned to be divorced, to be driven away with him, to be driven away with his children forever, as it is written: 'He drove out *et* Adam.'"

Male and Female

High mysteries ... The mysteries are explained below; these two verses are cited elsewhere as biblical indications of the secret arts of chiromancy and physiognomy. Such techniques were employed by the Merkavah mystics to ascertain whether a person was fit to receive esoteric teachings. "The book of the generations of Adam" was taken to mean "the book of human character and fate." "Male and female He created them" implied that chiromantic prediction varied according to sex, the right hand being the determining factor for the male, the left hand for the female. See *Ketem Paz* on this passage; Ramban on Genesis 5:2; Zohar 2:70a–b (*Raza de-Razin*), 75a, 77a; Scholem, *Kabbalah*, pp. 317–9; cf. *Sifra, Qedoshim* 4:12.

to make known the Glory on high, the mystery of faith The human being mirrors the structure of divinity, the ten *sefirot*, in which masculine and feminine are balanced. The *sefirot* constitute the mystery of faith, *raza di-meheimanuta*, the belief system of Kabbalah. See *Bahir*, §82; Zohar 1:101b; 3:117a, 141b (*Idra Rabba*); Tishby, *Mishnat ha-Zohar* 1:155–61; above, Introduction, §6.

heaven and earth ... Adam ... Rabbi Shim'on proves the correspondence between Adam's creation and the creation of heaven and earth by verbal analogy, a common technique of interpretation (*gezerah shavah*). The microcosm motif is ancient and widespread; see Altmann, *Studies*, pp. 19–28; and for rabbinic parallels, *Tanḥuma, Fequdei*, §3; *Avot de-Rabbi Natan*, Chap. 31; cf. Zohar 1:134b.

the mystery of our Mishnah Cf. Talmud, *Bava Batra* 74b: Rabbi Judah said in the name of Rav, "Everything that the Blessed Holy One created in His world He created male and female"; cf. Zohar 2:144b. Rabbi Shim'on's formulation does not appear in the Mishnah or the Talmud; he is referring to a secret, mystical Mishnah known only to him and his fellow kabbalists; see above, Introduction, n. 83.

Blessings are found only . . . Cf. Talmud, *Yevamot* 62b: Rabbi Tanhum said in the name of Rabbi Hanilai, "Any man who does not have a wife is without joy, without blessing, without goodness." Cf. Zohar 1:165a; 3:74b; Talmud, *Sotah* 17a.

when male and female are as one Cf. Talmud, *Yevamot* 63a: Rabbi El'azar said, "Any man [*adam*] who does not have a wife is not an *adam*, as it is said: 'Male and female He created them . . . and He called their name Adam.'" Rabbi Shim'on is also alluding to the original androgynous nature of Adam, a theme that informs the Zohar's psychology and theosophy. See *Bereshit Rabba* 8:1: Rabbi Jeremiah son of El'azar said, "When the Blessed Holy One created Adam He created him androgynous, as it is said: 'Male and female He created them.'" Rabbi Shemu'el son of Naḥman said, "When the Blessed Holy One created Adam He created him with a double face. Then He sawed him apart and gave him two backs, one on this side and one on that side." Cf. Talmud, *Berakhot* 61a; *Eruvin* 18a; Plato, *Symposium*, 189d–190d; Philo, *De Opificio Mundi*, §§24, 76; Ginzberg, *Legends*, 5:88–9, n. 42. The Zohar refers to this myth frequently; see 1:34b–35a, 37b (and *Ketem Paz*, ad loc.), 165a; 2:55a, 231a–b; 3:10b, 19a, 44b; *Zohar Hadash, Balaq*, 55c–d; *Shir ha-Shirim*, 66c. An essential component of the "mystery of faith" is that the sefirotic realm is androgynous. *Tif'eret* and *Shekhinah* are the masculine and feminine aspects of God, and the language of this myth is applied to them; see Zohar 1:30b–31a; 3:142b (*Idra Rabba*), 204a, 296a (*Idra Zuta*); cf. Gikatilla, *Sha'arei Orah*, p. 115. From their union all souls are born, and these souls too, in their original nature, are androgynous; see 1:85b, 91b, 108a; 2:246a; 3:43a–b, 283b. It is only because of Adam's sin that our androgynous nature has been lost; see 3:43b, 117a; *Zohar Hadash* 60b. Any man or woman who remains single is only "half a body" (*pelag gufa*); see 3:7b, 57b, 296a (*Idra Zuta*). But by joining together and engendering new life, each couple extends the chain of being. The inner purpose of human sexuality is to regain wholeness and manifest the oneness of God; see 3:7a, 81a–b; Tishby, *Mishnat ha-Zohar* 2:607–26; June Singer, *Androgyny*, pp. 144–63.

After the Flood (Midrash ha-Ne'elam)

Rabi   Rabbi Judah the *Nasi* (Patriarch), who lived in the second–third centuries and redacted the Mishnah. He was so highly esteemed that he was called *Rabi*, the Rabbi.

the aroma of his actions   Noah's bold statement is a delight to God. Cf. *Midrash Tehillim* 2:2: Rabbi Isaac said, "One person says to another, 'Why are you doing that?' and the other gets angry. But the righteous say to the Blessed Holy One, 'Why?' and he does not get angry; they are not punished. Why not? Because they have sought good not for themselves but for Israel." Cf. *Bereshit Rabba* 33:3; Talmud, *Mo'ed Qatan* 16b.

Therefore he commanded ...   The divine command to the people of Israel to offer sacrifices is expanded.

You are called Compassionate!   "*YHVH, YHVH*, a compassionate God" (Exodus 34:6).

Seeing this, Noah presented offerings   to atone for his selfish behavior.

Abraham thought there were ten   This explanation derives from *Bereshit Rabba* 49:13.

Moses also shielded   Cf. *Devarim Rabbah* 11:3, where Moses and Noah are contrasted, and *Mekhilta, Pisha*, §1.

Israel has sinned   by worshiping the Golden Calf.

overtaken by trembling   The Hebrew root of "implore," *ḥlḥ*, is here associated with *ḥil*, "to writhe, tremble." This midrashic wordplay is found in Talmud, *Berakhot* 32a.

the book that You have written   the Book of Life.

did not allow the attribute of Judgment ...   Cf. *Bereshit Rabba* 33:3: Rabbi Shemu'el son of Naḥman said, "Woe to the wicked, who turn the divine attribute of Compassion into the attribute of Judgment.... Happy are the righteous, who turn the divine attribute of Judgment into the attribute of Compassion."

He just built the ark ...   Since Noah failed to stand up to God and plead for the world, he is implicated in the holocaust. That is why Isaiah calls the Flood "the waters of Noah" (Isaiah 54:9): "Indeed, 'the waters of Noah'! They were named after him because he did not plead for mercy for the world" (Zohar 3:15a; cf. 1:67b).

Abram, the Soul-Breath (Midrash ha-Ne'elam)

Abram   the original form of Abraham's name; see Genesis 17:4–5.

soul-breaths of the righteous   Hebrew, *nishmotan shel zaddiqim*. In the Bible *neshamah* means "breath"; see Genesis 2:7: "He blew into his nostrils the breath of life [*nishmat ḥayyim*]." In the Zohar *neshamah* refers to a spiritual essence, the highest level of soul. This *neshamah* is sometimes correlated with the breath: "The *neshamah* of a human being ... leaves him every single night. In the morning she returns to him and dwells in his nostrils" (*Zohar Hadash, Rut* 90d [*Midrash ha-Ne'elam*]; cf. *Zohar Hadash, Noah,* 22a [*Midrash ha-Ne'elam*]; Zohar 2:155a; Jellinek, *Beit ha-Midrash* [Jerusalem, 1967], 3:137). According to Zohar 1:235a and 2:95b, *neshamot* are emanated by a divine breath.

carved from the bedrock of the Throne of Glory literally, "hewn out from beneath the Throne of Glory." In Talmud, *Shabbat* 152b, the souls of the righteous are said to be "hidden beneath the Throne of Glory" after death; cf. *Avot de-Rabbi Natan,* Chap. 12. The Zohar teaches that the soul has been created out of the substance of the Throne, which here refers to *Shekhinah,* mother of the soul; cf. Zohar 1:125b (*Midrash ha-Ne'elam*); *Zohar Hadash, Bereshit* 10d (*Midrash ha-Ne'elam*); Werblowsky, "Philo and the Zohar," *JJS* 10 (1959): 38–9.

her the soul-breath.

seven blessings the seven blessings pronounced in Genesis 12:2–3; cf. Zohar 1:78a (*Sitrei Torah*). Traditionally, seven blessings are recited at a marriage ceremony.

Avram, this is the soul-breath ... Employing the philosophical method of allegory, the *Midrash ha-Ne'elam* (the earliest stratum of the Zohar) weaves a drama of the fate of Avram, the soul-breath; see above, Introduction, n. 11.

the mirror that shines Hebrew, *ispaqlareya ha-me'irah.* In Talmud, *Yevamot* 49b, this image denotes the highest medium of prophecy. In the Zohar it designates *Tif'eret,* the Blessed Holy One, the central *sefirah* and divine mate of *Shekhinah.* The soul-breath is born from the union of *Tif'eret,* her father, and *Shekhinah,* her mother.

And even so even though the soul is far from her divine source.

'As long as the soul breathes within me ...' from the closing lines of *Elohai neshamah,* recited upon awakening.

Deviser of Evil Hebrew, *yezer ha-ra,* "the evil impulse, inclination." The root of *yzr* means "to fashion, devise," as in Genesis 8:21, quoted in the following lines.

Lot, who was cursed In Aramaic the verb *lut* means "to curse."

what Rabbi Isaac has said as reported in Zohar 1:35b.

challenge the soul-breath literally, "accuse" (Hebrew, *meqatreg*). The Deviser of Evil and the soul-breath battle for control of the human body; cf. *Zohar Hadash, Ki Teze* 58d: "All the limbs of the body are in torment, caught between the soul-breath and the Deviser of Evil."

Abram's Descent into Egypt

The main character here is Abraham the Patriarch, not the soul-breath.

to the depths of which Abraham descended Having discovered the mystery of faith, the mystical union of the divine realm, Abraham "had to know all those levels that are connected below" (Zohar 1:81b), the dark underside of wisdom. This wisdom of Egypt includes magic and alchemy. Abraham's descent symbolizes his exploration of *Sitra Aḥra*, "the Other Side," the Abyss. This dangerous psychic journey is the crucible of Abraham's spiritual transformation.

When Adam reached that level According to Kabbalah, Adam's sin was a misapprehension of the unity of God. Deceived by the serpent of false knowledge, he separated *Shekhinah* from the other *sefirot* instead of preserving their unity through pure contemplation. This tragic separation left *Shekhinah* vulnerable, enabling the demonic powers to take control of Her. Ever since, She has ruled the world under the aspect of the Tree of Death. See Zohar 1:35b, 52a–b, 221a–b; and above, "Adam's Sin." On the relation between *Shekhinah* and the demonic see Scholem, *Von der mystischen Gestalt der Gottheit*, pp. 183–6 (Hebrew translation: *Pirqei Yesod*, pp. 300–3); Tishby, *Mishnat ha-Zohar* 1:222–6.

The spelling implies 'her tent.' The Hebrew word in the verse is *ohaloh*, "his tent," but the suffix *o*, "his," is spelled here *oh* and can be read *ah*, "her." *Bereshit Rabba* 36:4 takes this to mean that Noah shamed himself in his wife's tent. The Zohar, expanding on the midrash, transfers Noah's sin to the divine feminine: *Shekhinah*. Noah was really trying to repair the damage caused by Adam, to reunite *Shekhinah* with the higher *sefirot*. However, intoxicated by the wine of false imagining, he blundered and "uncovered the breach of the world" (Zohar 1:73a–b; cf. Recanati, *Commentary on the Torah*, p. 20b).

the high rung he had grasped before Through his discovery of God and his own loving nature, Abraham had attained the rung of *Ḥesed*, Love, the first of the seven lower *sefirot*; cf. *Bahir*, §§135, 191.

rose to his full stature Cf. Mishnah, *Avot* 5:4: "Abraham was tested ten times, and he withstood them all, revealing how great was his love."

the Negev, the South, the high sphere The Negev is the southern region of the land of Israel and comes to mean "south." The *sefirah* of *Ḥesed*, Abraham's rung, is identified with south in the Zohar; cf. 1:80a.

refined as in the refining or smelting of precious metals, and as in alchemy. Cf. Cordovero's comment: "As silver is refined within lead, so holiness is refined through the power of the demonic" (*Or ha-Ḥammah*, ad loc.). The Zohar refers to alchemical transmutation in several passages; see *Encyclopaedia Judaica*, s.v. "alchemy."

partaken of the Blessed Holy One Abraham's descent into Egypt and safe return is a rite of passage. Having confronted and experienced the Abyss, he is transmuted into a divine hero, apotheosized as *Ḥesed*, the Love of God.

Openings

Abraham was sitting ... Sarah heard ... Three messengers from God appear to tell Abraham that Sarah, ninety years old and barren, will conceive and bear a son. Sarah overhears the fantastic promise.

Blessed be the Presence of YHVH wherever He is! Cf. Talmud, *Hagigah* 13b: "It is written: 'Blessed be the Presence of *YHVH* in His place' because no one knows his place." Cf. *Bahir*, §131: " 'Blessed be the Presence of *YHVH* in His place.' What is the Presence of *YHVH*? A parable. To what can this be compared? To a king who had a queen in his chamber over whom all his soldiers delighted. They had children who came every day to see the king and praise him. They said to him, 'Where is our mother?' He said, 'You cannot see her now.' They said, 'May she be blessed wherever she is!' "

How, then, can you say ... Rabbi Judah addresses his question directly to the Bible and then presents the answer himself.

Her husband is the Blessed Holy One! Proverbs 31:10–31, which describes the "woman of valor," is understood by the Zohar as a hymn to *Shekhinah*, the feminine aspect of God. Her husband is *Tif'eret*, the Blessed Holy One, a more transcendent *sefirah*; cf. *Va-Yiqra Rabbah*, 11:8.

to the degree that one opens the gates of imagination! literally, "according to what one imagines [or "estimates"] in his heart." The Hebrew word *sha'ar*, "gate," is here associated with the verb *sha'er*, "to imagine, estimate." Imagination provides the human being access to God, though, as Rabbi Judah goes on to say, all imaginative representations fall short of God's true being. Cf. the line in "The Song of the Presence," ascribed to Rabbi Judah the *Hasid* (twelfth century): "They have portrayed You in many visions; You remain one through all imaginings."

The relation between visions of the divine realm and human imagination is pointed out by Hai Gaon (tenth century) and Hanan'el son of Hushi'el (eleventh century). Hai, describing the heavenly ascent of the Merkavah mystics, writes: "... not that they actually ascend to heaven, but rather, they see and gaze within the recesses of their hearts [or "minds"; see the following note]." Hanan'el, perhaps borrowing from Hai, says: "The Blessed Holy One reveals His Presence to those who fear and love Him, through speculation of the mind [*be-'ovanta de-libba*]"; cf. Talmud, *Megillah* 24b. For the sources see Reuven Margaliot's comment in his edition of the Zohar, ad loc. Cf. Moses de León's statement in his *Mishkan ha-'Edut*: "They saw the King of Hosts in their mind" (cited by Scholem, *Major Trends*, p. 397, n. 151).

in one's heart-mind Aramaic, *be-libbeih*. *Lev*, usually translated "heart," also means "mind" in the Bible.

these gates, these spheres on high the *sefirot*, stages of emanation through which the Unknown becomes known.

Neshamah the soul-breath, the spiritual essence of the human being.

Neshamah of neshamah The human *neshamah* is of divine origin; the Blessed Holy One is the essence of this essence. Here "Blessed Holy One" refers not to *Tif'eret* but to *Ein Sof*, the Infinite, who becomes known through the *sefirot*. The phrase *"neshamah of neshamah"* derives from Solomon ibn Gabirol's *Keter Malkhut:* "You are alive but not through soul [*nefesh*] or *neshamah*, for You are *neshamah* of *neshamah*"; cf. above, "How to Look at Torah"; Talmud, *Berakhot* 10a; *Midrash Tehillim* 103:5.

openings for neshamah The *sefirot* are openings for the human *neshamah* to approach the hidden God, and openings for *Neshamah* of *neshamah* to manifest.

opening within opening, level beyond level The *sefirot* are revealed one by one as the mystic journeys within and beyond.

'The opening of the tent' Rabbi Shim'on connects his teaching with Genesis 18:10.

the opening of Righteousness . . . the first opening *Shekhinah* is the opening of the divine tent, the first *sefirah* one encounters upon entering the divine realm; cf. *Bahir*, §63; Zohar 1:7b, 79b. She is also called *Zedeq*, Righteousness or Justice; see *Bahir*, §§74–75, 120.

all other high openings come into view All the other *sefirot* are reflected in *Shekhinah*. Entering Her, the mystic's awareness and consciousness expand.

Now that Israel is in exile, this opening is unknown Israel's historical exile symbolizes cosmic dysfunction. The unity of the *sefirot* has been ruptured. All the higher openings have closed shut and vanished, leaving *Shekhinah* Herself in exile: alienated from the higher realms and unknown on earth.

the soaring spheres the higher *sefirot*.

All these The various "spirits" in the verse represent the higher *sefirot*.

the Opening of the Tent *Shekhinah*.

the good news that a child would be born to Sarah.

this sphere *Shekhinah*, the Opening of the Tent.

'Sarah heard the Opening of the Tent' The clause is often translated: "Sarah was listening at the opening of the tent." The Hebrew, however, employs no preposition before "the opening." Taking advantage of this ellipsis, Rabbi Shim'on reads the words with mystical literalness: "Sarah heard the Opening of the Tent." She heard *Shekhinah*, who was revealing to Abraham that Sarah would soon give birth.

An Offering to God

removes him from the world Satan and the angel of death are two manifestations of *Sitra Aḥra*, "the Other Side," the demonic; cf. Talmud, *Bava Batra* 16a.

To gladden the poor   Cf. *Zohar Hadash, Rut,* 87b (*Midrash ha-Ne'elam*): "The Blessed Holy One enjoys the food that one gives to a poor person because that food satisfies the poor person and makes him happy." Cf. *Zavva'at R. Eli'ezer,* §27.

His broken vessels   Cf. Psalms 34:19: "*YHVH* is close to the broken-hearted." The Midrash calls such supplicants "broken utensils" (*Vayiqra Rabba* 7:2). In the Zohar it is the poor who are God's broken vessels. They are compared to *Shekhinah* because, like Her, they have nothing at all of their own (3:113b). As She is provided for by the other *sefirot,* so we must provide for the poor, and "anyone who mistreats a poor person mistreats *Shekhinah*" (2:86b).

The members of the Academy of Heaven   The souls of the righteous reside in heaven, imbibe the deepest secrets of Torah, and defend the human species.

You are called Compassionate and Gracious   "*YHVH, YHVH,* a God compassionate and gracious, slow to anger, abounding in love" (Exodus 34:6).

It is love that sustains the world!   If there are no deeds of love, the world will collapse.

the Accuser   Satan.

He was kindhearted to all creatures   Abraham's devotion to God and love of his fellow creatures elevated him to the rung of *Hesed,* the *sefirah* of Love; cf. above, "Abram's Descent into Egypt," "Guests in the *Sukkah.*"

all the great people of his time   Cf. *Bereshit Rabba* 53:10: Rabbi Judah said, " 'A great feast' means a feast of the great. Og [King of Bashan] and all the great ones were there."

Now we have learned   apparently a new teaching.

no one believed that she had given birth   since she was ninety years old and barren until then; cf. Talmud, *Bava Mezi'a* 87a; *Pirqei de-Rabbi Eli'ezer,* Chap. 52.

and gave nothing to me   Most printed editions read "to You," i.e., to God; however the earliest editions (Mantua and Cremona) read: "to me," i.e., to Satan.

not even a single dove . . .   Cf. Talmud, *Sanhedrin* 89b: Rabbi Yohanan said in the name of Rabbi Yose son of Zimra, "Satan said in the presence of the Blessed Holy One, 'Master of the world! You bestowed upon this old man the fruit of the womb at the age of one hundred! From his entire feast could he not offer a single dove or pigeon to You?' " Cf. *Bereshit Rabba* 55:4. Leviticus 5:7 specifies doves or pigeons as the offering that a poor person may bring if he cannot afford a sheep.

But he held his ground   Satan would not leave God's presence or relent until . . .

that Isaac be brought as an offering   The Talmud (loc. cit.) suggests that God commanded Abraham to offer up Isaac in order to prove to Satan that Abraham was a loyal servant. Here the tone is different. The binding of

Isaac is a punishment for Abraham's selfishness and neglect of the poor, a substitute offering to God; cf. *Bereshit Rabba* 55:5, where Micah 6:7 is cited.

Sarah would die in anguish as related in the Midrash (*Tanḥuma, Va-Yera,* §23; *Pirqei de-Rabbi Eli'ezer,* Chap. 32).

he brought about Abraham brought about.

The Binding of Abraham and Isaac

devarim things.

Elohim a divine name; see below.

We have learned in the Talmud, *Megillah* 10b.

the lowest of all the higher spheres . . . Devarim *Shekhinah*, the last of the ten *sefirot,* is called *davar,* "word" of God; see Zohar 1:1b; 3:191a, 193b. Through Her the ineffable divine essence is mediated and expressed. *Davar* means both "word" and "thing." Here the plural, *devarim,* is cited from the verse and applied to *Shekhinah.*

'I am not a man of devarim' At the beginning of his career, Moses denied that he was connected with *Shekhinah.* Later, however, he is described as Her partner; cf. above, "The Birth of Moses"; Zohar 1:192b.

Elohim . . . The Deviser of Evil came to accuse him *Elohim* has a wide range of meaning in the Zohar. Already in rabbinic literature it is distinguished from *YHVH* and applied specifically to *din,* the divine attribute of judgment; see *Sifrei,* Deuteronomy, §26. Similarly in the Zohar *Elohim* often refers to the *sefirah* of *Din* or *Gevurah,* Judgment or Power. Sometimes it refers to *Binah,* the Divine Mother, situated above *Gevurah* (see above, "The Creation of *Elohim*"), while elsewhere it is a name for *Shekhinah,* since She is said to lean toward the left, toward *Din. Elohim* also refers to various powers that originate in *Din;* see Zohar 1:111b; 3:8a, 200a. In this passage *Elohim* refers both to *Din* (cf. 3:18a) and the Deviser of Evil, a harsh manifestation of *Din* who appears outside the divine realm, after the sphere of *Shekhinah.* According to Talmud, *Sanhedrin* 89b, when Satan accused Abraham of neglecting God, God responded by commanding Abraham to sacrifice Isaac and thereby prove his devotion and zeal; see above, "An Offering to God," where Rabbi Shim'on alters the talmudic account and suggests that the binding of Isaac is a punishment, not a test. Here Rabbi Shim'on presents a more paradoxical view: the Deviser of Evil is working for *Elohim;* his accusation is really part of God's plan, a mystical, psychological challenge to Abraham.

reflect Aramaic, *le-'istakkala.* In earlier mystical literature this verb means "to contemplate"; see Scholem, *Kabbalah,* p. 369; cf. *Bereshit Rabba* 2:4. In the Zohar it often appears in the context of mystical search or mystical exegesis; see 1:10a, 34b; 3:151b, 224a, 270b (*Matnitin*); *Zohar Ḥadash, Bereshit* 11d, 15b; *Noaḥ,* 23d (*Midrash ha-Ne'elam*); *Va-'Etḥannan,* 58d (*Qav ha-Middah*).

Isaac was already thirty-seven years old as related in the Midrash (*Tanhuma, Va-Yera,* §23).

Rigor Aramaic, *dina* (Hebrew, *din*). Abraham had attained the level of *Hesed,* Love, through his devotion and goodness. However, he was one-sided; he had to balance Hesed with *Din,* strict judgment and rigor. This new dimension would round out his personality and make him a complete human being in the image of God; cf. *Bereshit Rabba* 78:8; Zohar 1:230b; 2:257a; 3:18a; Moses de León, *Sod Eser Sefirot Belimah,* p. 372.

Water was crowned with Fire Water and Fire represent the pair of opposite *sefirot, Hesed* and *Din. Hesed* is free-flowing love; *Din,* the purgative power of judgment and rigor. Their conjunction symbolizes Abraham's wholeness.

to ordain it in its domain Abraham's attainment has cosmic effects. By manifesting *Din,* he conducts the power of that *sefirah* into the world.

That is why 'Elohim tested Abraham' ... Cf. *Bereshit Rabba* 55:1: "... test after test, elevation after elevation, in order to test them in the world, to elevate them in the world ... so that the attribute of Judgment be arrayed in the world"; cf. Zohar 3:18a.

One was judged and one executed judgment following the reading of *Ketem Paz,* ad loc. Isaac submits to Abraham, and together they enact the drama of the *sefirot.*

to challenge Aramaic, *le-qatrega,* "to accuse."

et Abraham On the word *et* see above, "Adam's Sin," note on "*et* Adam."

Isaac ... the sphere of low power *Et* indicates Isaac because of the midrashic principle noted above (ibid.) and because in the Zohar *et* refers to *Shekhinah,* the lowest sphere, "the sphere of low power"; see above, "Adam's Sin," note on "*Et,* precisely!" Isaac was destined to rise to the sphere of high power (*Din, Gevurah*), but at this stage he was unfulfilled and inhabiting the lower sphere of *Shekhinah.*

he was arrayed in his own sphere alongside Abraham Having undergone Judgment, Isaac manifests *Din* alongside Abraham, who manifests *Hesed*; cf. Zohar 1:133b.

Thus the battle was joined Abraham and Isaac, *Hesed* and *Din,* have completed each other but have not yet been reconciled. Their dialectical relationship awaits a synthesis.

until Jacob appeared ... Jacob, the third and decisive Patriarch, represents the *sefirah* of *Tif'eret,* Beauty and harmony. He was able to balance the polar qualities of *Hesed* and *Din,* Abraham and Isaac. He is called Israel, the father of the Jewish people, who are enjoined to realize the divine plan on earth.

Jacob's Journey (Sitrei Torah)

the hidden nexus   the realm of the ten *sefirot*.

the sealed secret   the deepest recesses of the *sefirot: Keter, Hokhmah,* and *Binah.*

a zohar   an effulgence, a splendor; cf. above, "The Creation of *Elohim.*"

shining as a mirror   The *zohar* is the first ray of *Tif'eret,* Beauty, the central *sefirah. Tif'eret* is also called "the mirror that shines"; cf. above, "Abram, the Soul-Breath."

embracing two colors   *Tif'eret* includes and balances the two polar *sefirot, Hesed* and *Din,* Love and Judgment. Their colors are white and red; *Tif'eret* is green, the color of harmony and life.

purple   *Tif'eret* is the King, the *Blessed Holy One;* so royal purple is also His color; cf. Zohar 2:135a; 3:141b (*Idra Rabba*).

flashing, disappearing   Hebrew, *razo va-shov,* "racing back and forth." The phrase first occurs in Ezekiel 1:14, describing the prophet's vision of the heavenly creatures. The Zohar applies this image to mystical vision; cf. *Sefer Yezirah* 1:6, 8; *Zohar Hadash, Yitro,* 39d; *Shir ha-Shirim,* 62a; *Sheqel ha-Qodesh,* p. 113; above, Introduction, nn. 116–7, 142; and the intriguing reference to cannabis in the context of a fleeting comprehension of the knowledge of God: *Zohar Hadash, Bereshit* 16a (*Midrash ha-Ne'elam*).

In this zohar dwells the one who dwells ...   *Ein Sof,* the Infinite, manifests through *Tif'eret,* who thus provides a name for the Ineffable. Moses de León may also be alluding to his own concealment within the Zohar. His pseudepigraphic technique provides him with a pseudonym; cf. above, Introduction, §5.

the Voice of Jacob   Cf. Genesis 27:22. *Tif'eret* is called both Voice and Jacob. He mediates the ineffable essence of the divine into the phenomenon of raw speech: voice. (Individual words are not articulated until *Shekhinah* appears; She is called Speech and Word.) *Tif'eret* is represented by Jacob, the third Patriarch, who balanced Abraham and Isaac; see the end of the previous selection.

Here dwells YHVH ...   the divine name given to *Tif'eret,* who is also called the Blessed Holy One and Compassion (*Rahamim*); cf. *Sifrei,* Deuteronomy, §26, where *YHVH* is associated with the attribute of *Rahamim. Tif'eret* is the focus of all the lower *sefirot,* the various sides and dimensions.

perfection of the Patriarchs   Cf. the end of the previous selection; *Targum Onqelos* on Genesis 25:27; and *Bereshit Rabba* 76:1: "The chosen one among the Patriarchs is Jacob, as it is said: 'For *Yah* has chosen Jacob for Himself' (Psalms 135:4)."

At first, Jacob; later, Israel   After wrestling with the divine, Jacob was given the name Israel; see Genesis 32:25–29, and below.

the End of Thought   *Shekhinah,* the last *sefirah,* is the consummation of the process of emanation, which begins with the appearance of *Hokhmah,*

Wisdom and Thought. She is therefore called both Lower Wisdom and the End of Thought. Mystical ascent begins with Her.

Written Torah *Tif'eret.*

Oral Torah *Shekhinah,* the mouth of the *sefirot,* who mediates revelation to the lower worlds; see Scholem, *On the Kabbalah,* pp. 47–8.

Be'er The root letters mean both "to explain" and "a well."

Sheva, Seven the Divine Mother, *Binah,* who gives birth to the seven lower *sefirot.* Six of these flow into the seventh, *Shekhinah,* and manifest through Her.

"It took him sheva, seven, years . . ." for Solomon to build the Temple. The Temple symbolizes *Binah,* who contains seven years: the seven lower *sefirot;* cf. Zohar 2:31a.

the Mighty Voice Cf. Deuteronomy 5:19. *Binah,* the Mighty Voice, is the source of *Tif'eret,* the Voice of Jacob; cf. Zohar 1:50b.

Be'er Sheva *Shekhinah* is the *be'er,* the well and explanation, of *Binah,* who is *Sheva.* Thus *Be'er Sheva* in the Jacob story refers to *Shekhinah,* the first stage of his mystical journey.

this gateway to faith *Shekhinah,* the opening to the realm of the *sefirot,* which are the object of mystical faith; cf. above, "Openings."

entering in peace and emerging in peace The same phrase appears in rabbinic literature to describe Rabbi Akiva's successful journey into the mystical orchard; see Tosefta, *Hagigah* 2:4; *Shir ha-Shirim Rabbah* 1:28.

Adam entered . . . Here we find another perspective on Adam's sin: he was seduced by demonic and sexual forces; cf. Zohar 1:140b; 2:245a; and above, "Adam's Sin," "Abram's Descent into Egypt."

that whore of a woman Lilit, the demonic feminine, who seduces men to sin. In the Zohar she is identified with the serpent; see below; cf. Tishby, *Mishnat ha-Zohar* 1:301–7; Patai, *The Hebrew Goddess,* pp. 180–225; Scholem, *Kabbalah,* pp. 356–61.

". . . within his tent" Cf. above, "Abram's Descent into Egypt."

Abraham entered See ibid.

Isaac entered . . . Isaac's journey to a foreign country is interpreted as a descent into the demonic realm; cf. Zohar 1:140b.

the other side the demonic sphere. Lilit and *Shekhinah* are reverse sides of each other; see above, "Seduction Above and Below."

Be'er Sheva *Shekhinah.*

Haran, the side of the woman of whoredom Lilit, the dark side of the feminine. The Zohar associates *Haran* with *haron,* "wrath"; cf. 1:78b (*Sitrei Torah*).

The secret of secrets a veiled description of the genesis of the demonic.

the scorching noon of Isaac Isaac represents the *sefirah* of *Din* or *Gevurah,* Judgment or Power. This *sefirah* is meant to balance *Hesed,* Love. If, however, its fire and power rage out of control, the results can be catastrophic.

the dregs of wine Wine is a symbol of *Din* or *Gevurah* because of its innate power. The dregs are the source of a dangerous concoction that gives rise to chaos and evil.

red as a rose Red symbolizes the power of the left and the demonic.

Sama'el Satan

his female Lilit. The Zohar avoids mentioning her name.

Just as it is... In the sefirotic realm *Tif'eret* and *Shekhinah* are male and female; if they are not united, holiness cannot function.

Serpent, Woman of Whoredom, End of All Flesh The Zohar links sin, lust, and death. All these are the work of Lilit acting in consort with Sama'el. The phrase "woman of whoredom" is from Hosea 1:2; "end of all flesh" is from the story of the Flood, Genesis 6:13; cf. Zohar 1:62b–63b.

she grabs him and kisses him an Aramaic rendering of Proverbs 7:13, which describes a prostitute's advances.

the venom of vipers Cf. Job 20:14.

fabric from Egypt Cf. Proverbs 7:16: the prostitute's invitation. On the reading adopted here see *Ketem Paz*, ad loc.

forty adornments minus one corresponding to the number of lashes administered by the court according to rabbinic law; see Deuteronomy 25:3; Mishnah, *Makkot* 3:10. Lilit's allurements soon turn into punishments.

ascends, denounces him... Cf. Talmud, *Bava Batra* 16a, where Satan's itinerary is described: "He descends and leads astray, ascends and arouses [God's] anger, obtains permission and takes the soul."

turns into a powerful warrior Lilit becomes Sama'el.

He is full of fearsome eyes Sama'el is also the angel of death. Cf. Talmud, *Avodah Zarah* 20b: "It has been said of the angel of death that he is completely full of eyes. When a sick person is about to die, he stands above the head of the bed. In his hand is a drawn sword with a bitter drop suspended. When the sick person sees him, he is frightened and opens his mouth. The angel flings the drop inside. From this drop he dies; from this drop he turns putrid; from this drop his face turns green."

Jacob descended to her He exposed himself to demonic and sexual temptation as part of his journey of transformation. Cf. Zohar 2:163a, where a king tests his son by instructing a prostitute to try to seduce him. There the parable symbolizes the encounter with the Deviser of Evil. Here Lilit serves the same function in a more dramatic and mythological setting.

Haran see above.

"And a man wrestled with him" In Genesis this man is a superhuman power; see Genesis 32:29. *Midrash Tanhuma, Va-Yishlah*, §8 identifies him with Sama'el.

raised... called Israel Jacob's struggle with the demonic, his prevailing over Lilit and Sama'el, clear the way for his ascent to *Tif'eret*, the *sefirah* of wholeness and balance. Having attained perfection, he receives a new name:

Israel, "for you have struggled with superhuman and with human beings, and you have prevailed" (Genesis 32:29).

"The center bar ..." from the description of the Tabernacle built by the Children of Israel in the desert, which symbolizes the structure of the *sefirot*. *Tif'eret* is the center bar, balancing right and left, joining the higher and lower *sefirot;* cf. Zohar 1:1b. Jacob, now centered and whole, manifests *Tif'eret Yisra'el*, the Beauty of Israel.

Joseph's Dream

levels within levels the *sefirot* and the entire chain of being.

these absorbing those the lower absorbing the flow of life (literally, "sucking") from the higher.

these on the right, those on the left Life is a balance between the flow of love and the force of limitation, the *sefirot* of *Hesed* and *Din*, right and left.

from a single aspect, through two well-known levels Prophecy is the result of emanation. The pair of lower *sefirot, Nezah* and *Hod*, Endurance and Majesty, are the channels of inspiration, the field of prophetic vision; cf. Zohar 2:251b; 3:35a.

the mirror that does not shine *Shekhinah*, the lowest *sefirah*, is the medium through which the prophet sees his vision. She is called *ispaqlareya*, "mirror" or "speculum," but one that is not clear. The divine essence must be filtered even for a prophet; otherwise it would be overwhelming. Cf. Talmud, *Yevamot* 49b: It has been taught: "All the prophets gazed through a mirror that does not shine; Moses our Rabbi gazed through a mirror that shines." Cf. 1 Corinthians 13:12: "For now we see through a glass darkly, but then face to face." *Tif'eret*, the *sefirah* of Jacob and Moses, is called "the mirror that shines"; see above, "Abram, the Soul-Breath."

a mirror in which all colors appear The Hebrew word *mar'ah* means both "vision" and " mirror." *Shekhinah* is a mirror reflecting all the other *sefirot* to the gaze of the prophet, though not with full clarity; cf. Zohar 1:88b.

one-sixtieth of prophecy Cf. Talmud, *Berakhot* 57b: "Fire is one-sixtieth of hell; honey is one-sixtieth of manna; the Sabbath is one-sixtieth of the world that is coming; sleep is one-sixtieth of death; a dream is one-sixtieth of prophecy." (*Berakhot* 55a–57b contains a wealth of material on dreams and interpretation.) Cf. Maimonides, *Guide of the Perplexed* 2:36: "The action of the imaginative faculty in the state of sleep is also its action in the state of prophecy; there is, however, a deficiency in it and it does not reach its ultimate term." Averroes alludes to a *hadith* according to which Muhammed defined a dream as the forty-sixth part of prophecy (*Epitome* 67:4–11; 84:11).

the sixth level from the level of prophecy From the level of prophecy to the level of dream there are six stages: the *sefirot Nezah, Hod, Yesod*, and *Shekhinah*, and the angels Michael and Gabriel.

Gabriel In the Book of Daniel Gabriel is the angel who interprets dreams (Daniel 8:16; 9:22). In Merkavah mysticism he is one of the four archangels. Here he appears as the prince of dreams.

already been said elsewhere in the Zohar: 1:149b.

false imaginings intermingling… Gabriel is located beneath *Shekhinah*, outside the realm of the purely divine; so demonic forces are in the vicinity. It is these forces who smuggle false images into the dream material; see Zohar 1:130a–b. Cf. Talmud, *Berakhot* 55a: Rabbi Yohanan said in the name of Rabbi Shim'on son of Yohai, "As there can be no grain without straw, so there can be no dream without absurdities."

follow the interpretation of the mouth of the interpreter; see *Berakhot* 55b.

that lower level Gabriel.

Speech commands that level *Shekhinah* is the realm of Speech: She expresses divine language; cf. Zohar 3:261a. She rules over Gabriel; thus "Speech commands that level." Human interpretation is effective because its words activate the divine realm of Speech, who then translates the dream into reality.

enthrone and accept the Kingdom of Heaven by reciting the *Shema:* "Hear O Israel! *YHVH* is our God; *YHVH* is One" (Deuteronomy 6:4); see *Berakhot* 4b.

a verse of mercy, as the Comrades have established The verse is Psalms 31:6: "Into Your hand I entrust my spirit; You redeem me, *YHVH*, faithful God." The Comrades (Aramaic, *ḥavrayya*) are the rabbis of the Talmud; see *Berakhot* 5a.

each one on its own path A soul receives what it is prepared to receive, and ascends as high as its nature and conduct allow.

She the soul.

things corresponding to the mind's reflections corresponding to the impressions left in the dreamer's mind from the day that has ended. Cf. *Berakhot* 55b: Rabbi Shemu'el son of Naḥman said, quoting Rabbi Yonatan, "A person is shown only what is suggested by the reflections of his mind."

Dream … vision … prophecy Gabriel, *Shekhinah*, *Nezaḥ* and *Hod*.

From here we learn … Cf. Zohar 1:200a: "One who dreams a dream should discuss it in the presence of people who love him, so that their will may work in his favor and their utterances be good. Then will and word become completely good."

for twenty-two years it was delayed The dream that Joseph told his brothers is related in Genesis 37:7: "We were binding sheaves in the field, when suddenly my sheaf stood upright; and behold, your sheaves gathered around and bowed down to mine!" Talmud, *Berakhot* 55b reckons that it took twenty-two years for this dream to be fulfilled, i.e., for Joseph's brothers to bow down to him; see Genesis 42:6.

they provoked accusations against him Their hatred had cosmic impact, stimulating demonic forces to delay the fulfillment of the dream.

then he revealed the dream to them see the note before last.

Suddenly . . . sealed their own fate! Their spontaneous, angry reaction revealed the correct reading of the dream. By expressing it in words, they guaranteed the dream's fulfillment.

Seduction Above and Below

"Though she urged him" Genesis 39:10 reads: "Though she urged Joseph." Later in this passage the Zohar cites the verse correctly twice. Here Moses de León may be altering the biblical text intentionally in order to leave the object of the seduction unspecified in accord with his midrashic message: Beware of the alien woman, the temptress, the Deviser of Evil, who seduces everyone day after day.

for the Name within her Hebrew, *li-shemah*, "for her name," for her own sake. This is the ideal mode of study: to engage in Torah without selfish motives, purely as an end in itself; see Mishnah, *Avot* 6:1; Talmud, *Sukkah* 49b, *Ta'anit* 7a, *Sanhedrin* 97b. For the kabbalist, Torah is the Name of God; see above, Introduction, n. 112. The goal of mystical study is to learn this Name, to recite it constantly, to address and encounter the Infinite.

'Long life she offers . . .' Cf. *Sifrei*, Deuteronomy, §48.

on the right side of Torah with pure intention, for the Name within her; cf. Rashi on Talmud, *Shabbat* 63a: "those who walk on her right side—engaged in Torah for her own sake."

the world that is coming On the mystical significance of this phrase see below, end of notes to "*Qorban* and *Olah*."

he still obtains . . . riches and honor Cf. Talmud, *Shabbat* 63a; Zohar 1:184b.

his face shone Cf. Jerusalem Talmud, *Shabbat* 8:1, 11a; *Pirqei de-Rabbi Eli'ezer*, Chap. 2; *Kitvei Ramban* 2:305–6; Zohar 2:15a; 3:163a.

He would pray for the other as Rav Safra prayed, according to Talmud, *Berakhot* 17a. Cf. *Pesaḥim* 50b: Rabbi Judah said, quoting Rav: "A person should always engage in Torah and *mizvot* even if not for their own sake, because by doing them not for their own sake, he will eventually do them for their own sake."

turned pale . . . 'This one is conceiving sinful thoughts!' Cf. Talmud, *Shabbat* 33a: "Dropsy is a sign of sin; paleness is a sign of blind hatred"; cf. *Yevamot* 60b; Rashi and Tosafot, ad loc. In Zohar 3:193b Rabbi Shim'on quotes a different formulation: "Paleness is a sign of sin." He cites the Book of Wisdom of King Solomon as his source, but the Apocryphal *Wisdom of Solomon* contains no such statement. Rabbi Shim'on is relying on one of the imaginary sources in his Celestial Library; see above, Introduction, §5.

and they will pass away Cf. *Avot de-Rabbi Natan,* Chap. 20: Rabbi Hananya, Assistant to the Priests, said, "Anyone who meditates on words of Torah . . . the imaginings of the Deviser of Evil are removed from him."

pull it toward Torah Cf. Talmud, *Sukkah* 52b: It was taught in the school of Yishma'el: "If you run into the repulsive one [the Deviser of Evil] drag him to the house of study!" Cf. *Qiddushin,* 30b; and *Sifrei,* Deuteronomy, §45: "The Blessed Holy One said to Israel, 'My children, I created the Deviser of Evil for you; no one is worse than he. . . . Engage in words of Torah, and he will have no power over you; keep away from words of Torah, and he will control you."

mizvah a divine command.

the Other Side The demonic is the opposite of the holy. It is both masculine and feminine, Sama'el and Lilit. It moves back and forth between heaven and earth, demanding strict judgment from God and tempting human beings to sin.

as was done to Job Satan received God's permission to test Job's character and faith; see Job 1:6–12; 2:1–6.

when the Blessed Holy One stands in judgment on *Rosh ha-Shanah,* the First of the Year, and *Yom Kippur,* the Day of Atonement.

A shofar on Rosh ha-Shanah The *shofar,* a ram's horn, is a device to confound Satan. "It is written: 'He will swallow up death forever' (Isaiah 25:8), and it is written: 'On that day a great *shofar* shall be blown' (Isaiah 27:13). When Satan hears the sound of the *shofar* the first time, he is a little frightened. When they repeat it, he says, 'That must be the *shofar* of "a great *shofar* shall be blown." My time has come to be swallowed up!' He trembles, becomes confused, and has no time to make accusations" (a midrash quoted in the *Arukh,* s.v. "*arev*"; cf. Talmud, *Rosh ha-Shanah* 16a–b).

on Yom Kippur a scapegoat ... This has been established This ritual of atonement is described in Leviticus 16:7–22. Aaron casts lots over two he-goats. One is designated as a sin offering to *YHVH;* the other is designated for Azazel, a demonic power. This second goat is sent off to the wilderness to carry away the sins of Israel. Cf. the Babylonian Akitu ritual of offering a goat as a substitute for a human being to Ereshkigal, the goddess of the Abyss.

The late Midrash *Pirqei de-Rabbi Eli'ezer* (Chap. 46) says: "They gave him [Satan] a bribe on *Yom Kippur* so that he would not interfere with Israel's sacrifice." Rabbi El'azar draws on the midrashic passage here and then alludes to his source with the formula: "This has been established." The Zohar returns to the same motif frequently. In several passages it suggests that by means of this device the demonic accuser is transformed into an advocate of Israel; see 1:174b; 3:102a, 203a; Tishby, *Mishnat ha-Zohar* 2:206–10.

the mystery of faith the realm of the *sefirot,* the content of mystical faith and experience, the goal of Torah study.

All is one ... From a mystical perspective, the holy and the demonic are the two sides of existence. Lilit is the "nakedness of *Shekhinah*" (Zohar 1:27b [*Tiqqunei Zohar*]; see Patai, *The Hebrew Goddess*, pp. 218, 222–5; above, "Abram's Descent into Egypt," note on "When Adam reached that level."

When this evil side comes down Cf. Talmud, *Bava Batra* 16a: "He [Satan] descends and leads astray, ascends and arouses [God's] anger, obtains permission and takes the soul."

until she is given power reading *lah*, "to her," instead of *leih*, "to it, to him"; see *Ketem Paz*, ad loc. There is abundant erotic imagery in the Zohar, but this passage is unusual and daring. The feminine aspect of the demonic, Lilit, attempts to seduce God into lying with her so that she can obtain power (or "authority"; Aramaic, *reshu*) to rule the world. In the Zohar Joseph represents the *sefirah* of *Yesod*, Foundation, which corresponds to the phallus in the human body; see Zohar 2:258a; 3:296a (*Idra Zuta*). Joseph attained *Yesod* as a result of his model behavior in this biblical narrative. By withstanding sexual temptation, he became the archetype of righteous conduct and self-control: Joseph the *Zaddiq*, the Righteous; cf. Talmud, *Yoma* 35b; Ginzberg, *Legends* 5:324–5, n. 3; and Proverbs 10:25: "The *zaddiq* is the *yesod* ["foundation"] of the world" (So the verse is understood midrashically and kabbalistically; see above, Introduction, n. 131).

Normally the *sefirah* of *Yesod* channels all divine energy to *Shekhinah* (also called *Malkhut*, "Kingdom"); it is through *Yesod* that the union between *Tif'eret* and *Shekhinah* is consummated. Since *Yesod*, i.e., Joseph, is the conveyor of power, Lilit tries to seduce Him. If she is successful, she will take the place of *Shekhinah*, receive the potency of *Yesod* herself, and tyrannize the world; cf. 3:69a.

Something else . . . an unclean woman Impure sexual behavior promotes the power of the demonic; see *Ketem Paz*, ad loc.; Zohar 2:60b–61a.

"It is all one path" Rabbi Abba indicates that his own interpretation is not in conflict with that just offered by Rabbi El'azar. He is about to speak about psychological evil, the Deviser of Evil who works within the human being, rather than mythological evil, Lilit, who attempts to seduce man and God. But "it is all one path," above and below, Lilit and the Deviser of Evil.

'to lie beside her' in hell . . . Cf. *Bereshit Rabba* 87:6; Talmud, *Yoma* 35b.

punished in excrement Cf. Talmud, *Gittin* 57a. Here Moses de León lashes out at the unbelievers of his time; cf. above, Introduction, §§2, 4.

to turn himself around "to turn in *teshuvah*." *Teshuvah* means turning back to God, reorienting one's life to focus on the divine.

that is the work a person should do Cf. Mishnah, *Avot* 2:20: Rabbi Tarfon says, "The day is short; the work is great; the workers are lazy; the reward is abundant; the Master of the house is pressing."

as strong as a lion See *Avot* 5:24: Judah son of Teima says, "Be powerful as a leopard, swift as an eagle, fleet as a gazelle, and strong as a lion, to carry out the will of your Father in Heaven."

the Deviser of Evil ... curls his hair   Cf. *Bereshit Rabba* 22:6: Rabbi Ammi said, "The Deviser of Evil does not walk on the side but in the middle of the street. When he sees someone painting his eyes, fixing his hair, swinging his heel like a dandy, he says, 'This one is mine!' " Cf. ibid. 84:7.

"The righteous are destined ... The wicked ..."   See Talmud, *Sukkah* 52a.

as it is said ...   The entire psalm is a plea for deliverance from evil enemies.

Jacob's Garment of Days

a herald ... no one hears his message!   Cf. Mishnah, *Avot* 6:2: Rabbi Joshua son of Levi said, "Every single day a divine echo reverberates from Mt. Sinai declaring: 'Woe to humankind for the humiliation of Torah!' " While alluding to this tradition, Rabbi Judah goes on to create a new ancient tradition: "It has been taught ..."

its place   among the other days.

the outlaw spirit   "the outside spirit," the demonic.

missing from the total   of fulfilled days.

When those days draw near to the Holy King   when one is about to die, as indicated in the verse: "The days of Israel drew near to die." Cf. Zohar 1:221b: " 'The days of Israel drew near to die.' ... Happy is the person whose days draw near to the King without shame, with no day excluded because of a sin committed thereon."

and they become a radiant garment for his soul!   To enter and experience higher dimensions of reality, one's soul must be clothed in a garment of splendor. Such a garment is woven out of days lived in goodness or out of the good deeds themselves; cf. Zohar 1:66a, 226b; 2:229b; 3:69a. Parallels appear in Islamic and Iranian eschatology and also in Mahayana Buddhism, where it is said of Buddha that upon attaining nirvana "he has, as it were, a special body created from his good deeds" (see Scholem, *Tarbiz* 24 [1955]: 305; *Pirqei Yesod*, pp. 371–2).

the mystery of our Mishnah   What follows is a kabbalistic homily with no basis in the Mishnah. The Zohar employs this formula to conceal the recent character of the teaching and present it as ancient tradition; see above, Introduction, §5; cf. *Bereshit Rabba* 19:6; *Pirqei de-Rabbi Eli'ezer*, Chap. 14.

the radiant garment ... had faded away   Adam and Eve's sin was so great that their entire fabric of days was ruined.

garments of skin   According to the Zohar, Adam and Eve were originally clothed in garments of "light" (*or*, spelled with an *alef*) befitting their high spiritual nature. As a result of the primordial sin, they fell into a lower, physical form and were clothed in garments of "skin" (*or*, spelled with an *ayin*);

see *Bereshit Rabba* 20:12; Zohar 1:36b; 2:229b; 3:261b; cf. Origen, *Contra Celsum* 4:40; above, "The Hidden Light." Here the radiant garment of days represents the garments of light.

'He came into days' Hebrew, *ba ba-yamim.* The phrase is usually translated: "advanced in days," "advanced in years." Literally, however, it means "came into days." Cf. above, Introduction, n. 115.

No garment was left for him to wear Job is a target of criticism in the Zohar because he denied resurrection and dared to question God's justice; see *Zohar Hadash, Rut,* 75d (*Midrash ha-Ne'elam*); cf. Talmud, *Bava Batra* 16a; Maimonides, *Guide of the Perplexed* 3:23. In the Midrash Job is often contrasted with Abraham.

All who have a garment will be resurrected, as it is written . . . Job, who denied resurrection, has no garment. God's answer to him out of the whirlwind reveals that without such a garment one cannot rise from the dead. Cf. *Bereshit Rabba* 95:1.

crowned . . . with crowns worn by the Patriarchs . . . Cf. Talmud, *Berakhot* 17a: "A pearl in the mouth of Rav: '[In] the world that is coming . . . the righteous sit with crowns on their heads and bask in the splendor of *Shekhinah.*'" The "crowns worn by the Patriarchs" are their respective *sefirot: Hesed, Gevurah,* and *Tif'eret.* The "stream that flows" is the flow of emanation that fills *Shekhinah,* who is the mystical Garden of Eden.

'satisfy your soul with sparkling flashes' The phrase is normally translated: "satisfy your thirst [*nefesh*] in parched places [*zahzahot*]." According to the Zohar, the *zahzahot* enlighten the righteous soul in the world that is coming; see 2:97a, 142b, 210b. A theory of ten *zahzahot* is presented by a later contemporary of Moses de León, David son of Judah the Hasid, in his *Book of Mirrors.* According to him, the *zahzahot* are the first sparks of emanation within *Keter,* the highest *sefirah.* See the conclusion of the verse in Isaiah.

He attained . . . Jacob's life was the culmination of the days and lives of the Patriarchs. Upon his death, he was arrayed in the *sefirah* of *Tif'eret,* Beauty, which harmonizes the *sefirot* of Abraham and Isaac, *Hesed* and *Gevurah;* cf. above, "The Binding of Abraham and Isaac," "Jacob's Journey"; *Sifrei,* Deuteronomy, §312. The seven lower *sefirot* are the seven primordial days of Creation; see above, "Guests in the *Sukkah.*"

The Birth of Moses

Gabriel One of the angels serving *Shekhinah;* cf. *Tanhuma, Va-Yeshev,* §2; *Pirqei de-Rabbi Eli'ezer,* Chap. 38; Zohar 1:184a.

the Communion of Israel Hebrew, *Keneset Yisra'el,* "Community of Israel." This is a name of *Shekhinah,* the divine counterpart of the people of Israel; see above, "How to Look at Torah." *Shekhinah* is "the house of Levi" because She emanates from the *sefirah* of *Din*, Judgment, who is called Levi. She is mild judgment, while *Din* is strict judgment, located on the left side of the sefirotic tree.

"daughter of Levi" refers to the soul-breath   The *neshamah*, soul-breath, is the fruit of the union of *Tif'eret* and *Shekhinah*, the divine couple. *Tif'eret* expresses His passion for *Shekhinah* through the left side, Levi; so the soul-breath is called "daughter of Levi." In Zohar 2:19a "daughter of Levi" refers to *Shekhinah* Herself, who emanates from Levi. *Shekhinah* is the mother of the soul-breath; both are daughters of Levi.

from the Garden   the Garden of Eden, where all soul-breaths await their bodies. "Garden" may also refer to the mystical Garden of Eden, *Shekhinah*, mother of all soul-breaths; cf. above, "Abram, the Soul-Breath," "The Gift of Dwelling."

"A man" is Amram . . .   The Zohar now offers a literal interpretation of the verse. Amram and Yocheved, both from the tribe of Levi, are Moses' parents.

A daughter of the Voice, a divine echo   Hebrew, *bat qol*, a voice from heaven revealing God's will. Amram is directed by God to unite with Yocheved. In the Midrash it is not a daughter of the Voice but Amram's own daughter, Miriam, who urges him to have another child with his wife, Yocheved. Yocheved, herself, is referred to as *bat ql*, "daughter of 130," i.e., 130 years old; see *Shemot Rabbah* 1:17, 23; Talmud, *Sotah* 12a. Moses de León loves to transpose midrashic traditions.

Shekhinah was present . . .   Cf. *Sotah* 17a: Rabbi Akiva expounded: "A man and a woman: if they are pure, *Shekhinah* is between them; if not, fire consumes them." Cf. Zohar 2:19a: "Amram was not worthy to give birth to Moses until he had partaken of *Shekhinah*. Then he fathered Moses."

Shekhinah never left the son   Moses became an intimate partner of *Shekhinah*; see below.

"Make yourselves holy and you will be holy"   Engage in sex in holiness, and the fruit of your union will be holy; cf. Talmud, *Shevu'ot* 18b; Zohar 1:112a (*Midrash ha-Ne'elam*).

A human being who makes himself holy . . .   Cf. Talmud, *Yoma* 39a: Our rabbis have taught: " 'Make yourselves holy and you will be holy.' If a person makes himself a little holy, he is made very holy. If he makes himself holy below, he is made holy from above. If he makes himself holy in this world, he is made holy in the world that is coming."

Their desire focused on joining Shekhinah . . .   For the mystic, sex is not merely a personal act; it is an occasion for communion with God; cf. Zohar 1:49b–50a; 2:89a–b; 3:81a–b, 168a. See Cordovero's comment on this passage (*Or ha-Hammah*, ad loc.): "Their desire, both his and hers, was to unite *Shekhinah*. He focused on *Tif'eret*, and his wife on *Malkhut* [*Shekhinah*]. His union was to join *Shekhinah*; she focused correspondingly on being *Shekhinah* and uniting

236

with Her Husband, *Tif'eret*." This corresponds to the Tantric ritual of *maith-una*, in which the human couple focuses on identification with their divine models; see Eliade, *Yoga: Immortality and Freedom* (New York, 1958), pp. 200–73; Agehananda Bharati, *The Tantric Tradition* (London, 1965); cf. above, "Male and Female."

cleave to the Other Side the demonic. One can attach himself to either side.

Shekhinah joined with him constantly Talmud, Shabbat 87a, indicates that Moses stopped having sexual relations with his wife once he received the Torah at Mt. Sinai because from then on he was in constant communication with *Shekhinah*. The Zohar teaches that Moses and *Shekhinah* were actually united in marriage. Moses rose to the *sefirah* of *Tif'eret* while still in his body and thus assumed the role of the divine husband. This is the hidden meaning of the phrase "Moses, the man of God" (Deuteronomy 33:1). *Shekhinah* is called the Bride of Moses; see Zohar 1:21b–22a; 236b; 3:148a; cf. *Pesiqta de-Rav Kahana* 1:1; *Midrash Tehillim* 90:5; Liebes, "*Peraqim*," pp. 182–3.

he was born circumcised See Talmud, *Sotah* 12a; *Shemot Rabbah* 1:24.

the secret of the covenant the sign of circumcision. See Genesis 17:11: "You shall circumcise the flesh of your foreskin, and that shall be a sign of the covenant between Me and you."

'Say of the righteous one that he is good' The righteous one, *zaddiq*, is one of the names for the *sefirah* of *Yesod*, Foundation, corresponding to the phallus in the human body. *Yesod* is also called "good" in the Zohar; here the secret of the covenant is found.

She saw the radiance of Shekhinah Cf. *Sotah* 12b; *Shemot Rabbah* 1:28, where it is said in the name of Rabbi Yose son of Hanina that Pharaoh's daughter saw *Shekhinah* when she opened the basket containing baby Moses; see Exodus 2:5–6.

the whole house was filled with light! . . . See *Sotah* 12a; *Shemot Rabbah* 1:24.

'God saw . . .' That is how good he was: he was everything! On the primordial light see above, "The Hidden Light." This light is a metaphor for cosmic consciousness. Experiencing it, Adam not only saw "from one end of the world to the other"; he extended from one end of the world to the other; cf. Zohar 3:117a. He had full awareness. This awareness and light had been lost to humanity since the expulsion from the Garden, but now that Moses is born, there is a new vessel for that light to shine through into the world; he is as good and pure as the primordial light. Born of a spiritual-physical union, he is a constant partner of *Shekhinah*; his awareness is unbounded; he is everything!

What is the point of saying "three months"? This detail seems unnecessary and provides Rabbi Judah with the starting point for another mystical midrash.

was not recognized until 'three months,' . . . 'On the third new

moon'   Rabbi Judah connects the "three months" of Exodus 2:2 with the "third new moon" of Exodus 19:1. Moses' state of enlightenment was fully revealed only at Sinai.

Elohim ... YHVH   *Shekhinah* and *Tif'eret;* see above, "Is There Anyone Like Moses?"

Moses and the Blazing Bush (Midrash ha-Ne'elam)

One who comes close to fire is burned   Cf. Talmud, *Ketubbot* 111b: "Is it possible to cleave to *Shekhinah?* Is it not written: 'For *YHVH* your God is a consuming fire' (Deuteronomy 4:24)?"

the dense cloud   Cf. Deuteronomy 4:11: "The mountain was ablaze with flames to the heart of heaven, dark with densest clouds."

The Angel of YHVH   *Shekhinah,* who is given this name because She transmits the power and blessing of the *sefirot;* cf. Zohar 1:166a; *Shemot Rabbah* 2:8; 32:8.

in the light of wisdom   in relation to the *sefirot.*

Why is it written ...   The literal sense of the verse is too mundane to satisfy Rabbi Abba's mystical yearning. "The water" must mean more than the Nile River, from which Moses was drawn by Pharaoh's daughter. It is really a symbol of *Hesed,* the free-flowing love of God. This was Moses' source; so he could confront fire, which in Rabbi Abba's view refers to *Gevurah,* the power of God. Moses was able to harmonize the two polarities. He attained the rung of *Tif'eret,* Beauty, the central *sefirah.*

the place Moses was hewn   Normally, according to the *Midrash ha-Ne'elam,* human souls are hewn from the Throne of Glory, *Shekhinah;* see above, "Abram the Soul-Breath." Moses had a higher source. Cordovero (*Or ha-Hammah,* ad loc.) suggests *Hokhmah,* which stands above *Hesed.* Cf. Zohar 1:22a.

arrayed in all ten spheres   Moses' perfection is symbolized by his intimate relation with *Shekhinah* and his attainment of *Tif'eret;* but according to Rabbi Yohanan, he was invested with all ten *sefirot.* He had full awareness of God and displayed all the divine qualities.

Not just a loyal member of My household   as the phrase could be understood; cf. the King James' Version: "who is faithful in all mine house."

Happy is the share ...   Cf. *Sifrei,* Numbers, §68: "Happy is the mortal human who is given such a promise: anytime he wanted to, he could converse with Him."

Who was that? Balaam   Balaam was the soothsayer from Aram invited by King Balak of Moab to curse the people of Israel before they entered the Promised Land; see Numbers 22–24. The Midrash compares him to Moses: "God raised up Moses for Israel and Balaam for the nations of the world" (*Bemidbar Rabbah* 20:1; cf. *Tanhuma, Balaq,* §1). The midrash quoted here (from *Sifrei,* Deuteronomy, §357) is more striking: Balaam was as great as Moses! The rabbis are perplexed and have to wait for the master, Rabbi Shim'on, to offer the true, mystical explanation of this bizarre midrash.

Black resin mixed with finest balsam? How could Balaam possibly be associated with Moses? Thirteen rivers of balsam await the righteous in the world that is coming, according to the Talmud (*Ta'anit* 25a; Jerusalem Talmud, *Avodah Zarah* 3:1, 42c; *Bereshit Rabba* 62:2). In the Zohar the rivers of balsam are the fragrant flow of emanation from *Binah*, the Divine Mother, to *Shekhinah*, Her daughter; see Zohar 3:181a. Moses, arrayed in all the *sefirot*, bathes in these rivers.

Black resin is the ultimate impurity. The Aramaic phrase, *qotifa de-qarnetei*, is characteristic of the Zohar's style. *Qotifa* is a variation on *qetaf*, which means resin from the balsam tree. *Qarnetei* is a neologism, its meaning unknown; cf. Zohar 2:175b; and Spanish, *carantona:* "ugly, false face." The phrase has been interpreted variously to mean: "a chamber pot" (Cordovero, *Or ha-Hammah*, ad loc.); "cedar resin" (Vital, *Derekh Emet*); "a bunch of resin, dark and black" (Galante, *Or ha-Hammah*). One must invent new words to adequately describe the gross impurity of Balaam.

Moses worked wonders ... Balaam worked black magic ... Aramaic, *ishtammash* means "made use of," but it is also a technical term for theurgic practice. See Mishnah, *Avot* 1:13: [Hillel] said, "One who makes theurgic use [*de-'ishtammash*] of the crown [i.e., the name *YHVH*] has no share in the world that is coming." Cf. above, "The Hidden Light."

Moses worked wonders with the holy crown. Because of his status in the *sefirot*, he was able to use the name *YHVH* to work wonders for Israel. Balaam's powers of magic also derived from crowns, but not holy crowns. The lower, or nethermost, crowns are the demonic powers located outside the realm of the *sefirot* and their corresponding names. Their potency derives from the fact that they are fed from the drippings of the juice of *Shekhinah;* see Zohar 3:209b. This accords with Rabbi Shim'on's first image: Balaam is black resin from the balsam tree; Moses is pure essence of balsam.

If you think he was any higher, go ask his ass! Balaam's ass makes a fool of him on the way to see Balak, king of Moab. She sees the Angel of *YHVH*, while he, the great sorcerer, sees nothing; see Numbers 22:21–35; Zohar 3:209b. On one level, Rabbi Shim'on's closing words are a mocking reference to this episode. But they also allude to Balaam's method of attaining prophetic powers. According to the Zohar, Balaam was able to draw down upon himself the impure spirit by having sexual relations with his ass; see Zohar 1:125b; 3:207a; *Sheqel ha-Qodesh*, p. 18; cf. Talmud, *Sanhedrin* 105b.

kissed his hands as a sign of veneration and thanks. This is a frequent custom among the *Havrayya*, the Comrades of the Zohar; see 1:83b, 133a, 250b; above, "Colors and Enlightenment," "Manna and Wisdom," "The Golden Calf," "The Wedding Celebration." Cf. Talmud, *Berakhot* 8b; *Bereshit Rabba* 74:2; Bacher, *REJ* 22 (1891): 137–8; 23 (1891): 133–4.

The coveting in my heart has disappeared ... Aramaic, *hamida de-libba'i nefaq le-var.* The Aramaic root *hmd* means "to desire, covet." The sentence may mean: "The yearning in my heart [to know the true meaning of this midrash] has been satisfied." The translation in the text conveys the role played by Kabbalah in Spain: reassuring the Jews that although the Christians were politically, economically, and socially in power, the Jews were God's chosen people and thus ultimately higher; see above, Introduction, §4. Rabbi Shim'on's midrash on the midrash has just this effect on Rabbi Yose, and he responds by thanking the master for helping him see the true state of affairs; cf. Zohar 3:119b, 221b. He no longer has a desire to covet the power and position of the gentiles, for Israel is high and the idolaters are low. Idolaters refers to Spanish Christians; cf. 2:163b; 3:119b. Balaam is the archetype of the non-Jewish prophet and may stand for Jesus, claimed to be the successor to Moses but here unmasked as a sorcerer. (See, however, Ginzberg, *Legends,* 6:123–4, n. 722, who rejects this interpretation in regard to rabbinic literature; cf. Urbach, *Tarbiz* 25 [1956]: 281–4.) In another passage Rabbi Shim'on declares: "I am a servant of the Blessed Holy One ... I do not rely upon a son of divinity, but rather, on the God of heaven" (see above, Introduction, n. 48). There is no need to covet Christian theology. As the closing lines of this passage indicate, the Jews are God's children and have a direct line themselves.

Moses was one of a kind On the special quality of Moses' prophecy see *Vayiqra Rabba* 1:14; Maimonides, *Guide of the Perplexed* 2:36, 45.

Moses was worried ... Cf. *Shemot Rabbah* 2:10.

His children ... children literally, "sons."

Moses and His Father-in-Law

Moses returned to YHVH Moses' first attempt at convincing Pharaoh to let the people go was a failure. Not only did Pharaoh refuse; he punished the Israelites with harsh labor as a result of Moses' demand. The people themselves were angry with Moses. Frustrated, he addresses God in bold terms.

Adonai ... Elohim "My Lord," "God." Both these words are names of *Shekhinah,* the feminine Divine Presence; *YHVH* refers to *Tif'eret,* a higher *sefirah.* In rabbinic literature a distinction is made between *Elohim* and *YHVH,* the former indicating the divine attribute of judgment; the latter, the attribute of compassion; see *Sifrei,* Deuteronomy, §26. In the Zohar *Shekhinah (Elohim)* executes judgment, and *Tif'eret* is called Compassion. The various divine names appearing in these verses stimulate Rabbi Yose to weave a mystical midrash.

husband of Elohim literally, "the man of *Elohim*" (Deuteronomy 33:1), which for the Zohar means "the husband of *Shekhinah [Elohim]*"; see above, "The Birth of Moses," note on "*Shekhinah* joined with him constantly." Moses is on such intimate terms with *Shekhinah* that he is called Her husband.

Therefore he is allowed to speak to Her as he wishes.

It is instructive to compare this passage with a midrash on these verses (*Shemot Rabbah* 6:1): Rabbi Shim'on son of Yohai said, "Why did he [Moses] criticize the ways of the Blessed Holy One? ... As a result, the attribute of Judgment sought to harm Moses, as it is written: '*Elohim* spoke to Moses.' However, since the Blessed Holy One saw that he had spoken up because of the suffering of Israel, He continued to deal with him through the attribute of Compassion, as it is written: 'He said to him, "I am *YHVH*." ' "

The Zohar passage is obviously built on the midrash; following its example, Rabbi Yose divides Exodus 6:2 into two sentences with two different subjects: "*Elohim* spoke ... He [*YHVH*] said ..." Here the similarity ends, however. According to Rabbi Yose, Moses is forgiven not because he was standing up for Israel, but because he is a member of the divine family, the husband of *Elohim*.

Do you not know that I am King? The man's wife is the daughter of the king. Rabbi Yose does not spell this out, but it is clear from the context and the second parable, below. This cryptic style is characteristic of the Zohar. The reader is puzzled and forced to search the text, to involve himself.

as if it were possible a common rabbinic expression used to tone down radically anthropomorphic statements.

He said, "Adonai ..." Moses addresses *Shekhinah*.

Elohim spoke to Moses *Shekhinah* begins to answer; cf. the midrash quoted above: "The attribute of Judgment sought to harm Moses, as it is written: '*Elohim* spoke to Moses.' "

He said to him, "I am YHVH ... You have spoken these words against Me!" Impugning *Shekhinah* is an affront to *YHVH*, the King, and He takes up the word.

El Shaddai One of the oldest names of God. The full name appears in the Bible only in connection with the Patriarchs, as the verse indicates.

different from the ones above *YHVH, Adonai, Elohim.*

It is like a king who had a daughter ... Cf. *Bahir*, §63: "A parable. There was a king within the innermost chambers. There were thirty-two chambers in all, and each had its own path. Is it fitting for a king that everyone enter his chamber by following his paths? Surely not! Is it fitting for him to display his pearls and gems, his hidden, precious treasures? Surely not! What did he do? He designated the daughter and included all the paths in her, in her garments. He who wants to enter, let him look here." Cf. above, "Openings."

Mistress Matronita Aramaic, *qerosponya matronita.* The second word means "matron, queen"; the first seems to be a neologism, which Cordovero (*Or ha-Hammah,* ad loc.) says indicates her power. Cf. Margaliot's note in his edition of the Zohar, 2:278b.

Similarly, God said to Moses ... El Shaddai Explaining the parable, Rabbi Yose indicates that *El Shaddai* is *Shekhinah*. When She was the unmarried daughter of God, Her Father employed Her as the medium for contacting His dear friends, the Patriarchs. All their visions and communications were channeled through Her.

How dare you open with words such as these, i.e., "*Adonai,* why did You wrong this people? . . . You have certainly not delivered Your people!" Cf. *Shemot Rabbah* 6:3: Rabbi Me'ir said, "A parable. There was a king of flesh and blood who married off his daughter. He called a certain townsman to be the marriage broker. This townsman began to speak presumptuously toward the king. The king said, 'Who made you so presumptuous? It was I myself who made you the marriage broker!' Similarly, the Blessed Holy One said to Moses, 'Who caused you to talk like this? It was I who made you great!' "

In this midrash the daughter is Torah, who is to be married to Israel at Mt. Sinai; Moses is merely the agent. In the Zohar the wedding is between Moses and *Shekhinah,* the daughter of God. Moses has married into divinity but has not yet learned how to behave properly.

I did not speak with them on the same level I have spoken with you The Patriarchs had visions of *Shekhinah.* Moses, however, had come to know *Shekhinah* intimately and was now Her husband. He had attained the *sefirah* of *Tif'eret,* the level of speaking with God face to face. Moses alone had direct knowledge and experience of *YHVH,* the Ineffable Name, the essence of Being.

Colors and Enlightenment

'I have appeared to Abraham, to Isaac, and to Jacob through *El Shaddai,* but by My name *YHVH,* I was not known to them' (Exodus 6:3).

The word should be spoken Rabbi El'azar's proposed emendation reflects the traditional Jewish view that language is the essential medium of revelation. "*YHVH* spoke to you out of the fire; you hear a voice of words, but an image you do not see—nothing but voice" (Deuteronomy 4:12). Moses beheld "the image of *YHVH*" (Numbers 12:8), and several theophanies are vividly described by the prophets, but it is the Word of *YHVH* that informs divine-human encounter throughout the Bible. Rabbi El'azar is surprised that God would say, "I have appeared" to the Patriarchs; He should have said, "I have spoken." El'azar's father, Rabbi Shim'on, reveals the secret meaning of appearance.

mystery of faith the realm of the *sefirot;* cf. above, "Male and Female." The *sefirot* are experienced as colored lights: vision takes the place of sound, and one who has seen believes.

Colors of El Shaddai, colors in a cosmic prism *El Shaddai* is a name of *Shekhinah;* cf. the previous selection. She is described as *ḥeizu,* which in Aramaic means "vision," but in the Zohar expands in meaning to include "mirror"; see 1:183a; 2:267a; cf. Hebrew, *mar'ah,* above, "Joseph's Dream." Through Her mirror, or prism, the lights of the higher *sefirot* are reflected or refracted. Encountering *Shekhinah*, the Patriarchs saw this display of colors, the spectrum of God's personality. On color symbolism in Kabbalah see Scholem, *Judaica* 3:98–151; cf. Idel's forthcoming Hebrew article, "The Use of Lights and Colors in Kabbalistic Prayer."

But the colors above ... The Patriarchs saw the *sefirot* as reflected in *Shekhinah;* they could not look at them directly. Moses, however, was united with *Shekhinah* and rose higher to discover the hidden lights and colors, the *sefirot* themselves. He knew *YHVH: Tif'eret* and the entire sefirotic realm.

through those that are revealed through the prism of *Shekhinah*.

zohar "brilliance, splendor."

Who is enlightened? ... The enlightened (*maskilim*) are the mystics; cf. above, "The Creation of *Elohim*." Through meditation, they discover "words [or "things"; Aramaic, *millin*] that human beings cannot mouth." Cf. the teaching of Todros Abulafia, a contemporary of Moses de León: "There are things grasped and attained by thought that the mouth cannot express" (*Sha'ar ha-Razim*). "Words that human beings cannot mouth" may also refer to the Ineffable Name, *YHVH*, in its various spellings and permutations, which was a focus of kabbalistic meditation; cf. *Bahir*, §139; Zohar 2:262a.

by himself, from himself Aramaic, *mi-garmeih*.

The sky of Moses ... the *sefirah* of Moses, *Tif'eret*, which forms the center of the *sefirot*. Its name is *YHVH*.

this zohar of his is concealed and not revealed The *zohar* of Moses is the "splendor" of his *sefirah*, *Tif'eret*. The words may also allude to another secret: the Zohar of Moses de León is concealed and disguised as an ancient work; see above, Introduction, §5.

the sky that does not shine *Shekhinah*, the *sefirah* who has no light of her own but reflects all higher *sefirot;* cf. above, "Joseph's Dream."

the hidden colors the higher *sefirot* themselves.

A shining light *Hesed*, Love, whose color is white.

A glowing light *Din, Gevurah*, the Power of Judgment, bright red.

A purple light *Tif'eret*, who harmonizes and includes all the sefirotic lights. He is the King, the Blessed Holy One; His color is royal purple; cf. above, "Jacob's Journey."

A light that does not shine *Shekhinah*, who has no light of Her own.

The secret is: the eye Cf. Talmud, *Derekh Erez Zuta*, Chap. 9: "In the name of Samuel the Small: 'This world is like a human eyeball. The white in it is like the ocean, which surrounds the whole world. The black in it is the world itself. The hole in the black is the Holy Temple, may it be rebuilt quickly in our days and in the days of all Israel. Amen!' "

Three colors the white of the sclera, the color of the iris, the black hole of the pupil.

a light that does not shine The black hole of the pupil leads to total blackness, the color of *Shekhinah*, who absorbs all the *sefirot;* cf. Zohar 1:226a.

images of the colors that are hidden   Beyond the colors of the eye are higher, spiritual colors.

These were shown . . .   The Patriarchs were shown the colors of *Shekhinah.*

those hidden ones that glow   the higher *sefirot* themselves.

close your eye and roll your eyeball   a technique for seeing the hidden colors. By closing one's eyes and pressing with the finger on the eyeball until it is moved to the side, colors of the spectrum appear. These are the hidden colors. See Cordovero and Galante, *Or ha-Hammah,* ad loc.; Tishby, *Mishnat ha-Zohar* 1:175; cf. above, "The Hidden Light"; Zohar 1:18b, 97a–b *(Sitrei Torah);* 2:43b; *Sheqel ha-Qodesh,* pp. 123–4; Scholem, *Judaica,* 3:137; Blumenthal, *Understanding Jewish Mysticism,* p. 136.

for they are high and concealed   the hidden colors, the higher *sefirot.*

Moses attained . . .   See Talmud, *Yevamot* 49b: It has been taught: "All the prophets gazed through a mirror that does not shine; Moses our Rabbi gazed through a mirror that shines." According to the Zohar, *Tif'eret,* the *sefirah* of Moses, is the mirror that shines with the full splendor of all the *sefirot. Shekhinah* is the mirror that does not shine with any of Her own light, though She reflects the higher colors; cf. above, "Abram the Soul-Breath," "Joseph's Dream." Note how Rabbi Shim'on alters the rabbinic teaching: "The rest of humanity [not only the prophets, have attained or see through] that mirror that does not shine."

El Shaddai   *Shekhinah.*

My name YHVH . . . high colors   The Ineffable Name, *YHVH,* pulsates with the full brilliance and colors of all the *sefirot.* Moses knew this name and saw these colors. Rabbi Shim'on is alluding to the technique of meditating on *YHVH.* The kabbalists are called "contemplators of His name" (Zohar 2:262a). The letters of the name *YHVH* represent all ten *sefirot* from *Keter* to *Shekhinah.* As the kabbalist meditates on these letters, he climbs the sefirotic ladder and sees the lights and colors of God. "One who wants to contemplate Me, let him gaze into My colors" (2:90b).

The world will be an orphan without you!   Cf. Rabbi Akiva's exclamation at the death of Rabbi Eliezer ben Hyrcanus *(Avot de-Rabbi Natan,* Chap. 25): "You have left the whole generation orphaned!" Cf. Zohar 3:100b, 232b, 236a; *Zohar Hadash, Bereshit* 7a, 19c *(Midrash ha-Ne'elam).*

Pharaoh, Israel, and God

It has been said   in the Midrash: *Shemot Rabbah* 21:5.

'Pharaoh drew [them] near!'   In the verse in Exodus the word *hiqriv* is difficult to translate. The root, *qrv,* means "close, near, to draw near." *Hiqriv* appears to be a transitive verb; so it cannot mean simply "approached." The biblical commentators offer various interpretations: brought his camp near (Ibn Ezra); brought himself near, i.e., rushed ahead (Rashi); offered sacrifices to *Ba'al Zefon* (*Targum Yonatan, Mekhilta*). In *Shemot Rabbah* Rabbi Joshua son of Abin takes *hiqriv* to mean that Pharaoh drew Israel near to *teshuvah,* "turning back" to God. Rabbi Yose adopts this startling interpretation and expands on it.

'When your chastisement falls upon them' Isaiah 26:16; the conclusion of the verse quoted above.

His scourge God employs the enemies of Israel as a means of punishment; cf. Isaiah 10:5: "Ah! Assyria, rod of My anger! My fury is a staff in their hand!"

A parable: the dove and the hawk Rabbi Yose merely indicates the parable with these words, assuming that his audience is familiar with the story, which appears in *Midrash Rabbah* on Song of Songs 2:14: "O my dove, in the clefts of the rock . . ." I have included the entire parable from the Midrash in brackets.

This has already been said in the Midrash; see the first note. Rabbi Yose emphasizes that this is not a new teaching but an old tradition.

Manna and Wisdom

He has heard your grumbling See Exodus 16:3: "If only we had died by the hand of *YHVH* in the land of Eygpt, when we sat by the pot of meat, when we ate our fill of bread! For you have brought us out into this desert to starve this whole congregation to death!"

in the cloud the cloud by which *YHVH* guided the Children of Israel along the way and in which He revealed Himself to Moses and Aaron; see Exodus 13:21–22; 24:15–18; 34:5; Leviticus 16:2; Numbers 11:25.

"What is it?" Hebrew, *man hu. Man* means "what" and "manna"; so the phrase can also be translated: "It is manna." The question "What is it?" represents a folk etymology of manna.

the Holy Ancient One the primal, most ancient manifestation of *Ein Sof,* the Infinite, through *Keter,* Its Crown.

the Impatient One Aramaic, *ze'eir appin;* literally, "short-faced," but meaning "short-tempered, impatient"; cf. Proverbs 14:17. The term designates the *sefirot* from *Hokhmah* to *Yesod. Keter,* the highest *sefirah,* is pure compassion and therefore described as *arikh anpin,* "long-faced, long-suffering, slow to anger"; cf. Exodus 34:6. The lower *sefirot* are characterized by a tension between different aspects of the divine: right and left, love and rigor. Relative to *Keter,* they are impatient.

the Orchard of Holy Apple Trees *Shekhinah*. The apple trees are the *sefirot* from *Hesed* to *Yesod,* which fill Her. The image originates in the Talmud as a midrashic comment on Genesis 27:27: " '. . . as the fragrance of a field that

YHVH has blessed.' Rabbi Judah son of Samuel son of Sheilat said in the name of Rav, 'As the fragrance of a field of apple trees' " (*Ta'anit* 29b); cf. Zohar 1:142b; Azriel of Gerona, *Perush ha-'Aggadot*, pp. 35–7.

angel bread Hebrew, *leḥem abbirim*, "bread of powerful beings." The verse describes the manna from heaven. In Talmud, *Yoma* 75b Rabbi Akiva takes the phrase to mean "bread that the ministering angels eat." The Zohar adopts this view and sees the manna as a product of divine emanation; cf. Ramban on Exodus 16:6.

The Comrades Aramaic, *ḥavrayya*, "companions, colleagues, comrades"; the circle of rabbis who gather around Rabbi Shim'on son of Yoḥai, the Master. They constantly engage Torah, searching for her mystical secrets.

engage Aramaic, *mishtaddelei*. The word has a wide range of meaning: "exert effort, strive, wrestle, win favor, be enticed, be sedulous." In the Zohar it often appears in the context of Torah study.

two balancing one Apparently, this means that the nourishment of the Comrades is half as holy or potent as the manna itself. The cryptic phrase, however, soon yields a different meaning.

When Israel entered the covenant, or the world of *sefirot*.

by uncovering the holy marking by being circumcised. Circumcision is the sign of the covenant with God; see Genesis 17: 10–11. According to the Zohar, the Jewish male who undergoes this rite achieves a mystical bond with the *sefirah* of *Yesod*; see Zohar 1:216a: "Everyone who is circumcised and enters this holy covenant, who partakes of this inheritance and guards this covenant, enters and joins himself to the body of the King and enters this *Zaddiq* ["Righteous one," i.e., *Yesod*]."

One midrashic tradition teaches that the Children of Israel failed to observe the rite of circumcision in Egypt, except for the tribe of Levi (*Shemot Rabbah* 19:6). Rabbi Shim'on concludes that only when they had been circumcised were they pure enough to eat the manna.

they went into the bread called Maẓẓah the unleavened bread baked by the Children of Israel during their exodus from Egypt; see Exodus 12: 8, 34, 39. *Maẓẓah* is a symbol of *Shekhinah*, the first taste of the world of *sefirot*. Israel's journey from Egypt to Sinai is a spiritual journey into the divine realm; cf. Zohar 2:183b.

literally: from Heaven! Heaven is a name of *Tif'eret*, the divine partner of *Shekhinah*. The manna came from this higher *sefirah*.

nourished from an even higher sphere ... The mystical Comrades, striving to attain wisdom, are nourished from the *sefirah* of Wisdom, *Hokhmah*, which is higher than Heaven (*Tif'eret*), the source of manna. Now the meaning of the phrase above, "two balancing one," becomes surprisingly clear: the food of the Comrades is twice as holy (not half as holy) as manna!

why are they weaker ...? The weak physical condition of the Comrades is referred to several times in the Zohar; see 2:143a, 198b, 225a–b; cf. 3:160a.

The food that comes from heaven and earth   ordinary food that grows from the ground and is fed by rain.

coarse and dense   of a material nature.

the sphere where Judgment is found   *Shekhinah*, who provides for the world according to the conduct of human beings.

This is the food that Israel ate   *mazẓah*, of a higher spiritual nature than ordinary food.

entering deepest of all ...   Manna is even more spiritual than *mazẓah* since it derives from Heaven (*Tif'eret*). This food bypasses the body and nourishes the soul. Cf. Deuteronomy 8:3: "He fed you manna, which neither you nor your fathers had ever known, in order to teach you that the human does not live on bread alone, but rather on everything that proceeds from the mouth of *YHVH*." Cf. *Wisdom of Solomon* 16:26: "that Your sons whom You love, O Lord, might learn that it is not the varieties of fruit that nourish a human, but that Your word preserves those who trust in You." On manna as the "word of *YHVH*" see *Mekhilta, Va-Yassa*, §5 (ed. Hayyim Horovitz and Israel Rabin [Jerusalem, 1970]), p. 172; and Philo (*Deterius*, §118): "Manna is the divine Logos." For the Zohar it is the food of the Comrades, higher than manna, that comes from *Hokhmah*, Divine Wisdom or Logos.

spirit ... soul-breath   Aramaic, *ruḥa, nishmeta* (corresponding to Hebrew, *ruaḥ, neshamah*): the higher levels of soul. The lower level is called *nefesh*, "soul."

the clarity of the word   Aramaic, *bariru de-millah*, "the clearness of the word," the clarification of the word, the teaching stated explicitly.

Torah derives from Wisdom on high   Cf. *Zohar Hadash, Bereshit* 15b (*Midrash ha-Ne'elam*): "Torah emanated from supernal Wisdom." Cf. *Bereshit Rabba* 17:5: "Torah is an unripe fruit of supernal Wisdom."

enter the source of her roots ...   The Comrades penetrate to the essence of Torah, the roots of the Tree of Life. Climbing the ladder of *sefirot*, they contact the source of revelation, Primordial Torah: *Hokhmah*, the *sefirah* of Wisdom.

the world that is coming   see below, "*Qorban* and *Olah*."

as it is written: "Choose life, that you and your seed may live, by loving *YHVH* your God, by heeding His voice, by cleaving to Him. For that is your life and the expanse [literally, "length"] of your days ..." (Deuteronomy 30:19–20). "The expanse of your days" is the world that is coming; see *Tanḥuma, Zav*, §14.

Is There Anyone Like Moses?

Elohim   one of the names of God; see below.

the Presence Aramaic, *yeqara da,* "this honor, this glory," the honor of experiencing *Shekhinah,* the Presence of God. *Targum Onqelos* employs *yeqara* to translate *kevod YHVH,* "the Presence [or "Glory"] of YHVH."

Elohim *Shekhinah.*

This is the origin of the saying ... In Talmud, *Shabbat* 104a, Resh Laqish is quoted as saying: "If one comes to make himself impure, they open the door for him. If one comes to purify himself, they help him." The proof text there, however, is not Exodus 19:3, adduced here by Rabbi Yose, but Proverbs 3:34: "He will defy the defiant and give grace to the humble." Rabbi Yose has discovered or invented a new origin for the saying: Moses' ascent to *Elohim* and the response of *YHVH.*

What is written next? 'YHVH ...' Having attained the level of *Shekhinah* (*Elohim*), Moses is addressed by Her divine partner, *Tif'eret,* the central *sefirah,* who is called *YHVH.*

One who desires ... Rabbi Yose offers a mystical paraphrase of the talmudic saying.

to dwell in the palace of the King; cf. Maimonides' parable in *Guide of the Perplexed* 3:51.

markings of the beyond Aramaic, *reshimin di-le-'eila,* "markings of above," heavenly signs. Cordovero (*Or ha-Ḥammah,* ad loc.) explains the phrase as referring to a ray of light from the *sefirot* that protects the mystic; cf. Zohar 1:104a; 3:76a. Galante (*Or ha-Ḥammah,* ad loc.) says that the markings are letters of the name *YHVH* that identify the kabbalist as a servant of the Holy King and guarantee a safe mystical journey. *Reshimin* may also refer to lines on the palms or the forehead; see Zohar 2:70b (*Raza de-Razin*), 77a. The Merkavah mystics used chiromancy and physiognomy to determine whether one could be initiated into the mysteries; see above, "Male and Female," note on "high mysteries."

Whoever displays that sign ... The image is drawn from the heavenly ascent of the Merkavah mystic, who had to display a seal with a holy name in order to be admitted to each of the palaces of heaven. Note how Rabbi Isaac has expanded the discussion: It is not only Moses who can approach God directly; any kabbalist who possesses markings of the beyond may ascend and dwell in His Presence. The verse from Psalms is the proof text.

Happy is Moses! This verse was written for him Rabbi Judah disagrees with Rabbi Isaac and claims that the verse from Psalms refers only to Moses. These two interpretations reflect two different answers to one of the unspoken questions of Kabbalah: Is it possible for the kabbalist to experience God directly, as Moses did?

Of him it is written ... Here two verses are combined: Exodus 20:18; 24:2.

All of Israel Saw the Letters

Anokhi the first word spoken by God at Mt. Sinai. It means "I." "I am *YHVH*, your God" (Exodus 20:2).

these letters the letters of *Anokhi*.

a spark *boziẓa*, a neologism based on Aramaic, *boziṇa* ("lamp"), and perhaps modeled after Hebrew, *niẓoẓ* ("spark"). The spark is the first impulse of emanation and revelation; cf. above, "The Creation of *Elohim*"; and Gottlieb, *Meḥqarim*, pp. 179–82.

to engrave the letters on the tablets of stone. See Exodus 32:16: "The tablets were the work of God; the writing was the writing of God, engraved upon the tablets."

A flowing measure Aramaic, *meshaḥta*, which in the Zohar means both "measure" and "oil"; cf. *Zohar Ḥadash, Va-'Etḥannan*, 57a–b (*Qav ha-Middah*). The *meshaḥta* is the measured flow of divine light initiated by the spark.

ten cubits … comets, seventy-one The numbers derive from the *gimatriyya* ("numerical value") of the letters of *Anokhi*. *Yod*, the final letter, is equal to ten; the other three letters (*alef, nun, khaf*) add up to seventy-one.

on this side … on the other side … on every side of the tablets. According to one talmudic tradition, all four sides of each stone tablet were engraved; see Jerusalem Talmud, *Sheqalim* 6:1, 49d, in the name of Rabbi Simai; Ginzberg, *Legends*, 6:49, n. 258; cf. Exodus 32:15.

from the side of the South … to the East … to the North Cf. *Shemot Rabbah* 5:9, where it is said that at Sinai the voice of God moved from the South to the North to the East to the West in order to amaze Israel. The people ran from one direction to the next to find the voice. Finally they exclaimed: "Wisdom, where can she be found?" (Job 28:12).

flaming letters Cf. Jerusalem Talmud, *Sheqalim*, loc. cit.: Rabbi Pinḥas said in the name of Rabbi Shim'on son of Laqish, "The Torah that the Blessed Holy One gave to Moses was given to him thus: white fire engraved with black fire …"; cf. *Mekhilta, Ba-Ḥodesh*, §9, *Shir ha-Shirim Rabbah* 1:13.

from the flowing measure of the spark Revelation is a mode of emanation. Silver and gold are often symbols of *Ḥesed* and *Gevurah*, the love and power of God. These two *sefirot* are balanced and refined in *Tif'eret*, the Voice of *YHVH*. This voice is transformed into speech through *Shekhinah*, the mouth of the *sefirot*. The entire process can be imagined as the birth of divine language. At Creation, and again at Sinai, God manifests through the alchemy of letters.

The Old Man and the Beautiful Maiden (Sava de-Mishpatim)

the Tower of Tyre *migdal de-zor*. This name has an interesting etymology. Talmud, *Megillah* 6a, records the original name of the city Caesarea as *migdal shir,* the Tower of Shir. The reading *migdal zor,* the Tower of Tyre, appears in several manuscripts and in *Ein Ya'aqov,* a sixteenth-century collection of talmudic legends that reflects Spanish manuscript tradition. When Moses de León read *Megillah* in a Spanish manuscript of the Talmud, he found the reading *migdal zor.* Subsequently he selected it as the setting for the story of the Old Man. Actually both readings, *shir* and *zor,* are corruptions of the real original name of Caesarea, the Tower of Strato, named after its builder, King Strato of Sidon (fourth century B.C.E.). Cf. *sulma shel zor* in *Eruvin* 64b, *Shabbat* 26a.

the face of Shekhinah! Cf. Jerusalem Talmud, *Eruvin* 5:1, 22b: Rabbi Samuel said in the name of Rabbi Ze'eira, "Whoever receives the face of his teacher [i.e., welcomes him], it is as if he receives the face of *Shekhinah!*" Rabbi Yishma'el taught, "One who receives the face of his friend [*havero*], it is as if he receives the face of *Shekhinah!*" Cf. Genesis 33:10. The Zohar transforms the talmudic simile into a synonym for the *Havrayya,* the mystical Comrades, who "are called the face of *Shekhinah* because *Shekhinah* is hidden within them. She is concealed and they are revealed" (Zohar 2:163b).

an old man, a donkey driver Aramaic, *sava tayya'a* In the Talmud *tayya'a* means "an Arab"; in the Zohar it indicates a donkey driver; see Moritz Steinschneider, *Polemische und apologetische Literatur* (Leipzig, 1877), pp. 248–54; Scholem, *Major Trends,* pp. 165; 388, nn. 42, 46; *Kabbalah,* p. 227. The prophet Elijah appears as a *tayya'a* in Talmud, *Berakhot* 6b. For Elijah as *sava,* "an old man," see *Pesiqta de-Rav Kahana* 11:22; *Zohar Hadash, Lekh Lekha,* 25b (*Midrash ha-Ne'elam*); *Tosafot, Hullin* 6a; Scholem, *Das Buch Bahir,* p. 37, n. 6. The rabbis of the Zohar often encounter donkey drivers who amaze them; see 1:5a–7a; 2:145b, 155b–157a; 3:21a–23a; *Zohar Hadash, Rut,* 83a–d (*Midrash ha-Ne'elam*); cf. *Talmud, Hagigah* 14b; *Bereshit Rabba* 32:10. On the old man as archetype of wisdom, see Jung, *The Archetypes and the Collective Unconscious, Collected Works* 9:217–30.

'What is a serpent ... These riddles confuse not only Rabbi Yose; the cryptic language is intended to mystify the reader as well. Cf. Proverbs 30:18–9; and on the serpent, *Bereshit Rabba* 99:11: "All the animals go in pairs, while the serpent goes on the road all alone." Most of the images in the first two riddles allude to various stages in the process of *gilgul,* reincarnation, one of the most esoteric doctrines of the Zohar; see 2:99b–100a, 105b–106a; Scholem, *Kabbalah,* pp. 344–50. The riddle of the beautiful maiden is expounded below.

chaos ... empty *tohu, be-reiqanya. Tohu* appears in Genesis 1:2: "The earth was formless and void [*tohu va-vohu*]." *Targum Onqelos* translates *vohu* ("void") with the Aramaic word *reiqanya* ("empty"). Moses de León relies on *Targum Onqelos* as a thesaurus of Aramaic.

the way would not have been empty an allusion to the absence of *Shekhinah,* who accompanies one on the road if he is engaged in words of

Torah; see Talmud, *Eruvin* 54a; Zohar 1:164a, 230a; cf. Mishnah, *Avot* 3:3; *Berakhot* 6a.

bells of gold Aramaic, *zaggin de-dahava*. The old man's foolish riddles may be hiding mystical gems. Bells of gold were worn by Aaron, the high priest, on the hem of his robe: "On its hem make pomegranates of blue, purple, and crimson yarns, all around the hem, with bells of gold between them all around" (Exodus 28:33). *Targum Onqelos* translates "bells of gold" as *zaggin de-dahava*, and Moses de León borrowed the phrase from here; cf. Zohar 2:192b. The bell appears as a symbol for divine inspiration in Talmud, *Sotah* 9b: "*Shekhinah* was ringing before him like a bell." Cf. Jerusalem Talmud, *Sotah* 1:8, 17b: "When the Holy Spirit rested upon him, his hairs tingled like a bell." Both statements are midrashim on Judges 13:25: "The spirit of *YHVH* began to impel him," referring to Samson; cf. Zohar 3:188b.

Now two are three, and three are like one! The Old Man plus the two rabbis make a group of three who are joined together. This is one meaning of the Old Man's riddle. On another level, the riddle refers to three parts of the soul described later by the Old Man; see Zohar 2:100a; cf. 3:162a; above, Introduction, nn. 52–3.

to engage Torah Cf. above, "Manna and Wisdom," note on "engage." As the story proceeds, the Old Man describes his method of study.

'YHVH is on my side . . .' The Old Man is about to reveal secrets of Torah; he begins by invoking divine protection and help. In the presence of rabbis who have not proved themselves, he has some misgivings about the venture. The quotation also reflects Moses de León's own hesitancy to publish the secrets. For him, the human threat is posed by opponents of Kabbalah or by other kabbalists who might disapprove of his undertaking.

How good and pleasant and precious and high The four adjectives allude to the four levels of meaning in Torah, which the Old Man describes below.

'I have placed My bow in the cloud and it shall be a sign of the covenant between Me and the earth.' God gives a rainbow to Noah after the Flood. "When I cover the earth with clouds, the rainbow will appear in the clouds, and I will remember My covenant between Me and you and every living creature among all flesh, and the waters will never again become a flood destroying all flesh. When the rainbow is in the clouds I will see her and remember the covenant of eternity" (Genesis 9:13–16). Ezekiel compares the appearance of the image of the Presence of *YHVH* to "the appearance of the rainbow in the clouds on a day of rain" (Ezekiel 1:28), and in Talmud, *Hagigah* 16a, Rabbi Abba correlates the rainbow and the Presence; cf. Zohar 2:66b. In the Zohar Rainbow is one of the many names of *Shekhinah*, the feminine Presence of God; see 1:117a, 247a. She displays the colors of the *sefirot* (3:215a–b). At Sinai She appeared wrapped in a cloud.

We have learned that the Rainbow ... *Shekhinah*, the Rainbow, takes off Her garment, the cloud, and gives it to Moses. Shielded by this cloud, he ascends the mountain and encounters the beyond; cf. Zohar 1:66a; 2:229a; and Talmud, *Yoma* 4a: "Moses ascended in the cloud, was covered by the cloud, was made holy within the cloud, in order to receive Torah for Israel in holiness."

in the All Aramaic, *mi-kola*, "in everything," in the fullness of God; cf. above, "The Birth of Moses," note on "That is how good he was: he was everything!"

The Comrades Rabbi Hiyya and Rabbi Yose.

If we have come ... Cf. *Pesiqta de-Rav Kahana* 1:3; Talmud, *Shabbat* 41a; *Ketem Paz* on Zohar 1:6b.

Friends, Comrades Aramaic, *havrayya*.

rattle Aramaic, *aveid qish qish*, based on a folk saying quoted in Talmud, *Bava Mezi'a* 85b: "A coin in a bottle goes *qish qish*."

Even though I have said ... see Zohar 2:98b–99a; cf. Maimonides, *Guide of the Perplexed* 1, Introduction: "The subject matter will appear, flash, and then be hidden again."

A parable based on the Old Man's riddle of the beautiful maiden; see above, the beginning of the selection.

No one near the lover sees This is the meaning of the phrase in the riddle: "who has no eyes"; i.e., no eyes behold her.

he who is wise of heart Aramaic, *hakkima de-libba*, one of the terms for mystic in the Zohar; cf. 2:74a, 75a, 76a, 77a–b, 145a; and Exodus 31:6.

without a heart Hebrew, *hasar lev*. *Lev* means "heart, mind." "What does *hasar lev* mean? That he has no belief [*meheimanuta*]. For one who does not engage Torah has no belief and is totally defective" (Zohar 3:80a).

derasha the "search" for meaning and interpretation. *Derasha* (Hebrew, *derashah* or *midrash*) is the second level of meaning in Torah, after the literal sense. Through applying certain hermeneutical rules and with the help of imagination, the midrashic method expands the meaning of the Bible. The rabbis of the Talmud employ midrash constantly to discover/invent new interpretations.

words riddled with allegory ... Aramaic, *millin de-hidah*, "words of riddle," e.g., the Old Man's riddles. *Hidah* also means "allegory" in medieval Hebrew, and the Old Man is referring to the allegorical method of interpretation prevalent among Jewish and Christian philosophers and sometimes to be found in the Zohar; see above, "Abram, the Soul-Breath"; cf. Scholem, *On the Kabbalah*, pp. 50–62. Here this method is called *haggadah*, "telling," expounding Torah through allegory.

all her hidden secrets the mystical dimension of Torah, the highest level and deepest layer of meaning.

primordial days According to several rabbinic traditions, Torah existed before the creation of the world; see *Bereshit Rabba* 1:1; *Vayiqra Rabba* 19:1.

"Primordial days" also alludes to the six *sefirot* from *Hesed* to *Yesod*, who are called the six Days of Creation; see *Bahir*, §82; Zohar 3:94b. They flow into *Shekhinah* and transmit to Her the emanation of the "hidden ways," the thirty-two hidden paths of Wisdom; see *Sefer Yezirah* 1:1; *Bahir*, §63.

husband of Torah, master of the house One who is in love with Torah and has received her secret teachings is called her husband (Hebrew, *ba'al torah vadda'i*). The phrase "master of the house" (Aramaic, *ma'rei de-veita*) appears above, "Moses and His Father-in-Law," and in Zohar 1:236b, where it designates Moses, husband of *Shekhinah*. Here it is applied to any mystic who has mastered the secrets of Torah.

withholding nothing, concealing nothing This explains the cryptic phrase in the Old Man's riddle: "She adorns herself with adornments that are not." The initial encounter with Torah yields an apparent meaning that is only an adornment and a disguise. The mystic sees through this garment and discovers the naked reality of revelation; cf. above, "How to Look at Torah."

that word, that hint the word of Torah that first caught his attention.

nothing should be added ... taken away The text must be safeguarded to preserve the secrets it contains. Cf. Deuteronomy 13:1: "The entire word that I enjoin upon you—be careful to fulfill it; neither add to it nor take away from it."

Now the peshat of the verse, just like it is! The root *psht* means "to strip, make plain, explain"; cf. *Shemot Rabbah* 47:8. The *peshat* is the plain meaning and is sometimes contrasted with deeper layers of meaning; see above, "How to Look at Torah." Here, instead of making contrasts, the Old Man points to the paradox of mystical study. The *peshat* is the starting point, the word on the page. As meaning unfolds, layer by layer, one encounters the face of Torah. This is revelation, enlightenment. But in Kabbalah, enlightenment leads back to the word; the *peshat* reappears as the upshot. One emerges from the mystical experience of Torah with a profound appreciation of her form. Cf. the Zen *koan*: "First there is a mountain; then there is no mountain; then there is." By employing this hermeneutic of mystical literalness, Kabbalah bolstered tradition and resanctified the text, while simultaneously uncovering countless interfaces between word and imagination.

day or night Cf. *Pirqei de-Rabbi Eli'ezer*, Chap. 2; Zohar 2:15a (*Midrash ha-Ne'elam*).

Yeiva Sava Yeiva the Elder. He appears in Talmud, *Pesahim* 103b, *Bava Qamma* 49b. In Zohar 1:59a it is reported that Yeiva Sava heard someone say that circumcision is not an essential commandment. Yeiva gazed upon him, and the man turned into a heap of bones.

to awaken your awareness of these words Aramaic, *le-'it'ara millin illein*. Hebrew, *hit'orer* means "to wake up"; in medieval usage it means "to discuss, explain, deal with." The Zohar sometimes plays with the two meanings.

his punishment   for having said that his words were empty.
these verses   Proverbs 4:18, 12; Isaiah 60:21.

The Gift of Dwelling

have them take Me a gift   a contribution of precious raw materials for the construction of the *mishkan*, the Dwelling for God in the desert.

efod   a garment worn by the high priest over his robe, made of gold and a mixture of wool and linen; see Exodus 28:6–12.

breastpiece   a square tablet or pouch attached to the *efod*. It too was made of gold and a mixture of wool and linen. It was inlaid with twelve precious stones engraved with the names of the twelve tribes of Israel. In it were placed the *urim* and *tummim*, a device for obtaining oracles; see Exodus 28:15–30.

the plain by the Sea of Ginnosar   The Sea of Ginnosar is the Sea of Galilee, Lake Kinneret. The narrow plain on its northwestern shore is very fertile, "filled with the blessing of *YHVH*" (*Sifrei*, Deuteronomy, §355). Its fruit ripens quickly and is extremely sweet (*Bereshit Rabba* 99:12). Rabbi Shim'on son of Laqish (third century) is said to have gone out of his mind from eating a huge quantity of this fruit (Talmud, *Berakhot* 44a).

The shade   The *mishkan*, the Dwelling in the desert, is referred to as "shade" in *Shemot Rabbah* 34:1; cf. *Berakhot* 55a; Zohar 2:223b.

We have already established ...   The verse from Song of Songs is cited in the Midrash as an account of the construction of the *mishkan* and the Temple in Jerusalem; see *Pesiqta de-Rav Kahana* 1:2; *Shir ha-Shirim Rabbah* 3:16–17; *Targum* on the verse. Zohar 1:29a interprets the verse as an account of the emanation of the *sefirot*, identifying the palanquin as *Shekhinah*.

the Palace below ... like the Palace on high   *Shekhinah* is the last of the *sefirot*, the Palace below. She resembles Her mother, *Binah*, the Palace on high. According to Zohar 2:240a, the Dwelling constructed in the desert symbolizes a higher Dwelling, *Shekhinah*, who is sustained by the highest Dwelling, *Binah*; see *Tishby, Mishnat ha-Zohar* 2:183–94.

Garden of Eden   *Shekhinah* is called Garden of Eden, located above and beyond the physical Garden of Eden. In His Garden the Blessed Holy One communes with the souls of the righteous; cf. Zohar 3:84a. Eden means "pleasure, delight."

souls who have no body   apparently souls of the righteous who have died; see Cordovero and Galante, *Or ha-Hammah*, ad loc.; cf. Zohar 1:82b; 2:127b.

Delight of YHVH   Hebrew, *no'am YHVH*. *No'am* means "pleasantness, beauty." See Psalm 27:4: "One thing I ask of *YHVH*, that alone do I seek: to live in the house of *YHVH* all the days of my life, to gaze upon the beauty of *YHVH* [*no'am YHVH*] and to frequent His palace." In the Zohar *no'am YHVH* refers to *Binah*; cf. 1:197b. The souls of the righteous bask in Her light; cf. *Berakhot* 17a.

rivers of pure balsam Thirteen rivers of balsam await the righteous in the world that is coming; see above, "Moses and the Blazing Bush," note on "balsam." In the Zohar *Binah* is called both Balsam and the world that is coming; see above, "*Qorban* and *Olah*." Rivers of emanation flow from Her toward *Shekhinah* to delight the souls of the righteous; cf. Zohar 1:7a.

the Palanquin *Shekhinah.*

the trees of the Palanquin ... the *sefirot* from *Hesed* to *Yesod*, out of which the Palanquin (*Shekhinah*) is made; cf. Zohar 1:29a. Rabbi Shim'on yearns for the shade of these higher *sefirot*.

the synagogue which takes the place of the Dwelling; cf. Zohar 3:126a: "Every synagogue in the world is called a sanctuary." Cf. Talmud, *Megillah* 29a; *Mekhilta, Ba-Hodesh,* §11.

the level of Ẕaddiq *Zaddiq* means "righteous" and designates *Yesod*, the ninth *sefirah*, who joins with *Shekhinah.*

'Those who seek Me early will find Me' The first half of the verse reads: "I love those who love Me."

ascends very high! Cf. Zohar 2:140a, where the words "will find Me" intimate the attainment of *Shekhinah* and the higher *sefirah*, *Tif'eret.*

But we have learned ... in Talmud, *Berakhot* 6b. A quorum of ten, a *minyan*, is required for public prayer. The objection, then, is that God would be in no mood for union unless and until there is a *minyan*; cf. Zohar 1:201a; 3:126a.

one coupling Aramaic, *zivvuga ḥad.*

The verse does not read: 'There are not ten.' ... In *Berakhot* this verse is cited to prove the necessity of a *minyan*, a quorum of ten. Rabbi Shim'on points out that the verse specifies a single man, the partner of *Shekhinah*; cf. Zohar 3:126a.

'the man of Elohim' Moses is called "the man of Elohim" (Deuteronomy 33:1), which the Zohar takes to mean "the husband of *Shekhinah*"; see above, "Moses and His Father-in-Law." One who comes early to synagogue imitates Moses by joining with *Shekhinah.*

Ẕaddiq *Yesod*; see above.

the Tree of Life the *sefirah* of *Tif'eret*, who is called the Written Torah; cf. Genesis 2:9; Proverbs 3:18; Zohar 3:176a.

the Garden of Eden *Shekhinah*; see above.

the paths that guard this Tree paths of *Shekhinah*, the Oral Torah, which protect, preserve, and expand the Written Torah; see Galante, *Or ha-Hammah*, ad loc.; cf. Gikatilla, *Sha'arei Orah*, p. 52.

This has been established in Talmud, *Menaḥot* 29a: "It was taught in the school of Rabbi Yishma'el: Three things were too difficult for Moses to understand until the Blessed Holy One showed him with His finger: the *menorah*, [recognizing] the new moon, and [determining which] creeping creatures [were pure and which were impure]." Cf. Zohar 2:241a.

255

If this gift was given . . . The gift is *Shekhinah;* see Zohar 2:127a, 134b–135a, 147a. Moses alone possesses Her.

'Have them take My gift' Following the parable, Rabbi Abba offers a new interpretation of God's command in Exodus 25:2. The words no longer mean: "Have them take Me a gift," but rather: "Have them take My gift." The gift, *Shekhinah,* is given *by* God, not *to* God. She is the Queen, wedded to Moses but dwelling among all the people. Cf. *Vayiqra Rabba* 30:12: Rabbi Judah opened, quoting Rabbi Shim'on son of Pazzi, "It does not say: 'Have them take a gift,' but rather: 'Have them take Me.' It is Me you are taking!'"

'I place My Dwelling in your midst!' Leviticus 26:11, which Rabbi Abba joins to the verse from Exodus to support his interpretation. The Dwelling, the *mishkan,* is *Shekhinah,* the Queen. Cf. *Tanhuma, Naso,* §22: Rabbi Joshua son of Levi said, "Once the *mishkan* was set up, *Shekhinah* descended and dwelled among them."

'Moses consummated . . . the Bride of Moses Hebrew, *kallot Mosheh.* The Midrash connects the verb *kallot,* "to complete," with the noun *kallah,* "bride," indicating that Israel is the bride of God (*Pesiqta de-Rav Kahana* 1:1). Rabbi Abba adopts this pun but reassigns the roles: the bride is *Shekhinah,* who is married to Moses, the husband of *Elohim.* Half human, half divine, Moses consummates the *hieros gamos,* the rite of the Blessed Holy One. This bold, mythical scenario recurs frequently in the Zohar; see 1:239a; 2:5b, 235a, 238a; 3:4b, 148a. On the plene and defective spelling of *kallot* see *Minhat Shai* on the verse, and 3:254a (*Ra'aya Meheimna*). The reader is left wondering: Whom does the king in the parable represent: God or Moses?

vibrating Aramaic, *mekhashkesha.* Cf. Talmud, *Sotah* 9b: "*Shekhinah* was ringing [*mesqashqeshet*] before him like a bell"; Jerusalem Talmud, *Sotah* 1:8, 17b: "When the Holy Spirit rested upon him, his hairs tingled [*meqishot*] like a bell."

A generation like this will not arise . . . *Bereshit Rabba* 35:2 compares the generation of Rabbi Shim'on to that of King Hezekiah. According to Talmud, *Sanhedrin* 94a, God wanted to make King Hezekiah the Messiah. The Zohar asserts that Rabbi Shim'on's generation is the holiest one that will ever be, until Messiah appears; cf. 3:159a, 206a, 241b. Because of this, even the deepest mystical secrets can be revealed by Rabbi Shim'on and the *havrayya;* see 3:236b; cf. Liebes, *"Ha-Mashiah shel ha-Zohar,"* pp. 143–44.

Torah has been restored to her ancientry! Aramaic, *le-'attiquteha,* to her ancient, original state and authority. Rabbi Shim'on is paraphrasing the talmudic statement (*Qiddushin* 66a): "He restored Torah to her oldness [*le-yoshnah,* i.e., her former condition]"; cf. *Yoma* 69b. His exclamation cryptically conveys the goal and method of the Zohar: to reinstate the authority of tradition by creating new ancient mythical teachings and transmitting them through talmudic figures; see Introduction, §§4–5.

The Secret of Sabbath

She is Sabbath! *Shekhinah* is the Sabbath Queen entering the palace of time on Friday evening at sunset. As the seventh *sefirah* below *Binah*, *Shekhinah* is the seventh primordial day, the hypostatization of the seventh day of the week. For the various sefirotic associations of the Sabbath see Tishby, *Mishnat ha-Zohar* 2:490–4.

United in the secret of One *Shekhinah* and Her angels of escort join together in preparation for Her encounter with the King. Cf. Zohar 2:131b: ". . . those supernal maidens who decorate themselves together with Matronita [*Shekhinah*] and decorate Her to escort Her into the presence of the King."

to draw down upon Her the secret of One This secret of One is *Tif'eret*, the Holy King, joined together with the *sefirot* surrounding Him. *Shekhinah* and *Tif'eret* must each be whole before their union: "The Blessed Holy One [*Tif'eret*], One up above, does not sit on His Throne of Glory [*Shekhinah*] until She becomes like Him through the secret of One: One in One. We have already established the secret meaning of: '*YHVH* is One and His Name is One' (Zechariah 14:9)" (Zohar 2:135a).

The holy throne of Glory *Shekhinah;* cf. above, "Abram, the Soul-Breath."

the High Holy King *Tif'eret.*

the Other Side Aramaic, *sitra ahra*, the demonic realm, which threatens *Shekhinah* on the weekdays. Once the Sabbath begins, however, She is safe and provides blessing openly to the world; cf. Zohar 1:75b.

She is crowned over and over to face the Holy King The Sabbath is referred to as Queen in the Talmud; see *Shabbat* 119a: "Rabbi Hanina used to wrap himself in a garment and stand close to sunset as Sabbath entered and say: 'Come, let us go out to greet Sabbath, the Queen!' Rabbi Yannai would put on special clothes as Sabbath entered and say: 'Come, O Bride! Come, O Bride!' " Here in the Zohar, the Sabbath Queen is *Shekhinah;* She prepares to meet King *Tif'eret.* The Sabbath is God's wedding celebration; see Zohar 3:105a.

All powers of wrath . . . Once Sabbath has entered, the power of strict judgment disappears. According to Talmud, *Sanhedrin* 65b, even the wicked in hell are granted rest on the Sabbath; *Midrash Tehillim* 92:5 states that on the first Sabbath "demons ceased from the world." Cf. Zohar 2:88b; 3:288b (*Idra Zuta*); and 1:48a: "Come and see: As Sabbath enters and the day is sanctified, the Canopy of Peace spreads over the world. Who is the Canopy of Peace? It is Sabbath. Then all spirits and whirlwinds and demons and the whole dimension of impurity—all of them are hidden away, entering the eye of the millstone of the hollow of the Great Abyss. For once holiness has been aroused throughout the world, the spirit of impurity cannot be aroused. Rather, this one flees from that one, and the world is protected from on high."

She is crowned below ...   Israel's special relationship with the Sabbath is described in *Bereshit Rabba* 11:8: Rabbi Shim'on son of Yohai taught: "Sabbath said to the Blessed Holy One, 'Master of the worlds, all [the other days of the week] have a partner, but I have no partner!' The Blessed Holy One said to her, 'The Community of Israel is your partner.' " Israel shares in the sanctification of the Sabbath by observing and celebrating her; cf. *Tanna de-Vei Eliyahu*, §24: "How do you sanctify the Sabbath? With Bible, Mishnah, food, drink, and rest." In the Zohar's mythical drama, Israel helps prepare the Queen for union with the King.

all of them are crowned with new souls   According to Rabbi Shim'on son of Laqish (Talmud, *Beizah* 16a), "The Blessed Holy One gives an extra soul to a human being on the eve of Sabbath. When Sabbath leaves, it is taken from him." The Jewish philosophers of the Middle Ages disregarded this teaching or reinterpreted it rationalistically; see Tishby, *Mishnat ha-Zohar* 2:485–6; Abraham Joshua Heschel, *The Sabbath* (New York, 1966), p. 132, n. 5. The Zohar revels in the literalness of the image and embellishes it; see, e.g., 1:48a: "Come and see: When Israel blesses and invites this Canopy of Peace [*Shekhinah*, the Sabbath Queen], Supernal Holiness descends and spreads Her wings over Israel and covers them like a mother protecting her children. All evil types are raked up from the world, and Israel sits beneath the Holiness of their Lord. Then this Canopy of Peace gives new souls to Her children. Why? Because in Her, souls abide; from Her they come forth. When She comes down and spreads Her wings over Her children, She pours out new souls to every single one." Cf. 3:173a. The extra soul enables Israel to leave behind the turmoil of the week and experience the joy of Sabbath: "With this extra soul they forget all sadness and anger; only joy is present above and below" (2:204a; cf. 3:95a). "Every Friday evening, a human being sits in the world of souls" (2:136b).

beaming faces   Cf. *Bereshit Rabba* 11:2: "On the Sabbath, the light in a person's face is different than on all other days of the week."

ET YHVH   In the Zohar *et* is a name for *Shekhinah*, who expresses the fullness of divine speech, *alef* to *tav: et;* see above, "Adam's Sin." Here this interpretation is applied to the opening words of the Sabbath evening prayer, the *Barekhu*. The mystical meaning is that Israel is blessing *Shekhinah* first, and then *YHVH*. Crowning the Queen from below, Israel proclaims and initiates Her union with the King, *YHVH*. This passage from the Zohar is recited in the Sephardic liturgy on Sabbath Eve as an introduction to the *Barekhu*.

The Golden Calf

Moses took so long   See Exodus 24:18: "Moses remained on the mountain forty days and forty nights"; cf. Talmud, *Shabbat* 89a.

Elohim   "a god" or "gods."

mountains of light mountains in the East that catch the first rays of dawn.

the sun The Zohar is drawing a parallel between sun worship and the golden calf. In Egyptian mythology Nut, the sky goddess, is pictured as a cow rising and lifting the sun to heaven. The sun itself is called the "calf of gold" (see Henri Frankfort, *Before Philosophy* [Aylesbury, England, 1963], p. 28).

'Allah of the shining pearl' Cf. *al-durra al-baida,* "the white pearl," a Sufi expression for the first intelligence created by Allah at the beginning of the animate world.

the deputy in charge of the sun The archangel Raphael is appointed over the sun and administers its healing rays; see Zohar 2:254a; Reuven Margaliot, *Mal'akhei Elyon* (Jerusalem, 1964), p. 188, n. 36.

holy letters of the high holy Name *YHVH.* According to *Pirqei de-Rabbi Eli'ezer,* Chap. 6, three letters of the Name are inscribed on the heart of the sun itself; cf. *Zohar Hadash, Bereshit,* 17d (*Midrash ha-Ne'elam*); Jellinek, *Beit ha-Midrash,* 3:137.

the windows of heaven There are 365 (according to another version, 366) of these windows, through which the sun comes forth; see Jerusalem Talmud, *Rosh ha-Shanah* 2:5, 58a; *Shemot Rabbah* 15:22; *Pirqei de-Rabbi Eli'ezer,* loc. cit.

points of the sun Aramaic, *niqqudin de-shamsha,* points representing the poles of the axis of the sun; for the medieval usage see Eliezer Ben-Yehuda's *Dictionary* 5:3787b, s.v. *nequddah.* The Zohar may be alluding to the use of the astrolabe, an instrument used to determine the position of stars and planets. Originally devised by the Greeks, the astrolabe was further developed by Moslem astronomers. A description of one of the improved models was translated from Arabic into Spanish by a group of Jewish scholars working under the auspices of Alfonso X of Castile (1252–1284) during the lifetime of Moses de León. Two centuries later, the astrolabe facilitated oceanic navigation. See *Encyclopaedia Judaica,* s.v. "astrolabe." Another contemporary scientific instrument, a water clock, is described both in Zohar 1:92b and in the treatises commissioned by Alfonso; see Baer, *A History of the Jews in Christian Spain* 1:437, n. 24.

falsehood has no feet ... Cf. Talmud, *Shabbat* 104a: "Truth stands; falsehood does not stand." Cf. *Alfa Beita de-Rabbi Akiva,* ed. Adolf Jellinek, *Beit ha-Midrash* 3:51.

'only till I wink my eye' Hebrew, *ve-'ad argi'ah.* This rare form is explained midrashically below.

the Blessed Holy One does not want ... Cf. Talmud, *Avodah Zarah* 54b: Our rabbis have taught: Philosophers asked the Jewish elders in Rome, "If your God does not desire the worship of idols, why does he not destroy it?" They answered, "If they worshiped something that the world does not need, He would destroy it. But they worship the sun, the moon, the stars, and the constellations. Should the world be destroyed because of these fools? Rather, the world continues on its course, and in the future the fools who have acted corruptly will have to give an account."

Israel, who are the lip of truth: 'YHVH ... one' One of the central prayers in the liturgy is the *Shema*, which begins with the verse "Hear O Israel! *YHVH* is our God; *YHVH* is one" (Deuteronomy 6:4). By reciting this prayer every day, Israel proclaims the oneness of *YHVH* and thus proves itself to be the lip of truth. The Zohar attaches cosmic significance to the *Shema*. One who prays it with the proper *kavvanah* ("intention," mystical awareness and focus) unites all the *sefirot*. His desire then rises along with the *sefirot* to *Ein Sof*, the Infinite; see Zohar 2:133b–134b, 216b; Tishby, *Mishnat ha-Zohar* 2:276–9; cf. above, Introduction, n. 59.

they conclude: 'YHVH, your God, is truth' These are the words with which the reader concludes the *Shema* in public worship. The first three words are from the end of the last paragraph of the *Shema* (Numbers 15:41). "Truth" is the beginning of the next prayer in the liturgy. By reciting these words, the reader brings the total number of words in the *Shema* to 248, the traditional number of limbs in the body, as well as the number of positive commandments in the Torah; see *Tanhuma, Qedoshim*, §6; *Zohar Hadash, Aharei Mot*, 48a.

The verse should read: 'only for a moment' ... Hebrew, *ve'ad rega*. The reading 'only till I wink my eye,' *ve-'ad argi'ah*, is unusual; cf. Isaiah 51:4; Jeremiah 49:19. Why doesn't the verse employ the simpler word? There must be a deeper meaning.

they the tongue of falsehood.

when I will have rest ... The speaker is *Shekhinah*, the mystical Community of Israel who suffers along with Her people.

servitude Aramaic, *pulhana*. The same word is used above in the sense of "worship" and "rite." The false religious practices of the non-Jews constitute a burden for *Shekhinah* and Israel, and keep them in exile; cf. Zohar 1:177a: "Joy has departed from above and below. Israel goes into exile; they are under the power of other gods."

I can relax and take a wink Hebrew, *argi'ah*. Rabbi Hiyya takes the word to mean "relax, rest"; cf. Deuteronomy 28:65; Isaiah 34:14.

those who call 'God' him who is not God the idolaters who worship the sun and its deputy, or the Spanish Christians who worship Jesus as the Son of God.

hegemona In the Talmud the word means "prefect." Rabbi El'azar was involved in the Roman administration of Palestine; see Talmud, *Bava Mezi'a* 83b–84a. In medieval Hebrew *hegemon* means "cardinal" or "bishop." For a similar confrontation see above, Introduction, n. 38; cf. Leivy Smolar and Moshe Aberbach, "The Golden Calf Episode in Postbiblical Literature," *HUCA* 39 (1968): 91–116.

May your spirit deflate! Aramaic, *tippaḥ ruḥeiḥ*, "may his spirit [or "breath"] blow out," employing the third person euphemistically.

and springs forth from the midst of the earth Cf. Psalms 85:12: "Truth will spring forth from the earth."

"will be established forever ..." Rabbi El'azar does not spell out the second half of the verse.

join with Shekhinah, engaging in Torah The pursuit of Torah draws down the Divine Presence. Cf. Talmud, *Berakhot* 6a: Ravin son of Rabbi Adda said, quoting Rabbi Isaac, "Two who are sitting engaged in Torah, *Shekhinah* is with them." Cf. Mishnah, *Avot* 3:3.

'... of all His good words ...' The verse concludes: "that He spoke through Moses, His servant." As is sometimes the case, the unquoted portion of the verse is relevant to the midrashic interpretation.

it would be better for the world to have never been created! because then God's threats to punish the world, His bad words, would have been carried out.

He does not want to carry out a bad word Cf. *Tanḥuma, Va-Yera,* §13: Rabbi Shemu'el son of Naḥman said, "If He threatened in a moment of anger to bring evil, He relents."

Mother comes ... *Shekhinah* comes and intercedes on behalf of Her children, counterbalancing the wrathful aspect of God. For other references to *Shekhinah* as Mother see Zohar 2:14b *(Midrash ha-Ne'elam)*; 3:262a, 296a *(Idra Zuta)*; *Zohar Ḥadash, Shir ha-Shirim,* 65b; *Eikhah,* 91a *(Midrash ha-Ne'elam)*; above, "The Secret of Sabbath," note on "all of them are crowned with new souls."

'Go down ...' See the passages from Exodus at the beginning of this selection.

He penetrated him Aramaic, *anqid leih.*

Moses was instantly roused, and he seized the arm ... Cf. Talmud, *Berakhot* 32a: Rabbi El'azar said, "As soon as He said, 'Leave Me alone and I will destroy them!' (Deuteronomy 9:14), Moses said, 'This matter depends on me!' Immediately he stood and emboldened himself in prayer and begged for mercy." "Now leave Me alone! My anger will blaze against them and I will consume them, and I will make you into a great nation!" (Exodus 32:10). Rabbi Abbahu said, "If the verse were not written, it would be impossible to say! This shows that Moses grasped the Blessed Holy One like a man grasping his friend by the garment, and said before Him: 'Master of the world! I will not leave You alone until You pardon and forgive them!' " Cf. *Shemot Rabbah* 42:10: " 'Now leave Me alone!' Moses said, 'It is because the Blessed Holy One wants me to appease Him concerning Israel; that is why He is saying, "Now leave Me alone!" ' " Cf. *Shemot Rabbah* 44:8; Rashi on Exodus 32:10. Rabbi Yose's bold statement here in the Zohar has precedents in the Midrash, but note that

Moses seizes God's arm, not His garment. Moses assumes the role of *Shekhinah*.

'Remember Abraham!' This is the right arm Abraham symbolizes *Hesed*, the *sefirah* of Love, the right arm of God; see above, "Abram's Descent into Egypt." By reminding God of *Hesed*, Moses prevents the execution of the harsh decree.

the clarity of the word Aramaic, *barira de-millah*; cf. above, "Manna and Wisdom."

the Holy Light Aramaic, *bozina qaddisha*, "the holy lamp," Rabbi Shim-'on's title in the Zohar; see Zohar 1:4a: "*Bozina Qaddisha*, who lit up the world"; cf. 2:86b. Cf. the talmudic phrase *bozina di-nehora*, "a lamp of light," applied to Rabbi Abbahu (*Ketubbot* 17a; see Rashi, ad loc.); cf. *Avot de-Rabbi Natan*, Chap. 25.

a sign in their faces showing that they were troubled, having failed to perceive the clarity of the word. Cf. Zohar 3:157a: "I see in your face that there is something troubling you inside"; cf. 3:6a; *Zohar Hadash, Shir ha-Shirim*, 72a.

pass away from the world Cf. Talmud, *Yevamot* 62b: "Rabbi Akiva had 12,000 pairs of students between Gabbat and Antipatris. All of them died in a single season because they did not show respect to one another."

in her in Torah.

Abraham loves Isaac; Isaac, Abraham ... Jacob ... The Patriarchs symbolize different *sefirot*: Abraham is *Hesed*, balancing Isaac, *Gevurah*; Jacob is *Tif'eret*, the harmony of all the spheres. See above, "The Binding of Abraham and Isaac," "Jacob's Journey."

their spirit, their breath of life! Aramaic, *ruhaihu*. The Zohar defines a kiss as "the joining of *ruha* to *ruha*" (2:124b; cf. 2:254a, 256b; *Zohar Hadash, Shir ha-Shirim*, 60c [*Midrash ha-Ne'elam*], 64b).

whispered to me Esoteric teachings are transmitted by whisper; cf. *Bereshit Rabba* 3:4; *Zohar Hadash, Bereshit*, 19d (*Midrash ha-Ne'elam*).

the Head of the Academy of the Garden of Eden A heavenly academy of departed scholars is mentioned several times in the Talmud, e.g., *Berakhot* 18b; *Bava Mezi'a* 86a. According to Zohar 1:7a, the Academy of Heaven is located in the supernal Garden of Eden. It serves as the source for various mystical secrets in the Zohar; see particularly 3:161b–174a, 197b. The head of the academy is Metatron; see *Zohar Hadash, Yitro*, 36b; Jellinek, *Beit ha-Midrash* 3:136–7; Scholem, *Devarim be-Go*, p. 281; Margaliot, *Mal'akhei Elyon*, pp. 98–100; *Encyclopaedia Judaica*, s.v. "Academy on High."

And when the time comes that we see face to face ... Rabbi Shim'on looks forward to a time of full revelation, when secrets can be taught openly. Cf. Zohar 3:130b (*Idra Rabba*): "In the days of King Messiah they will not have to teach one to one"; cf. Jeremiah 31:33; Maimonides, *Mishneh Torah, Hilkhot Teshuvah* 9:2. One hears in the background the voice of Moses de León and his isolated circle of kabbalists who envision a time when revelation is conveyed "in a language that everyone talks, that they can speak to one another with no one able to accuse" (1:89a [*Sitrei Torah*]). The phrase "face to face" may refer to awareness of God (see Genesis 32:31; Exodus 33:11; Zohar 1:96b; cf. 1 Corinthians 13:12) or to Moses de León's desire to take off the mask of Rabbi Shim'on and be revealed to his readers (see above, Introduction, §5 and n. 107). The claim of agreement and approval, both human and divine, is expressed frequently in the Zohar; see above, "Threshing Out the Secrets," "The Wedding Celebration"; Zohar 1:96b; 3:203a; cf. 1:22b (*Tiqqunei Zohar*). On the theme of future recognition see 1:217b; 2:217b.

the mixed multitude According to the Midrash (*Shemot Rabbah* 42:6), it was not Israel that sinned but rather the mixed multitude, the hordes who accompanied Israel out of Egypt (see Exodus 12:38). They demanded that Aaron make a god and caused the innocent Children of Israel to sin. The Zohar adopts this apologetic explanation; cf. 2:45b.

the real Elohim, the Glory of Israel *Shekhinah*. She is often called *Elohim* and *Kavod* ("Glory"); cf. Zohar 2:237a.

'Glory has gone into exile' Words spoken by the wife of Pinhas as she lay dying in childbirth after having heard that her husband had been killed and the Ark of *Elohim* captured by the Philistines.

they drew Shekhinah into exile along with them According to Rabbi Shim'on (Talmud, *Megillah* 29a), "Wherever they [Israel] went in exile, *Shekhinah* was with them." The theme of the exile of *Shekhinah* is prominent in the Zohar; see above, "God, Israel, and *Shekhinah*"; Tishby, *Mishnat ha-Zohar* 1:228–31. Here the exile of both Israel and *Shekhinah* is linked to the sin of the golden calf; cf. Talmud, *Sanhedrin* 102a: Rabbi Isaac said, "Every single punishment that comes upon the world has within it one twenty-fourth of the overbalance of a pound [i.e., a tiny bit] of the first calf." At Sinai Israel had returned to a state of paradisiac purity (Talmud, *Shabbat* 146a), but with the sin of the golden calf, they cast themselves back into exile; cf. Zohar 2:193b; and above, "Adam's Sin."

within the dregs of wine Wine is a symbol of the *sefirah* of *Din* (*Gevurah*) because of its innate power. The dregs are the source of evil. Here Rabbi Shim'on offers a veiled description of the birth of the demonic; cf. above, "Jacob's Journey."

the primordial demon Aramaic, *mazziqa qadma'ah*, the hypostatization of all demonic forces, as opposed to *adam qadma'ah*, Primordial Adam, the personification of all holy, divine forces; see above, "The Hidden Light."

disguised in the form of a man . . . The demonic power appears in the form of Sama'el, Evil Adam (see Zohar 2:112a). His goal is to take control of *Shekhinah*, the holy place, and thereby rule the world.

he must clothe himself in a garment Any power of the beyond, whether holy or demonic, must assume physical form in order to enter and affect the physical world; cf. above, "How to Look at Torah."

The first garment . . . 'the image of a bull' According to the Midrash,

Israel worshiped the golden calf as an imitation of the bull in the divine chariot: "The Blessed Holy One said to him [Moses], 'I see them coming to Sinai and receiving My Torah. I descend on Sinai in My chariot of four animals. They focus their attention on the chariot and unhitch one of them and thus arouse My anger, as it is said: "the face of a bull on the left" [Ezekiel 1:10, the prophet's vision of the chariot], and it is written: "They exchanged their Glory for the image of a bull" (Psalms 106:20)' " (*Tanḥuma, Ki Tissa,* §21; cf. *Shemot Rabbah* 42:5; *Midrash Tehillim* 106:6, *Mekhilta, Va-Yehi Be-Shallaḥ,* §6; Ramban on Exodus 32:1; Ginzberg, *Legends,* 3:123; 6:52–3, n. 271; and Saul Lieberman's comment in Scholem, *Jewish Gnosticism,* pp. 122–3, n. 24).

Here Rabbi Shim'on associates the bull with the demonic, left side; cf. Zohar 2:6a, 64b, and 236b–237a, where the verse from Ezekiel is cited in connection with the golden calf. Gold symbolizes the holy left, the divine source of evil (*Bahir,* §52; Zohar 1:48a, 62b, 228a). The golden calf is the primordial demon's vehicle for entering the world. Note the reference to chariots in the previous line.

That is why Mother was not there   Rabbi Shim'on finally answers the question that was troubling Rabbi Yose and Rabbi Ḥiyya. He soon interrupts himself again, however, before spelling out the secret.

on the verge of Elohim   Aramaic, *vi-setar de-'lohim. Setar* means "edge" or "side"; it has various connotations in the Zohar. The golden calf had a divine element in it: the face of the bull from the left side of the chariot. However, when the left is separated from the whole, it turns demonic. The golden calf, worshiped as an embodiment of *Elohim,* was a false god and a threat to Holy *Elohim, Shekhinah.* Rabbi Shim'on is playing with various associations of *Elohim: Shekhinah, Gevurah* (the *sefirah* of the left side), and idolatry (see Talmud, *Sanhedrin* 56b; Zohar 3:113a); cf. above, "The Binding of Abraham and Isaac," note on *"Elohim...."*

penetrated him   Aramaic, *anqid leih.*

Faithful Shepherd   Aramaic, *ra'aya meheimna.* Cf. Numbers 27:17; *Mekhilta, Be-Shallaḥ,* §6; Ginzberg, *Legends* 5:414. This title appears several times in the Zohar; see 1:106a; 2:8b, 53b; cf. *Zohar Ḥadash, Bereshit* 15a (*Midrash ha-Ne'elam*): "I have not found a shepherd who sacrificed his life for his sheep like Moses." Soon after the Zohar's composition, another kabbalist wrote a book in a similar style entitled *Ra'aya Meheimna.* It contains mystical interpretations of the commandments transmitted by Moses, the Faithful Shepherd, to Rabbi Shim'on and his Comrades; see above, Introduction, n. 20.

The wisdom of Moses was in these three points ...   The three points indicate three *sefirot.* The first is *Ḥesed,* Love, the right arm of God; cf. above: " 'Remember Abraham!' This is the right arm." The second is *Din,* the *sefirah* of Judgment, the left arm of God. The third is *Tif'eret,* the trunk of the sefirotic tree, the beautiful body of the King. Moses is identified with this *sefirah;* see Zohar 3:181b. Cf. the expression *corpus domini,* above, Introduction, n. 46.

He could not move to any side at all!   By embracing God completely, Moses immobilized Him and saved Israel from His wrath.

the various points of the King   Aramaic, *minei niqqudin de-malka*. The phrase is intended to remind the reader of another set of points mentioned earlier: "the points of the sun," *niqqudin de-shamsha* (above). Those points were used to discover gold. Moses masters another set of points: the points of the King, the *sefirot*. *Tif'eret* (the body of the King and central *sefirah*) is symbolized by the sun. With his mystical knowledge, Moses performs spiritual alchemy and is transformed into a superhuman being.

to be firm   Aramaic, *yittaqqaf*, "to grab hold, be firm"; cf. above, "Mother comes and grabs hold" (*atqifat*). For the range of meaning see Zohar 1:142a, 170b, 190b, 202a; 2:13a, 109b, 140b, 155b; 3:94b, 203b, 208a, 291b (*Idra Zuta*).

If we have come into the world ...   Cf. above, "The Old Man and the Beautiful Maiden."

Then he cried   Rabbi Abba.

Rabbi   Rabbi Shim'on.

The Blessed Holy One is rejoicing now in this word   Cf. Zohar 1:4b: "We have learned: The moment a new word of Torah comes forth from the mouth of a human being, that word ascends and presents herself before the Blessed Holy One. He picks up that word and kisses her and crowns her with seventy crowns, all engraved!"

Qorban and *Olah,* Drawing Near and Ascending

qorban   an offering, a sacrifice. The root *qrv* means "to draw near."

Why qorban?   The final Hebrew letter, *nun*, seems superfluous.

Qorban, their drawing near   Rabbi Shim'on reads the word as *qeiruvan*. The final *nun* is understood as a pronominal suffix meaning "their." Thus the word means "their drawing near," the drawing near of the holy crowns, the *sefirot*. This interpretation originates in *Bahir*, §109: "Why is it called *qorban*? Because it draws near the holy forms [another reading: "the holy powers"]." The kabbalists of the thirteenth century relied on the *Bahir* and elaborated this particular teaching, as Rabbi Shim'on indicates: "This is well-known to the Comrades!" Cf. Zohar 1:89b; 3:5b, 8a.

The *qorban* is a sacrament, unifying all the aspects of divinity and symbolizing the ascent of the human soul on the ladder of the *sefirot*. Cf. the statement by an earlier thirteenth-century kabbalist: "The meaning of the *qorban* is to raise the low desire [the human desire] in order to draw it near and unite it with the desire of the upper worlds, which are His names [the *sefirot*], and then to draw the upper desire and the lower desire to one desire [the highest *sefirah*, called Desire]" (see Tishby, *Mishnat ha-Zohar* 2:197–8). Cf. the parable in Zohar 1:239b: "A human being who brings a gift to the king must ascend from level to level until he climbs from below to above, to the place where the king sits above all. Then it is known that a gift is being offered to the king, and that gift belongs to the king."

to perfect the Holy Name *YHVH,* whose letters symbolize the entire range of *sefirot;* see Zohar 1:162a (*Sitrei Torah*); 3:65b. By drawing near all the *sefirot,* the *qorban* unifies and spells out God's being. The Zohar's emphasis on the cosmic role of *qorban* is directed implicitly against Maimonides, who stated that the sacrifices were not pure divine service but rather a concession to Israel's idolatrous habits and environment; see *Guide of the Perplexed* 3:32; Tishby, *Mishnat ha-Zohar* 2:194–7. The kabbalists reacted strongly against this position, perceiving it as a rationalistic attack on tradition. Here Rabbi Shim-'on fights back by offering a mystical spiritualization of the *qorban.* The passage is a veiled description of the kabbalistic technique of *yihud,* the "unification" of the Name of God. Through this rite of contemplation, the mystic harmonizes all the *sefirot* and draws down divine blessing and compassion; cf. above, "Colors and Enlightenment." The ancient ritual of *qorban* serves as a metaphor for *yihud,* "the highest ritual of the Blessed Holy One" (Zohar 2:55b).

Therefore 'to YHVH,' not 'to Elohim' *YHVH* denotes the *sefirah* of *Rahamim* (*Tif'eret*), Compassion, while *Elohim* refers to *Din,* Judgment; cf. *Sifrei,* Deuteronomy, §26; above, "The Binding of Abraham and Isaac"; Zohar 2:108a; and Talmud, *Menahot* 110a: Rabbi Shim'on son of Azzai said, "Come and see what is written in the portion of *qorbanot:* There is no mention of *El* or *Elohim* but only *YHVH.* "

We must arouse Compassion! ... not Judgment! Rabbi Shim'on moves from exegesis to an impassioned plea to God and a directive to the Comrades on where to focus their meditation: on the name *YHVH.* This will insure harmony and compassion, whereas contemplation on the name *Elohim* will draw down strict judgment.

torah "teaching, instruction."

olah "that which goes up." The *olah* is a specific type of *qorban,* an offering totally consumed by fire, producing "a pleasing aroma" [*reiah nihoah*] for *YHVH* (Leviticus 1:9; cf. Genesis 8:21; Zohar 1:70a).

The bond of olah ... Aramaic, *qishshura de-'olah.* I have adopted the variant reading found in Zohar 2:239a; cf. Tishby, *Mishnat ha-Zohar* 1:119. The *olah* symbolizes *Shekhinah,* who rises up to *Binah,* the Holy of Holies, and thereby connects all the lower *sefirot* to their source; cf. 3:26a.

the joining of desire of priests, Levites, and Israel The pure desire of one who engages in the ritual of *olah* is joined to *Shekhinah.* Cf. above; and Zohar 1:51b: "After this blue light [*Shekhinah*] has consumed [the offerings] beneath it, priests, Levites, and Israel cleave to it; these by the joy of song, these by the desire of the heart, and these by prayer. The lamp is kindled above them; the lights join as one; the worlds are illumined; above and below are blessed. Then 'you who cleave to *YHVH* your God are alive, every one of you, today!' (Deuteronomy 4:4)." The three groups also represent three *sefirot:*

Hesed, Gevurah, and *Tif'eret,* who are elevated by the ritual; cf. 3:32a–b, 241a.

to Infinity   Hebrew, *ad ein sof.* The phrase can also be translated: "infinitely." *Ein Sof* (literally, "there is no end") is the designation of the Absolute, God as Infinite Being beyond the specific qualities of the *sefirot.* Rabbi Shim-'on states that the bond of *olah, Shekhinah* encompassing the desire of those down below and the *sefirot,* ascends to *Ein Sof;* cf. Zohar 2:213b, 216b, 259b.

the secrecy that cannot be grasped . . .   Infinity.

Primordial Nothingness   *Keter,* the highest *sefirah,* borders on Infinity and "cannot be counted" (Zohar 1:31b; 3:269a). It is "that which thought cannot comprehend" and is called "the annihilation of thought" (Azriel of Gerona, *Perush ha-'Aggadot,* ed. Tishby, pp. 40, 104). It is often referred to as Nothingness, though it "has more being than any other being in the world. But since it is simple and all other simple things are complex compared with its simplicity, in comparison it is called Nothing" (David son of Avraham ha-Lavan; see Scholem, *Kabbalah,* p. 95). Through the *sefirah* of Nothingness *(Ayin),* all other *sefirot* emanate; see above, Introduction, §6.

Beginning   the second *sefirah,* the first that can in any way be perceived: *Hokhmah,* Wisdom, the highest point; cf. above, "The Creation of *Elohim.*"

'the end of the matter'   Ecclesiastes 12:13; here a designation of *She-khinah,* last of the *sefirot.*

no end   *ein sof.*

All these lights and sparks are dependent on It but cannot comprehend   The *sefirot* are brought into being and sustained by the emanation of *Ein Sof,* but even they cannot comprehend Infinity. The reading "on It" follows the Constantinople edition of the Zohar; see Tishby, *Mishnat ha-Zohar* 1:119, 500.

the highest desire, concealed of all concealed   The highest *sefirah* is also called *Razon,* Will, Desire. It is supremely hidden and has an indescribable awareness of *Ein Sof.*

the highest point   Hokhmah, Wisdom.

the world that is coming   The rabbinic concept of *olam ha-ba* (Aramaic, *alma de-'atei*) is often understood as referring to the hereafter; it is usually translated as "the world to come." However, another interpretation is that "the world that is coming" is already in existence, occupying another dimension; see *Tanhuma, Va-Yiqra,* §8: "The wise call it *ha-'olam ha-ba* not because it is not now in existence, but for us who are today in this world it is still to come. So it is 'the world that comes' after a person leaves this world. But one who says that this world is destroyed and afterwards *ha-'olam ha-ba* will come—it is not so." Cf. Maimonides, *Mishneh Torah, Hilkhot Teshuvah* 8:8; and Julius Guttmann, *Philosophies of Judaism,* trans. David W. Silverman (New York, 1973), p. 37: " 'The world to come' does not succeed 'this world' in time, but exists from eternity as a reality outside and above time, to which the soul ascends." According to *Bahir,* §160, *olam ha-ba* means "the world that already came," the primordial light that shone before the creation of the world and was subsequently hidden away; cf. above, "The Hidden Light." The Zohar identifies *alma de-'atei* with the *sefirah* of *Binah*, the Divine Mother, the Who of meditation. She is "the world that is coming, constantly coming and never stopping" (3:290b [*Idra Zuta*]; cf. 1:92a–b; *Sheqel ha-Qodesh*, p. 30; above, Introduction, §6). Here Rabbi Shim'on indicates that *Binah* ascends with *Hokhmah* toward *Ein Sof.*

aroma Cf. the "pleasing aroma" of Leviticus 1:9, and *Shir ha-Shirim Rabbah* 1:20.

Guests in the *Sukkah*

the Festival of Sukkot the Festival of Booths.

the Communion of Israel Hebrew, *Keneset Yisra'el*, "the Community of Israel." In the Zohar this is a name of *Shekhinah*, the divine counterpart of the people of Israel who accompanies them wherever they go. Jeremiah's image of the people is transferred by Rabbi El'azar to *Shekhinah*.

'I remember the devotion' This is the cloud of Aaron According to Rabbi Eli'ezer (Talmud, *Sukkah* 11b), the verse "I lodged the Children of Israel in *sukkot*" refers to "clouds of glory" that surrounded the people on their journey through the desert. There were seven of these clouds, according to Rabbi Hosha'ya (*Bemidbar Rabbah* 1:2), and the Zohar identifies them with the seven *sefirot* below *Binah*. The first six of these were bound to the seventh, *Shekhinah*, who escorted Israel; cf. 3:103a. The "cloud of Aaron" is *Hesed* ("devotion"), the first of the seven, since Aaron was the high priest, and "priest" is a symbol of *Hesed*; cf. 1:256b. *Mekhilta, Va-Yassa*, §5 relates that at Aaron's death the clouds of glory disappeared.

five others The *sefirot* between *Hesed* and *Shekhinah*: *Gevurah, Tif'eret, Nezah, Hod,* and *Yesod.*

They decorated ... The six *sefirot* from *Hesed* to *Yesod* adorned *Shekhinah*, the bride of *YHVH*.

this dwelling the *sukkah*, the "booth."

the shade of faith Faith, *meheimanuta*, is the realm of the *sefirot*. *Shekhinah* absorbs them all. With Her wings, She covers the *sukkah* and those who dwell inside, providing a shade of faith; cf. Zohar 3:103a. In 2:135a *Shekhinah* Herself is called "a *sukkah* covering and protecting us"; cf. 1:48a.

Abraham and five other righteous heroes Abraham, Isaac, Jacob, Moses, Aaron, and Joseph all come to dwell in the *sukkah*. These figures represent the *sefirot* from *Hesed* to *Yesod*. (Here Moses and Aaron symbolize *Nezah* and *Hod*.).

King David Rabbi Abba adds a seventh figure: David, the ideal ruler "who followed the paths of Torah, carried out the commands of Torah, and conducted the kingdom [*malkhuta*] properly" (Zohar 3:113a). He is the representative and symbol of *Malkhut* (*Shekhinah*).

'Seven Days dwell in sukkot' The Days themselves dwell in the *sukkah*. These Days are the seven primordial Days of Creation: the seven lower *sefirot*, *Hesed* to *Shekhinah;* cf. Zohar 2:186b. Their presence in the *sukkah* is symbolized by the appearance of Abraham, Isaac, Jacob, Moses, Aaron, Joseph, and David, their historical manifestations.

'Seven days' it says, not 'For seven days' Rabbi Abba reads the verse according to the method of mystical literalness; cf. above, Introduction, n. 115.

Similarly it is written: 'Six Days . . .' Rabbi Abba alludes to a teaching in *Bahir*, §82 (cf. §§57, 158): " 'Six days *YHVH* made heaven and earth.' It does not say: 'In six days.' This teaches us that each Day had its own power." The six days are not merely the time framework of Creation; they are the *sefirot* from *Hesed* to *Yesod*, the powers of Divinity that create the world. This interpretation from the *Bahir* appears numerous times in the Zohar, e.g., 1:247a; 2:89b; 3:94b, 298b. Here Rabbi Abba adapts it to the verse in Leviticus and then alludes to its original form.

guests Aramaic, *ushpizin*. The mythical guests come representing the *sefirot*, one day at a time.

Rav Hamnuna Sava Rabbi Hamnuna the Elder, a Babylonian teacher of the third century. The Talmud cites several prayers uttered and apparently composed by him (*Berakhot* 11b, 17a, 58a). In the Zohar he is frequently referred to as a great authority, and several original ritual acts are attributed to him; cf. 1:6a, 7b, 250a; 2:88a; 3:87b; Scholem, *Das Buch Bahir*, p. 68.

stand erect, recite a blessing "Blessed are You, *YHVH*, our God, King of the universe, who has sanctified us by His commandments and commanded us to dwell in the *sukkah*." This blessing is recited after the *qiddush*, the blessing over wine that inaugurates the festival; cf. Isadore Twersky, *Introduction to the Code of Maimonides (Mishneh Torah)* (New Haven, 1980), p. 120.

'Seven Days, dwell in sukkot!' Rav Hamnuna Sava addresses the verse to the guests (the righteous heroes, the *sefirot*, the Days), inviting them to dwell in the *sukkah*. This innovation of the Zohar was spread to wider circles by later, Lurianic Kabbalah and has become an integral part of the celebration of *Sukkot;* see *Hemdat Yamim, Sukkot*, Chap. 3; Tishby, *Mishnat ha-Zohar* 2:520–1.

guests of faith symbols of the *sefirot*.

the portion of Israel . . . the portion of YHVH . . . Cf. *Sifrei*, Deuteronomy, §312: "We do not know if the Blessed Holy One chose Jacob or if Jacob chose the Blessed Holy One."

in this world and the world that is coming One who observes and celebrates the Festival of *Sukkot* attains eternal life.

Nevertheless Aramaic, *im kol da*, adopting the reading preserved by Cordovero and the Cremona edition of the Zohar; see *Or ha-Hammah*, ad loc.;

Tishby, *Mishnat ha-Zohar* 2:559, 770. It is not enough to inherit eternal life; one must share the joy of *Sukkot* with the poor.

the portion of those guests ... By providing for the poor, one serves the sublime guests. Cf. above, "An Offering to God," where gladdening the poor is called "the portion of the Blessed Holy One."

'I will spread dung upon your faces ...' Maimonides quotes the same verse in a similar connection; see *Mishneh Torah, Hilkhot Yom Tov* 6:18: "When one eats and drinks [on a festival], he must feed the stranger, the orphan, and the widow along with the other unfortunate poor. But he who locks the doors of his courtyard and eats and drinks alone with his children and his wife and does not give food and drink to the poor and the embittered—this is not the joy of *mizvah* [divine commandment] but only the joy of his belly. Of ones such as these, it is written: 'Their sacrifices are like the food of mourners, all who partake of which are defiled. Their food is only for their appetite' (Hosea 9:4). This kind of joy is a disgrace to them, as it is said: 'I will spread dung upon your faces, the dung of your festal offerings.' " Rabbi Abba adds a literalistic midrash: " 'Your festal offerings,' not Mine!" God wants no part of a selfish meal. Cf. Zohar 2:88b.

Abraham used to stand at the crossroads ... Cf. *Avot de-Rabbi Natan,* Chap. 7: "[Abraham] would go around searching, and when he found wayfarers, he would bring them into his house. To one who was not used to eating wheat bread, he would feed wheat bread; to one who was not used to eating meat, he would feed meat; to one who was not used to drinking wine, he would give wine. Not only that; he went and built large storehouses on the roads and left food and drink there. Anyone who came and entered would eat and drink and bless heaven." Cf. Talmud, *Sotah* 10a–b; *Bereshit Rabba* 54:6. One time, Abraham neglected the poor and was severely punished; see above, "An Offering to God."

'Move away from the tents ...' In the Book of Numbers Moses tells the Children of Israel to move away from the tents of the rebels: Korah, Datan, and Aviram. Employing midrashic style, Rabbi Abba puts the words into Abraham's mouth.

'there is no place' In Mishnah, *Avot* 3:4, Rabbi Shim'on takes these words to mean that God, who is called *maqom,* "place," is not present.

Torah does not demand ... Cf. *Shemot Rabbah* 34:1: "The Blessed Holy One does not come to His creatures with excessive demands; He comes to a person only according to his capacity."

'Each according to what he can give ...' The verse describes the offerings one should bring on the three pilgrimage festivals, one of which is *Sukkot.*

the prime portion belongs to the guests Cf. *Zohar Hadash, Rut,* 87b (*Midrash ha-Ne'elam*): "This is what is right: to give of that food to the poor. The best way to fulfill the command is to give of the food that he himself is eating, from the finest that he desires." Cf. Maimonides, *Mishneh Torah, Hilkhot Issurei ha-Mizbeah* 7:11: "When he feeds one who is hungry, he should feed him the best and the sweetest that he cooked." Cf. *Zavva'at R. Eli'ezer*, §27.

'Then you will delight in YHVH' In the Book of Isaiah this promise is offered to anyone who observes and celebrates the Sabbath; cf. Talmud, *Shabbat* 118a; Zohar 2:88b. The verse is cited frequently in the Zohar.

Rabbi Shim'on interrupted … The Master interrupts his son, El'azar, to make a correction; he then continues the list himself. David was the warrior king; so this verse pertains to him. Moreover, he is the symbol of *Shekhinah* (see above), who is entrusted with all the weapons of King *Tif'eret* (Zohar 1:258a; 3:42b, 150a, 269b). She defends Her people and punishes the wicked.

What Isaac says is … Isaac represents the *sefirah* of *Gevurah*, Power, which is also symbolized by gold. Note that this verse is from the Book of Psalms, traditionally ascribed to King David!

Jacob says, 'Then your light will burst through' The Hebrew word *yibbaqa*, "will burst through," has the same letters as *ya'aqov*, Jacob. The preceding verse reads in part: "Share your bread with the hungry; take the wretched poor into your home."

'and satisfy … your soul with *zahzahot*.' Rabbi Shim'on may be alluding to the secret doctrine of *zahzahot*, "sparkling flashes" that illuminate the righteous soul in the world that is coming; cf. above, end of "Jacob's Garment of Days." The usual rendering is: "satisfy your thirst in parched places," which also fits the context.

'Your people, all of them are righteous … they will inherit the land forever; a sprout of My planting, the work of My hands, making Me glorious!' (Isaiah 60:21). This verse is cited over thirty times in the Zohar; cf. above, "The Old Man and the Beautiful Maiden." Here the point is that all of Israel are potentially righteous. By inviting the poor into the *sukkah* and treating them as holy guests, one welcomes the presence of the righteous heroes, the guests of faith. They, in turn, transmit divine blessings and invite this human being into the company of God.

God, Israel, and *Shekhinah*

mishkan "dwelling, abode"; see above, "The Gift of Dwelling."

seven sevenfold. The Zohar takes the word literally.

My mishkan is Shekhinah Both words have the same root: *shkhn*, "to dwell." *Shekhinah* is God's Indwelling Presence who accompanied Israel through the desert in the *mishkan*; cf. above, "The Gift of Dwelling."

My mishkan is My mashkon. The Midrash invents this play on words. The Tabernacle constructed by Israel in the desert and the Temple in Jerusalem are both referred to as *mishkan*, the dwelling place of God. But each is also a *mashkon*, a "pledge" offered by the people as a guarantee of their loyalty and observance of God's commands. "If they sin, the holy Temple will be seized on their account, as it is said: 'I will place my *mishkan* in your midst.' Do not read: 'My *mishkan*,' but rather: 'My *mashkon*' " (*Shemot Rabbah* 31:9; cf. 35:4; *Tanhuma, Fequdei*, §2). The Zohar adds the identification of *mishkan* with *Shekhinah*. She is seized on account of Israel's sins and banished into exile; see below.

My mashkon, literally Mine! After citing the midrashic play on words, the Zohar presents its own version: the *mashkon*, the pledge, is offered by God, not Israel. A parable . . .

His most precious possession *Shekhinah.*

has removed Himself from us by placing us in exile.

we guard that treasure of His Cordovero preserves a different reading: "We take [*natlin*, instead of *natrin*] that treasure of His." He comments: "We have taken hold of it almost illegally . . . He left Her and we took Her. It is as if She is oppressed by us" (*Or ha-Hammah*, ad loc.).

let Him come and dwell among us! We possess part of God's own being: His feminine half; this is the ultimate guarantee. Cf. *Zohar Hadash, Shir ha-Shirim* 65b: "Come and see: The Blessed Holy One placed His *Shekhinah* among Israel to sit over them like a mother over her children and to protect them on every side. As long as the Holy Mother sits over them, the Blessed Holy One comes to dwell with them because He never leaves Her. All supreme love is directed toward Her. Therefore He gave Her as a pledge in the midst of Israel, to make it known that He will never forget them or leave them. Why? Because that pledge is in their midst."

Even though Israel is now in exile . . . Cf. Talmud, *Megillah* 29a: Rabbi Shim'on son of Yohai says, "Come and see how beloved Israel is to the Blessed Holy One: Wherever they went in exile, *Shekhinah* was with them." This teaching is cited numerous times in the Zohar, e.g., 1:211a; 2:2b, 82a; 3:66a, 90b, 297b.

He took his bed a symbol of both intimacy and stability; cf. Baer, *A History of the Jews in Christian Spain* 1:205: "Besides the house or a small plot of ground remaining to the family, the only asset generally mentioned is the bed, the only permanent item, apparently, of all their property."

My Dwelling *Shekhinah.*

Here, My Bed *Shekhinah* is called Bed in the Zohar, indicating Her intimate relationship with *Tif'eret*, the Blessed Holy One; cf. 2:48b, 51a; 3:118b. Peter Damian (eleventh century) says that Mary was the golden couch upon which God, tired out by the actions of humanity and the angels, lay down to rest; see Patai, *The Hebrew Goddess*, pp. 258–9. Cf. Talmud, *Shabbat* 55b, where it is said that Jacob kept a bed in his tent for *Shekhinah*; cf. Rashi on Genesis 49:4.

the Sea of Tiberias the Sea of Galilee.

They rose at midnight Cf. Talmud, *Berakhot* 3b: Rabbi Shim'on the Hasid said, "There was a harp suspended above [King] David's bed. When midnight arrived, a north wind would come and blow upon it, and it played by itself. Immediately David would rise and engage in Torah until dawn appeared." In the Zohar this legendary custom is expanded into a ritual: all kabbalists are expected to rise at midnight and adorn *Shekhinah* with words of Torah and song; see Scholem, *On the Kabbalah*, pp. 146–50. This parallels the midnight vigil, common among Christian monks from early medieval times; Zohar 3:119a alludes to the Christian practice: "I have seen something similar among the nations of the world."

the Tree of Life Torah; cf. Proverbs 3:18: "She is a tree of life to those who hold fast to her." Tree of Life is also a name for *Tif'eret*, the Written Torah. "Everyone who engages Torah grasps the Tree of Life" (Zohar 3:176a). Cf. above, "The Gift of Dwelling."

the Tent the Tent of Meeting, the *mishkan*, symbolizing *Shekhinah*. Cf. *Encyclopaedia Judaica* 15:685.

exchanged His Glory Israel's worship of the golden calf was an affront to God; they exchanged His Glory, *Shekhinah*, for an idol. Cf. Psalms 106:20: "They exchanged their Glory for the image of a bull"; and above, "The Golden Calf."

let His pledge be placed in the hands of a trustee Israel has exchanged the Glory and thereby forfeited their claim to the pledge. Moses decides to transfer the pledge to a third party, thereby preventing its immediate return to God.

Because he was to Moses . . . See Talmud, *Bava Batra* 75a: "The face of Moses was like the face of the sun; the face of Joshua was like the face of the moon." Cf. Zohar 1:241b; 2:215a; *Zohar Hadash, Terumah* 43c. The moon is a symbol of *Shekhinah*, and Joshua shares that symbol with Her.

This has been established in Talmud, *Megillah* 29a; see above. There this verse is not connected with the teaching.

So, with Israel . . . The parable and the analogy do not correspond. In the parable the pledge is the son, who guarantees the king's faithfulness and love for the queen. In the analogy the pledge is *Shekhinah*, the Queen, who guarantees God's love for Israel, the son. Cordovero notes this discrepancy and tries to explain it away; see *Or ha-Hammah*, ad loc. Cf. Maimonides' remarks on the design of esoteric parables: *Guide of the Perplexed*, 1, Introduction (ed. Pines), p. 8; and above, the second parable in "The Gift of Dwelling." The Zohar is tingling the mind of the reader, subtly introducing some puzzling questions: Who is a pledge for whom? What is the relationship between Israel and *Shekhinah*, the mystical Community of Israel?

As it is written: 'My beloved . . .' Rabbi Isaac imitates the Midrash on Song of Songs, which interprets this and many other verses as love poetry between Israel and God; see *Shir ha-Shirim Rabbah* 2:20–22.

'There he stands behind our wall' in the synagogues and houses of study See *Shir ha-Shirim Rabbah* 2:21: " 'There he stands behind our wall,' behind the walls of synagogues and houses of study."

for indeed, a synagogue must have windows   Cf. Talmud, *Berakhot* 34b: Rabbi Ḥiyya son of Abba said, quoting Rabbi Yoḥanan, "A person should only pray in a house with windows, for it is said: 'There were windows in the upper chamber open toward Jerusalem [and three times a day he would get down on his knees and pray and offer grateful praise before his God]' (Daniel 6:11)." Cf. Zohar 2:59b (*Ra'aya Meheimna*), 251a.

on that day   on new moons, Sabbaths, and festivals.

and they say: 'This is the day ...'   This verse is from the *Hallel* (Psalms 113–118), recited on new moons and festivals.

'YHVH corrects the one whom He loves ...'   Cf. *Berakhot* 5a: Rava said, some say it was Rav Hisda, "If a person sees that suffering comes upon him, he should examine his deeds. ... If he examines and does not find [sufficient cause], he should assign the cause to neglect of Torah. ... If he assigns it and does not find [sufficient neglect], then he knows that these are sufferings of love [*yissurin shel ahavah*], as it is said '*YHVH* corrects the one whom He loves.'" Cf. Deuteronomy 8:5; *Sifrei*, Deuteronomy, §32.

'I have loved you ...'   This verse is spoken to Israel, represented by Jacob.

'But Esau I hated' ...   Cf. Zohar 2:17b (*Midrash ha-Ne'elam*): "What does 'I hated' mean? As it is written: 'He who withholds the rod hates his son' (Proverbs 13:24). I hated him and therefore withheld the rod from him"; cf. *Tanḥuma, Shemot*, §1. Esau symbolizes medieval Christendom; see Gerson Cohen, "Esau as Symbol," in *Jewish Medieval and Renaissance Studies*, ed. Alexander Altmann (Cambridge, 1967), pp. 27–9; cf. 2:188b, 237a; 3:32a. The passage here is a veiled commentary on the condition of the Jews in Christian Spain; see above, Introduction, §4; cf. the encounter between R. El'azar and a gentile, above, "The Golden Calf." Whereas Christianity claimed that Israel's poor condition was a sign of divine punishment for their rejection of Christ, the Zohar sees its people's sufferings as a sign of God's loving discipline. Esau's rise to power, on the other hand, is evidence that God has forsaken him and offers him no correction.

to share Myself with him   literally, "to give him a portion in Me."

'dread' ... thorns   Rabbi Yose associates the word *taqoz*, "dread," with *qoz*, "thorn."

Justice   Hebrew, *zedeq*, another name for *Shekhinah*. Cf. *Bahir*, §120: "*Zedeq* is *Shekhinah*." Ideally, She is joined to Her spouse, Compassion (*Raḥamim*, another name for *Tif'eret*). Then Justice is administered with love. However, in a time of sin or exile, She is divorced from Compassion and becomes a terrifying power: forces of evil overwhelm Her, wreaking havoc and punishment upon the world. Cf. Zohar 3:291b (*Idra Zuta*): "When the sins of the world abound and the Temple [*Shekhinah*] is defiled and the Male removes Himself from the Female and the mighty Serpent begins to be aroused, woe to the world, for then it is fed from this *Zedeq*. Bands of marauders are aroused throughout the world; many of the righteous are taken away from the world. Why all this? Because the Male removes Himself from the Female."

materialize literally, "come out and arise in the world."

forty-minus-one Forty lashes is the maximum punishment allowed by the Torah under the category of flogging (Deuteronomy 25:3); Mishnah, *Makkot* 3:10 reduces the number to thirty-nine. In the Zohar forty-minus-one becomes the number of powers of impurity (3:194a; *Zohar Hadash, Balaq* 55a) and the number of adornments worn by Lilit, the seducer to evil (above, "Jacob's Journey").

the Hollow of the Great Abyss the source of all demonic forces; cf. Zohar 2:65a, 141a, 163b, 267b.

'I shall not doom the world any more . . .' God's promise to Noah. Cf. Zohar 3:54a: "What does this mean: 'I shall not [doom the world] any more'? It means: 'I will not give any more to that Sword [the destructive aspect of *Shekhinah*] but only as much as the world can endure.' "

How can you say . . . addressing Torah directly.

Who is She? Release . . . Seven *Shekhinah* is the last of the seven lower *sefirot* and includes them all; so She is called Seven. She is also called *Shemittah*, "release" or "remission of debts," which was to take place every seven years according to Deuteronomy 15:1–3. The seven years symbolize the seven lower *sefirot*. *Shekhinah* executes divine punishment but also expresses divine forgiveness and remission.

as has been established Cf. above.

'Myself' Now I will confront you! Seven . . . Cf. *Bahir*, §66: Rabbi Rehumai said, "What does 'Myself' mean? The Blessed Holy One said, 'I will discipline you.' The Communion of Israel [*Shekhinah*] says, 'Do not imagine that I will plead for mercy for you. Rather, I Myself will discipline you.' " Cf. Ramban on Leviticus 26:16. *Shekhinah* is called "I" in the Zohar; She is the immediate presence of God; see 1:6b, 65b; 2:98a, 236b; Scholem, *Major Trends*, pp. 216–7.

received accepted the reprimand.

both of us go into exile Cf. Talmud, *Megillah* 29a: Rabbi Shim'on son of Yohai says, "Come and see how beloved Israel is to the Blessed Holy One: Wherever they went in exile, *Shekhinah* was with them."

"Myself" too, along with you! reading the verse: "I will discipline you and Myself!"

Seven, who will be banished along with you. Why? . . . See above, the opening lines of the selection. Cf. *Bahir*, §76: "A parable. To what can this be compared? To a king who had a beautiful wife. He had children by her; he loved them and raised them. They fell into evil ways; he hated them and hated their mother. Their mother went to them and said, 'My children, why have you acted like this? Now your father hates me and you!' They repented and returned to carry out the will of their father. Once their father saw this, he loved them as at first and remembered their mother." In several Zohar passages it is *Shekhinah* who takes the initiative and exiles Herself in order to comfort and protect Her children; see 1:134a, 210a; 2:216b; 3:297b; cf. 2:189a. For a discussion of the theme of the exile of *Shekhinah* see Tishby, *Mishnat ha-Zohar*, 1:228–31; cf. above, "Adam's Sin" and "The Golden Calf."

'For your crimes, your Mother was sent away' In Isaiah the mother is Israel personified. Here the mother is *Shekhinah*. Cf. Zohar 3:74a–b: "Come and see: As long as Israel is far from the palace of the King, the Queen is removed with them, as if it were possible. Why? Because She did not enforce the rules and strike the son, guiding him in the straight path. For the King never strikes His son; He leaves it all in the hands of the Queen, to administer the palace and discipline the son and lead him in the true path toward the King.... The secret of the word is: 'For your crimes, your Mother was sent away.' "

For a palace is worthless ... *Cf. Eikhah Rabbah* 5:20: "Is there such a thing as a king without a queen?" Cf. Zohar 3:5a: "A king without a queen is not a king."

This has already been said in Talmud, *Megillah* 29a, in the name of Rabbi Shim'on son of Yohai: "When they are destined to be redeemed, *Shekhinah* will be with them, as it is said: *"YHVH* your God will return your captivity' (Deuteronomy 30:3). It is not said: 'will bring forth' [*ve-heshiv*], but rather: 'will return' [*ve-shav*]. This teaches us that the Blessed Holy One will return with them from exile."

a certain cave in a field The Comrades sometimes come across caves where they discover words of Torah; cf. Zohar 2:13a; 3:149b–150a, 162a, 268b. According to rabbinic sources, Rabbi Shim'on and his son, El'azar, hid in a cave for twelve years; see Talmud, *Shabbat* 33b; *Bereshit Rabba* 79:6, and parallels cited there; above, Introduction, n. 84; cf. 1:11a–b; *Zohar Hadash, Ki Tavo,* 59c–60a. Such stories provided evidence for Moses de León's claim that the Zohar was composed by Rabbi Shim'on. Note that Rabbi Ḥiyya transmits a teaching of Rabbi El'azar.

The verse should read ... The verbs "strike" and "kill" seem to fit the context better.

My soul's beloved *Shekhinah.*

le-khallotam "so as to destroy them"; but Rabbi El'azar reads the word as it is spelled ...

spelled: le-khalltam, without the "o" The letter *vav*, denoting the "o", is not found in the biblical text. This abbreviated spelling allows the creation of a midrash.

the tanners' market notorious for its foul odor. See Talmud, *Qiddushin* 82b: "Woe to him who is a tanner by trade!" According to Mishnah, *Ketubbot* 9:10, a woman can demand a divorce from her husband if he is a tanner.

Le-khallatam, "Because of their bride" The abbreviated spelling enables Rabbi El'azar to insert an "a" for the "o" and read the word as *le-*

khallatam, "because of their bride," instead of *le-khallotam*, "so as to destroy them." Cf. *Minhat Shai* on Leviticus 26:44; for a similar play on words see above, the conclusion of "The Gift of Dwelling." This mystical midrash raises several questions: Whose bride is *Shekhinah*, Israel's or God's? What does it mean that *Shekhinah* is in our midst? What is the relationship between God, Israel, and *Shekhinah?* Cf. the third parable in this selection.

If I have come here ... Cf. above, "The Old Man and the Beautiful Maiden."

Threshing Out the Secrets (Idra Rabba)

How long will we sit on a one-legged stand? Aramaic, *bi-qeyama de-had samekha*, "a stand [or "pillar"] of one support." Rabbi Shim'on urges the Comrades to deepen and stabilize their understanding of the secrets. For an analysis of the question see Liebes, *"Peraqim,"* pp. 359–60; idem, *"Ha-Mashiah shel ha-Zohar,"* pp. 118–28, 204–5, 227–9. Cf. *Zohar Hadash, Bereshit,* 16a (*Midrash ha-Ne'elam*): "How long will we sit on one stand and be unable to proceed?"

'Time to act for YHVH! They have violated Your Torah!' Maimonides cites this verse in the Introduction to *Guide of the Perplexed* (ed. Pines, p. 16) as justification for his plan to reveal "concealed things." Here Rabbi Shim'on is about to reveal some of the deepest secrets of Kabbalah, and he opens with the same verse. The threat to tradition posed by unbelievers and radical rationalists demands a bold response; see above, Introduction, §§2, 4–5; cf. Talmud, *Berakhot* 54a, 63a; Jerusalem Talmud, *Berakhot* 9:3, 14d (in the name of Rabbi Shim'on); Zohar 1:116b; 2:155b; 3:62b.

The days are few ... Cf. Mishnah, *Avot* 2:20: Rabbi Tarfon says, "The day is short; the work is great; the workers are lazy; the reward is abundant; and the Master is pressing."

a herald cries out every day! Cf. Mishnah, *Avot* 6:2: Rabbi Joshua son of Levi said, "Every single day a divine echo reverberates from Mt. Sinai declaring: 'Woe to humankind for the humiliation of Torah!'" Cf. above, "Jacob's Garment of Days."

The Reapers of the Field are few Cf. Matthew 9:37; Luke 10:2: "The harvest is rich but the laborers are few." The Comrades are called Reapers of the Field (Aramaic, *mehazzedei haqla*) frequently in the Zohar: 1:156a (*Sitrei Torah*), 216a; 2:37a, 79b, 85b, 240b, 258a; 3:106a, 141b, 143a, 144a (*Idra Rabba*), 214b, 297a; *Zohar Hadash, Rut* 85d (*Midrash ha-Ne'elam*); see Liebes, *Ha-Mashiah shel ha-Zohar,"* pp. 146–8. Cordovero offers the following explanation of the name (in *Or ha-Hammah* on 3:106a): "The Reapers of the Field are the Comrades, masters of this wisdom, because *Malkhut* [*Shekhinah*] is called the Apple Field [see above, "Manna and Wisdom"], and She grows sprouts of secrets and new flowerings of Torah. Those who constantly create new interpretations of

Torah are harvesting Her." *Shekhinah* is the source of inspiration and kabbalistic creativity.

Only at the edge of the vineyard Even the Comrades have not succeeded in penetrating the secrets. They need the guidance of the Master, Rabbi Shim'on. Cf. Liebes, "*Ha-Mashiah shel ha-Zohar*," pp. 149–50.

the threshing house Aramaic, *bei idra. Idra* means "threshing floor." In the Midrash *idra de-'azharah* ("*idra* of enlightenment") refers to the hall of the Sanhedrin because the members convened in a semicircle, half the shape of the threshing circle; see *Shir ha-Shirim Rabbah* 7:6; Mishnah, *Sanhedrin* 4:3; cf. 1 Kings 22:10; 2 Chronicles 18:9; *Va-Yiqra Rabbah* 11:8; *Qohelet Rabbah* 1:30; *Zohar Hadash, Yitro* 36b. In *Shir ha-Shirim Rabbah* 5:7 the phrase "threshing floor of Torah" refers to an intensive study session. In the Zohar *idra* has a wide range of meanings: "threshing floor, room, assembly"; it is also a symbol of *Shekhinah* and other *sefirot*. The Zohar refers to this particular section (3:127b–145a) or to the event as *Idra*, Holy *Idra, Idra* of Rabbi Shim'on; see 3:79a, 145b, 288a, 291a, 292a, 295a (*Idra Zuta*). Later copyists and editors called it *Idra Rabba*, "The Great *Idra*," to distinguish it from another section (3:287b–296b) that they called *Idra Zuta*, "The Small *Idra*." For a full discussion of the term see Liebes, "*Peraqim*," pp. 93–107. Here the *idra* is the place where the secrets of Torah are threshed out. Cf. 3:148a: "I want to walk behind you and learn some of those sublime words that you taste every day from the Holy *Idra*." Cf. the statement by David son of Judah the Hasid, an early translator of the Zohar (fourteenth century): "This secret [is clear] ... to anyone who has entered the threshing house" (*Sefer Mar'ot ha-Zove'ot* [*The Book of Mirrors*], p. 116).

wearing coats of mail ... The Comrades are summoned to engage in the battle of Torah. Cf. Talmud, *Shabbat* 63a: " 'Gird your sword upon your thigh, O hero, your splendor and glory' (Psalms 45:4). Rav Kahana said to Mar son of Rav Huna, 'This refers to words of Torah.' " Cf. *Ta'anit* 7a: Rabbi Hanina said, "Just as one piece of iron sharpens another, so two scholars sharpen each other in the law." The Zohar elaborates the metaphor in 2:110a––b; 3:188a–189b.

your array Aramaic, *tiqquneikhon. Tiqqun* means "arrangement, adornment"; the root has various connotations in the Zohar; see, e.g., 3:135a (*Idra Rabba*); cf. *Targum Onqelos* to Exodus 33:6, where "their finery" is taken to mean "their weapons" (*tiqqun zeineihon*); cf. *Targum Yonatan* and Rashi, ad loc.; *Shemot Rabbah* 45:1; Zohar 1:52b; 2:194a.

Design, Wisdom ... Hands and Feet These words indicate various *sefirot*. Design, *eita*, is associated with the highest *sefirah, Keter*, in Zohar 3:133b (*Idra Rabba*). Wisdom, Intellect, and Knowledge appear in Exodus 35:31 and *Targum Onqelos*, ad loc. They correspond to *Hokhmah* and *Binah*, the second and third *sefirot*, and *Da'at*, which represents the hidden balancing power of the *sefirot*. Vision, *heizu*, refers to *Shekhinah*, who reflects all the *sefirot;* cf. above, "Colors and Enlightenment." The two Hands are *Hesed* and *Gevurah*, the arms of God; the two Feet, *Nezaḥ* and *Hod*, the legs of God. (On the *sefirot* see above, Introduction, §6.) The Comrades are instructed to equip themselves with sefirotic powers in preparation for the battle of Torah.

high holy ones In Daniel 7:18–27 this phrase refers to the people of Israel. Here it refers to the angels, who are eager to hear new words of Torah; cf. below; Talmud, *Hagigah* 14b; Zohar 2:41a; 3:128a, 135a (*Idra Rabba*). The Comrades are referred to as "high holy ones" in 1:95b; 2:130b, 176a, 265a; 3:72b, 290a (*Idra Zuta*). According to 1:90a (*Sitrei Torah*), all of Israel are comrades of the angels. Cf. *Qiddushin* 72a; *Nedarim* 20b; Zohar 1:12b.

Woe if I reveal . . . Cf. Talmud, *Bava Batra* 89b, where Rabbi Yohanan son of Zakkai says, concerning the details of illegal practices, "Woe to me if I say it! Woe to me if I do not say it! If I say it, the deceivers will learn. If I do not say it, the deceivers will say: 'Scholars are not expert in our practices.' " Cf. Zohar 1:11b: Rabbi Shim'on cried, and said, "Woe if I say it! Woe if I do not say it! If I say it, sinners will know how to worship their Lord. If I do not say it, the Comrades will be deprived of this word." Cf. 3:74b.

'The secret of YHVH . . .' Cf. Maimonides, *Guide of the Perplexed*, 1, Introduction (ed. Pines), p. 7.

crossed the threshold of the Dwelling literally, "entered the *idra* of the Dwelling." On *idra* see above; on this *idra*, whose account has apparently been lost, see Liebes, "*Ha-Mashiaḥ shel ha-Zohar*," pp. 153–4. *Shekhinah* is called both *Idra* (2:128b–129a) and Dwelling (above, "The Gift of Dwelling," "God, Israel, and *Shekhinah*"). In 2:172a *idra de-mashkena* refers to the highest heaven. Rabbi Abba's point is that the Comrades are not novices; they have entered the secret realms.

entered . . . emerged Early rabbinic literature speaks of four rabbis who entered *pardes* ("orchard" and "Paradise"), i.e., engaged in mystical contemplation on the divine chariot. Only Rabbi Akiva "entered in peace and emerged in peace" (Tosefta, *Hagigah* 2:4); see Scholem, *Jewish Gnosticism*, pp. 14–9; *Kabbalah*, pp. 13–4, 18. The Zohar employs the phrase "one who has entered and emerged" to designate the kabbalist who has entered the realm of the divine, discovered wisdom, and come out unscathed; see above, the end of the Introduction; 1:44a; 2:179a (*Sifra di-Zeni'uta*), 213b; 3:141a (*Idra Rabba*), 290a (*Idra Zuta*), 297a. Cf. above, "Jacob's Journey," where the phrase refers to a successful venture into the realm of the demonic.

Present were . . . There are ten rabbis present, including Rabbi Shim'on. Historically, a number of these figures lived several centuries apart from each other; see Tishby, *Mishnat ha-Zohar* 1:71–2 (Introduction).

on my breast Aramaic, *be-tuqpi*, according to the reading of the Mantua and Constantinople editions; see Tishby, *Mishnat ha-Zohar*, 1:29, 499. The word *tuqpa* illustrates Moses de León's peculiar method of utilizing his sources. *Tuqpa* means "strength," and it has this sense in the Zohar; see, e.g., 2:111a–b; 3:118b, 120a; *Zohar Ḥadash, Balaq*, 56a. Elsewhere in the Zohar, however, the word signifies "breast" or "bosom." This new twist of meaning is based on *Targum Onqelos* to Numbers 11:12, where the phrase "carry them in your bosom" is rendered: "bear them in your strength [*be-tuqpakh*]." Relying on this interpretation, Moses de León employs *tuqpa* to mean "breast"; cf. 2:96a, 113a–b; 3:234a; *Zohar Hadash, Balaq,* 55b; see Scholem, *Major Trends,* pp. 165, 389, n. 48; Liebes, *"Peraqim,"* p. 267. Sometimes it seems that both meanings are being played with; see 3:161a–b; *Zohar Hadash, Balaq,* 55a. Moses is playing hide-and-seek with his readers: hiding his sources while at the same time offering a correct interpretation of his weird Aramaic only to those who can track down those sources. In 3:201a Rabbi Shim'on says: "In Arabia they call a person's breast [*hadoi*] 'strength' [*koah*]." (Cf. Talmud, *Rosh ha-Shanah* 26a; *Bereshit Rabba* 36:1.) There is no such usage in Arabic. Moses is simply inventing an etymology for the new meaning of *tuqpa* to take the place of his secret source in the *Targum.*

'Cursed be the one who makes a carved or molten image . . .' Before beginning to reveal the secrets of Divinity, Rabbi Shim'on cites this verse as a warning against taking his words and symbolic images literally. Such a misunderstanding would be tantamount to idolatry. Cf. *Tiqqunei Zohar,* Preface, 6b; Gikatilla, *Sha'arei Orah,* pp. 4–5.

They all responded, "Amen!" The verse in Deuteronomy concludes: "The entire people responded, 'Amen!' " Moses de León may be changing the wording to fit the present context: the Comrades respond, "Amen!"

The Torah up above   *Tif'eret,* who is called the Written Torah.

if this Name is not arrayed perfectly   The Name *YHVH* must be recited with the proper *kavvanot* ("intentions," mystical awareness and focus). Otherwise, *Tif'eret* (the Torah up above, the *sefirah* corresponding to *YHVH*) is rendered incomplete. Cf. above, "*Qorban* and *Olah.*" For a different interpretation, see Liebes, *"Ha-Mashiah shel ha-Zohar,"* pp. 166–7.

addressed to the Ancient of Days   The Ancient of Days, *attiq yomin,* is described in Daniel 7:9. In the Zohar it is a name of *Keter,* the highest *sefirah.* "Your Torah" in this verse means the *sefirah* of *Tif'eret,* called Torah, which belongs to the Ancient of Days.

'Who is like you?' . . . 'Who is like You . . .?'   By means of selective citation, Rabbi Shim'on begins to draw an analogy between his own circle and God. This is spelled out as he proceeds. For a different interpretation, see Tishby, *Mishnat ha-Zohar* 1:29.

the other side   Aramaic, *sitra ahra.*

We are the sum of the whole!   Aramaic, *anan kelala de-khola.* Cf. Talmud, *Sukkah* 45b: In the name of Rabbi Shim'on son of Yohai: "I have seen the sublime humans, and they are few. If there are one thousand, I and my son are among them. If there are one hundred, I and my son are among them. If there are two, I and my son are they!" Cf. Jerusalem Talmud, *Berakhot* 9:3, 13d; *Bereshit Rabba* 35:2.

Now the pillars stand firm! Rabbi Shim'on and his two close Comrades embody the three pillars of the sefirotic world: right, left, and center. The seven other Comrades fill out the decade. By joining together to engage in secrets of Torah, Rabbi Shim'on and the Comrades correct the instability of the pillar; see the beginning of the selection.

their knees knocked, one against the other   The phrase is from Daniel 5:6, describing King Belshazzar's reaction when he saw the hand writing on the wall.

the Assembly on High   heavenly beings assembling to hear the secrets.

There it was right to be afraid   These words reflect Habakkuk's revelation of the stern manifestation of God, *Ze'eir Appin*, the Impatient One, the realm of *sefirot* from *Hokhmah* to *Yesod;* see below. Cf. *Bahir*, §69; Zohar 1:7b; and 3:138b (*Idra Rabba*); "It is written: 'I was afraid.' There it is right to fear, to be shattered in His Presence. This is said concerning *Ze'eir Appin*."

for us the word depends on love   Rabbi Shim'on's revelation, now being introduced, derives from a higher aspect of Divinity, the realm of *Keter*, above *Ze'eir Appin*. Here there is nothing but love; cf. Zohar 3:138b, 140b (*Idra Rabba*). There is no need to be afraid of revealing the secrets of this high realm; fear does not pertain. For other interpretations see Tishby, *Mishnat ha-Zohar*, 1:29; Liebes, "*Ha-Mashiah shel ha-Zohar*," pp. 156–9.

'Love your neighbor ...'   These verses are from Leviticus 19:18; Deuteronomy 6:5, 7:8; Malachi 1:2. The first verse does not appear in the printed editions; it is recorded by Cordovero (*Or ha-Hammah*, appendix to Leviticus).

It has been told   Rabbi Shim'on transmits a teaching.

the Will of the White Head   The White Head is *Keter*, who is pure love and compassion, untainted by judgment. Cf. Daniel 7:9: "The hair on His head was like clean wool." *Keter* is often called Will.

to manifest Its Glory   literally, "to make Glory for Its Glory."

the Blinding Flash   Aramaic, *bozina de-qardinuta;* see above, "The Creation of *Elohim*." This is the Zohar's name for the first impulse of emanation proceeding from *Ein Sof*, the Infinite, through *Keter*. The flash directs the entire process of emanation, providing its rhythm and measure; cf. 3:292b (*Idra Zuta*); *Zohar Hadash, Va-'Ethannan*, 56d–58d (*Qav ha-Middah*). The goal of meditation is to attain this flash and participate in the flow of being; see *Zohar Hadash*, 57d–58a, 58c–d.

one spark   Aramaic, *had nizoza*. This is the first point: *Hokhmah*, Wisdom.

370   This number recurs in the Zohar in various contexts; see 1:4b; 2:14a–b (*Midrash ha-Ne'elam*); 3:133b (*Idra Rabba*). Cf. 2:254b; 3:292b (*Idra Zuta*), where sparks fly in 320 directions and Divine Thought is cleansed of impurities.

A pure aura emerged   from *Keter*, who is called *avira*, the "aura" of *Ein Sof;* cf. above, "The Creation of *Elohim*."

one hard skull *Binah*, who proceeds from the spark of *Hokhmah*.

four sides The four sides (north, south, east, and west) symbolize four *sefirot* that emanate from *Binah*: *Din*, *Hesed*, *Tif'eret*, and *Shekhinah*.

Surrounded by this pure aura . . . *Hokhmah* is absorbed by its source. It does not dissolve there but rather remains hidden and transmits the power of further emanation to *Binah*.

the Ancient of Days *Keter*.

the breath breathed by the aura through the spark of *Hokhmah* into the skull of *Binah*.

fire *Din*, (*Gevurah*), the *sefirah* of Judgment.

air *Hesed*, Love.

What is fire doing here? How can there be fire above *Din*? The highest *sefirot* are not characterized by Judgment.

270 worlds . . . Judgment *Binah*, the product of the spark of *Hokhmah*, is the compassionate Divine Mother. However, She includes within Herself the roots of Judgment and gives birth to *Din*, the *sefirah* of Judgment. 270 may be an allusion to *ra*, "evil," which has the numerical equivalent of 270. According to Isaac son of Jacob Kohen, a contemporary of Moses de León, evil proceeds from *Binah*; see Scholem, *Kabbalah*, pp. 123–4. If 270 is an allusion to evil, then the number 370, above, may allude to the 270 evil realms plus the 100 holy realms of the *sefirot*. The Zohar often squares the decade of *sefirot* and refers to them as 100; see 1:87b, 172a; 2:127a, 185b, 200a.

Into this skull trickles dew . . . The dew is the flow of emanation; cf. above, "Manna and Wisdom."

constantly overflowing The Head overflows (literally, "is filled") with dew; cf. Song of Songs 5:2: "My head is filled with dew."

the dead are destined to come to life Cf. *Pirqei de-Rabbi Eli'ezer*, Chap. 34: "In the time to come, [the Blessed Holy One] will shake the hair of His head, as if it were possible, and bring down a reviving dew and bring the dead to life, as it is said: 'I am asleep, but my heart is awake . . . My head is filled with dew.' " Cf. Talmud, *Shabbat* 88b; Zohar 1:130b, 232a; 3:128b (*Idra Rabba*).

a white embracing all whites pure love and compassion.

the Head of the Impatient One *Binah*, the skull. The *sefirot* below *Keter*, from *Hokhmah* to *Yesod*, are referred to as the Impatient One (*Ze'eir Appin*; literally, "short-faced," but meaning "short-tempered, impatient"; cf. Proverbs 14:17). *Keter*, the White Head, the highest *sefirah*, is pure compassion and therefore described as *Arikh Anpin*, "long-faced, long-suffering, slow to anger"; cf. Exodus 34:6. The lower *sefirot* are characterized by a tension between different aspects of the divine: right and left, love and rigor. Relative to *Keter*, they are impatient.

red the color of Judgment.

Like this crystal . . . Cf. Zohar 3:128b (*Idra Rabba*): "The appearance of that dew is white, like the color of crystal gems in which all colors appear, as it is written [concerning the manna]: 'Its color was like the color of crystal' (Numbers 11:7)." Manna and dew are associated in Exodus 16:13–14; cf. above, "Manna and Wisdom." "Crystal dew" is mentioned in Zohar 2:176b (*Sifra di-Zeni'uta*); *Zohar Hadash, Aharei Mot* 48c.

the Patient One   Aramaic, *arikha de-anpin;* see above.

'Your dew is a dew of lights'   The first part of the verse is pertinent: "Your dead will live! Corpses will arise! Awake and shout for joy, you who dwell in the dust!"

the Apple Orchard   *Shekhinah;* see above, "Manna and Wisdom." The apple trees filling Her are the *sefirot* from *Hesed* to *Yesod,* especially *Hesed, Gevurah,* and *Tif'eret,* whose colors are white, red, and green, the colors of the apple (Zohar 3:287a [*Idra Zuta*]).

one-and-a-half million worlds ... the Impatient One   Since He receives only one-sixtieth of the ninety million worlds inside the skull, He is called *Ze'eir Appin,* literally, "short-faced, little-faced."

When necessary   When Judgment looms and the world needs compassion ...

long-suffering   Aramaic, *arikhin,* "long."

the Ancient of Ancients   the Ancient of Days, *Keter,* called *Arikh Anpin,* "long-suffering, the Patient One." Looking back to His source, the Impatient One is soothed and manifests the compassion overflowing from *Keter.* Cf. Zohar 3:136b (*Idra Rabba*): "When the Blessed Holy One is aroused to delight Himself with the righteous, the Face of the Ancient of Days shines into the face of the Impatient One. Its Forehead is revealed and shines to this forehead. Then it is called 'a time of favor' (Psalms 69:14). Whenever Judgment looms and the forehead of the Impatient One is revealed, the Forehead of the Ancient of Ancients is revealed; Judgment subsides and is not executed."

feels compassion   Aramaic, *hayeis,* also meaning "spares."

died   Rabbi Yeisa's death is foretold in Zohar 3:79a; cf. 1:217a; 2:61b.

a canopy   This canopy had been spread over Rabbi Shim'on and the Comrades while they threshed out the secrets; cf. 3:134b, 138b (*Idra Rabba*).

they settled down   The subject is either the Comrades, calmed by Rabbi Shim'on's word, or the angels, forced by his word to descend. The usual meaning of the Aramaic word *ishtakkekhu* accords with the first interpretation; the context, however, is ambiguous. Cf. the consequences of another word of Rabbi Shim'on, below.

something not revealed since ... Moses   The secrets disclosed here are divine revelation; cf. Talmud, *Hagigah* 14b; Jerusalem Talmud, *Hagigah* 2:1, 77b; *Va-Yiqra Rabbah* 16:4; *Tanhuma, Huqqat,* §8; *Avot de-Rabbi Natan* (2), Chap. 13; *Pirqei de-Rabbi Eli'ezer,* Chap. 2. Earlier, in 3:132b (*Idra Rabba*), Rabbi Shim'on states: "I see now what no human has seen since the day Moses ascended Mt. Sinai the second time. For I see my face shining like the light of the powerful sun. ... Moreover, I know that my face is shining, whereas Moses did not know and did not see, as it is written: 'Moses did not know that the skin of his face was radiant' (Exodus 34:29)."

'At the cost of his firstborn . . .' This curse was proclaimed by Joshua after the battle of Jericho against anyone who dared to rebuild the city. Here it is applied to Rabbi Shim'on's reconstruction of the divine realm.

All the more so there is no reason to mourn . . .

their souls joined the Divine They achieved *devequt*, communion with God, at the moment of death.

250 worlds On the Sabbath 250 worlds are filled with joyous song (Zohar 2:88b).

these ones the three Comrades.

departed by a kiss According to rabbinic sources, Moses, Aaron, Miriam, and the three Patriarchs all died by a kiss from God, not through the agency of the Angel of Death; see *Shir ha-Shirim Rabbah* 1:16; Talmud, *Bava Batra* 17a; Rashi, ad loc.; cf. Maimonides, *Guide of the Perplexed* 3:51; Zohar 1:125a. Here the Zohar confers this honor upon the three Comrades who died. Cf. Recanati, *Commentary on the Torah*, p. 38b, who cites this passage and adds: "Out of great *devequt*, their souls cleaved to the sublime soul [*Shekhinah*] until they died by a kiss."

Because . . . they had entered and not emerged These three Comrades were initiated into the mysteries but did not emerge successfully; see above: "some have entered; some have emerged." Cf. Zohar 3:141a (*Idra Rabba*): "Anyone who has entered and not emerged, it would be better for him if he had never been created!"

'You who cleave . . .' Their *devequt*, "cleaving" to God, assures the departed Comrades eternal life. The verse also applies to Rabbi Shim'on and the Comrades still with him who strive for *devequt*.

Wherever they looked, aromas arose This contrasts sharply with the talmudic description of what happened when Rabbi Shim'on and his son, El'azar, came out of the cave: "They saw people plowing and sowing. He [Rabbi Shim'on] said, 'They are forsaking eternal life [Torah] and engaging in temporal life!' Every place they gazed upon was immediately burnt" (Talmud, *Shabbat* 33b).

Everyone's face shone . . . as did Moses' face when he came down from Mt. Sinai; see Exodus 34:29–35; cf. above, note on "something not revealed . . ."

these three who had died.

threshing houses in the sky the chambers of the Heavenly Academy, where secrets are studied by angels and departed souls; see above, "The Golden Calf"; cf. *Zohar Hadash, Yitro* 36b; Zohar 3:185b.

mountains of pure balsam Thirteen rivers of Balsam await the righteous in the world that is coming; see above, "The Gift of Dwelling." Here the rivers are transformed into mountains; cf. Zohar 2:87b.

The seven of us are the eyes of YHVH The seven Comrades represent seven divine powers that conduct the world and watch over it; cf. Zohar 1:218a, 241a; 2:252a; 3:129b–130a, 136b–137b (*Idra Rabba*), 293b–294a (*Idra Zuta*); Corbin, *The Man of Light in Iranian Sufism*, pp. 52–4.

six lights   symbolizing the six *sefirot* from *Hesed* to *Yesod*.

the seventh of all   corresponding to *Binah*, the Divine Mother, who sustains all seven lower *sefirot* and is called Seven; see above, "Jacob's Journey." Rabbi Shim'on is *Bozina Qaddisha*, the Holy Light.

Sabbath, source of blessing for all six   Cf. Zohar 2:63b: Rabbi Judah said, "All six days are blessed by the seventh day."

'Sabbath for YHVH,' 'Holy to YHVH'   Exodus 20:10; 16:23.

The Rabbis Encounter a Child (Yanuqa)

the village of Sikhnin   in the Galilee.

Shema   the declaration of God's oneness that opens with the words: "Hear O Israel! YHVH is our God; YHVH is one" (Deuteronomy 6:4). The prayer consists of Deuteronomy 6:4–9; 11:13–21; Numbers 15:37–41. Traditionally it is recited every morning and evening. The Zohar attaches cosmic significance to the *Shema;* see above, "The Golden Calf," note on "Israel, who are the lip of truth . . ."

'Anyone who has not recited Shema . . .'   The proper time to recite the morning *Shema* is from the first traces of dawn until a quarter of the day has passed; see Mishnah, *Berakhot* 1:2. In rabbinic law a ban, *niddui*, involves isolation from, and enforced contempt by, the community at large. Various offenses are punishable by *niddui*, but failure to recite Shema is not specified as one of them; see Talmud, *Berakhot* 19a; Maimonides, *Mishneh Torah, Hilkhot Talmud Torah* 6:14. Maimonides includes among the offenders anyone who disregards a rabbinic prescription, and this may have inspired the formulation here. Note also Maimonides' comment: "Even if a minor bans him, the head of the court and all of Israel must treat him as banned."

engaged with a bride and groom   Cf. *Avot de-Rabbi Natan*, Chap. 4: "It happened once that Rabbi Judah son of Ila'i was sitting and teaching his students. A bride walked by without all that she needed. They cheered her up until she passed." Cf. Talmud, *Ketubbot* 17a. Rabbi Judah's teacher, Rabbi Tarfon, is said to have done more in a similar situation: "It happened once that Rabbi Tarfon was sitting and teaching his students. A bride passed by. He gave a command and had her brought into his house. He told his mother and his wife, 'Bathe her, anoint her, adorn her, dance in front of her until she goes to her husband's house' " (*Avot de-Rabbi Natan*, Chap. 41). The Zohar draws on these accounts but involves Rabbi Judah and Rabbi Isaac more directly. The rabbis may also be alluding to their mystical preoccupation with the union of the divine bride and groom, *Shekhinah* and *Tif'eret*. According to the Zohar, this union is the mystical purpose of reciting *Shema;* see Zohar 2:133b–134b;

Tishby, *Mishnat ha-Zohar* 2:276–9. It is interesting that five centuries later the Hasidim were charged by their orthodox opponents with failing to recite *Shema* at its proper time because they engaged so long in preparation and meditation; see Louis Jacobs, *Hasidic Prayer* (New York, 1973), pp. 46–53.

One who is busy doing a mizvah ... performing a divine commandment. Cf. Talmud, *Sukkah* 26a: Rabbi Hananya son of Aqavya said, "Scribes and their vendors and their vendors' vendors and all who are engaged in the work of heaven, including those who sell purple dye [for the fringes on a garment], are exempt from reciting *Shema* and the standing prayer and from donning *tefillin* [phylacteries] and from all the *mizvot* stated in the Torah. This fulfills the words of Rabbi Yose the Galilean, who said, 'One who is occupied with a *mizvah* is exempt from another *mizvah*.' "

by the smell of your clothes There are 248 words in the *Shema*, corresponding to the 248 limbs in the human body; see above, "The Golden Calf," note on "they conclude: *YHVH*. . . ." "Every person who recites *Shema* properly, every single word emanates to one of his limbs. But if a person does not recite *Shema* in the daytime and at night, every one of his limbs is filled with an evil spirit and with all kinds of evil disease" (*Zohar Hadash, Aharei Mot,* 48a; cf. ibid., *Rut* 90c–d [*Midrash ha-Ne'elam*]). In 3:188a the child makes another discovery with his sense of smell.

he blessed before he washed He said the blessing for washing the hands before washing them; cf. Talmud, *Pesahim* 7b. The accepted practice is to first wash and then bless; see *Arba'ah Turim, Orah Hayyim,* §158; *Shulhan Arukh,* ad loc.

Rabbi Shema'yah the Hasid Rabbi Shim'on, Master of the Comrades, who is occasionally referred to as *Hasid,* "pious one, devotee"; see Zohar 3:166a–b, 169b. On the interchange of the names Shema'yah and Shim'on, cf. Wilhelm Bacher, *Die Agada der palästinensischen Amoräer* (Hildesheim, 1965), 3:774, n. 5.

One who blesses with filthy hands ... Cf. Talmud, *Berakhot* 53b: Rabbi Zuhamai said, "Just as an offensive-looking priest is unfit for service, so filthy hands are unfit for blessing"; *Sotah* 4b: Rabbi El'azar said, "Whoever disregards the washing of hands is uprooted from the world." The child is more extreme. Cf. Matthew 15, Mark 7.

child Aramaic, *yanuqa,* "suckling, infant, child." There are children like this one running through the Zohar, catching the rabbis unawares with their startling wisdom; cf. 1:92b, 148a, 238b; 2:6b, 169b; 3:39a, 162a, 171a, 204b; *Zohar Hadash, Bereshit* 9a, 14d (*Midrash ha Ne'elam*); *Aharei Mot* 48a, 49a–b; *Rut* 77d, 84b–c (*Midrash ha-Ne'elam*); Jellinek, *Beit ha-Midrash,* 3:136–7; Scholem, *Devarim be-Go* 1:270–83. This section of the Zohar (3:186a–192a) is the most extended narrative of this type and is called *Yanuqa.*

inhabit the height of the world The ten fingers of the human hand symbolize the ten *sefirot.* Cf. *Sefer Yezirah* 1:3; *Bahir,* §124; Ramban on Exodus

30:19; Zohar 1:20b; 2:67a, 208a; 3:143a (*Idra Rabba*), 195b. On the phrase here cf. Talmud, *Berakhot* 6b.

one finger   the middle finger, as becomes clear below.

the finger that Moses raised   when he held up his hands to defeat the Amalekites; see Exodus 17:8–16. That Moses raised his middle finger seems to be an invention of the child. The sefirotic symbolism is spelled out below: the middle finger corresponds to *Tif'eret*, the *sefirah* of Moses. Thus by raising this finger, he invoked that *sefirah*; cf. Zohar 2:66a, 76b. Raising the middle finger is an ancient power symbol, a means of combating the evil eye. The child may be hinting that Moses made the gesture for this purpose; the evil eye is spoken of below. Cf. *Talmud, Berakhot* 55b; *Encyclopaedia Judaica*, s.v. "evil eye," col. 999; Desmond Morris et al., *Gestures, Their Origins and Distribution* (New York, 1979), pp. 81–2, 149, 152.

the Dwelling   the *mishkan*, the Tabernacle in the desert, which for the Zohar is a symbol of the *sefirot*; see 2:221a; Tishby, *Mishnat ha-Zohar* 2:183–94.

That center bar is one of those five   See *Baraita di-Melekhet ha-Mishkan*, Chap. 1; Talmud, *Shabbat* 98b; *Tosafot*, ad loc.; Rashi on Exodus 26:26.

Two on this side ...   The five bars represent the five *sefirot* from *Hesed* to *Hod*. The two on the right symbolize *Hesed* and *Nezah*; the two on the left, *Gevurah* and *Hod*. *Tif'eret* is the Center Bar, balancing the two sides. This central *sefirah* is associated with Jacob and Moses.

the five hundred years ...   Cf. *Bereshit Rabba* 15:6: Rabbi Judah son of Ila'i said, "It would take five hundred years to walk around the Tree of Life." Here the Zohar identifies the Tree of Life with *Yesod*, and the five hundred years with the five *sefirot* referred to above, which provide *Yesod* with the flow of emanation; cf. 1:18a, 35a.

The Holy Covenant is aroused ...   The Holy Covenant is *Yesod*, which corresponds to the phallus and the covenant of circumcision; cf. above, "The Birth of Moses." There are two variant readings here: "circumcised" (*itgezar*) instead of "aroused" (*it'ar*), and "astonishing" (*teima*) instead of "secret" (*setima*).

the blessings of the priest ...   The fingers transmit the blessing from the *sefirot*; cf. *Bahir*, §135; *Bemidbar Rabbah* 12:4.

Moses' hand was spread out ...   to draw down power from the *sefirot*; cf. Ramban on Exodus 17:12. On the use of the singular, "hand," see Exodus 17:11; Zohar 2:57a, 66a; *Minhat Shai* on Exodus 17:12.

paradigm   Aramaic, *dugma*, "example, model"; i.e., the *sefirot*.

All filth and all dirt heighten the Other Side   The Other Side, the Demonic, feeds on whatever is unclean; cf. Zohar 1:10b.

compulsory, a compulsory offering!   Hebrew, *hovah ve-hovah*. Cf. Talmud, *Hullin* 105a: Rabbi Isaac son of Ashyan said, "The first waters [i.e., washing before the meal] are a *mizvah*; the last waters [i.e., washing after the meal] are a *hovah*." The Zohar is playing with Hebrew, *hovah*, and Aramaic, *ḥova,* "sin." The water that washes the dirt from one's hands is offered to the Other Side as its portion of filth and evil, thus keeping it content; see Zohar 2:154b, 266b; *Zohar Ḥadash, Rut* 87b–c (*Midrash ha-Ne'elam*); Tishby, *Mishnat ha-Zohar* 1:67; cf. above, "Seduction Above and Below."

appears as a donkey driver Aramaic, *tayya'a;* cf. above, "The Old Man and the Beautiful Maiden."

never sees a donkey ... "Donkey" (*ḥamra*) also means "fool"; see Talmud, *Bava Batra* 74a, in the middle of a fantastic story about a *tayya'a.* In Zohar 3:275b (*Ra'aya Meheimna*) "donkey" (Hebrew, *ḥamor*) designates a talmudic scholar who does not know the secrets of Kabbalah; cf. Tishby, *Mishnat ha-Zohar* 2:385, n. 63; above, Introduction, n. 8.

this child is not a human being! Cf. Talmud, *Shabbat* 112b, where Rabbi Ḥizkiyah is astounded by the brilliance of his student, Rabbi Yoḥanan, and says, "This is not a human being!" Here the remark has other connotations as well; see below.

Just as they say: 'From a person's mouth ...' A similar formulation appears in Zohar 3:193b; cf. *Shir ha-Shirim Rabbah* 1:7. Here it is an insult.

We have learned: 'A person should not walk ...' Cf. Talmud, *Qiddushin* 31a: "Rav Huna son of Rabbi Joshua would not walk four cubits with his head uncovered. He said, '*Shekhinah* is above my head!'" This was considered a sign of exceptional piety; see *Shabbat* 118b; Maimonides, *Mishneh Torah, Hilkhot De'ot* 5:6; *Guide of the Perplexed* 3:52. *Sefer Ḥasidim* ("Book of the Pious," thirteenth century) counsels: "A person should not walk erect or with his head uncovered because *Shekhinah* is above his head" (§53). The child introduces the pietistic custom with the word *tenan,* "we have learned [in the Mishnah]," as if it were Mishnaic law.

a light is kindled above the light of the soul, which emanates from *Shekhinah.*

King Solomon traditionally the author of Ecclesiastes.

the two sides of the *sefirot,* represented by *Ḥesed* and *Gevurah,* the right and left arms of God.

towering, invincible rocks! Cf. Zohar 1:7a, 92b; 3:206a. Aramaic, *rama'in,* "high, towering," can also mean "deceivers, imposters"; cf. 2:71b–72a (*Raza de-Razin*); 3:51a, 203b; *Minḥat Shai* on Numbers 23:9; cf. "the village of Ra'min," the fictitious home of an anonymous Jew and another wonder child encountered by the rabbis on the road (1:63b; 3:39b).

I am the son of a great and precious fish The meaning becomes clear below.

as it is written ... for we have learned ... Cf. Talmud, *Berakhot* 20a: "Rabbi Yoḥanan used to go and sit at the gates of the bathhouse. He said, 'When the daughters of Israel come out from bathing, they will look at me, and they will have children as beautiful as I!' The rabbis said to him, 'Are you not afraid of the evil eye?' He said to them, 'I am descended from Joseph, who is immune to the evil eye. . . .' Rabbi Yose son of Rabbi Hanina said, '[We know this] from the following verse [from Jacob's blessing to the sons of Joseph]: "They shall multiply like fish in the midst of the earth." Just as fish of the sea are covered by water and are immune to the evil eye, so the descendants of Joseph are immune to the evil eye.' " The child is playful: taking what he wants from the talmudic passage, he adds his own cryptic reference to "a great and precious fish." The line in brackets ("so the descendants . . .") does not appear in the Zohar, thus forcing the reader to recall or locate the source.

Come, let us bless   the blessing after the meal, *Birkat ha-Mazon.*

generous   literally, "good."

Read it: 'will bless'   Cf. Talmud, *Sotah* 38b: Rabbi Joshua son of Levi said, "The cup of blessing should be given only to one who is generous, for it is said: 'One whose eye is generous will be blessed, because he gave of his own bread to the needy.' Do not read: 'will be blessed,' but rather: 'will bless.' " This midrashic twist appears several times in the Zohar in various contexts: 2:218a–b; 3:63b, 117b, 130a (*Idra Rabba*), 211b.

From the bread and food of my Torah . . .   Cf. *Shemot Rabbah* 47:8: " 'He [Moses] was there with *YHVH* forty days and forty nights; he ate no bread and drank no water' (Exodus 34:28). But from the bread of Torah he ate . . . from the water of Torah he drank."

We have learned   in Talmud, *Berakhot* 46a, in the name of Rabbi Shim-'on son of Yohai.

I am not master of the house, and you are not guests!   Rabbi Solomon ibn Adret (thirteenth century) notes in his commentary on the passage in *Berakhot*: "If the meal is solely in honor of the guests, they are called 'the masters of the meal,' and the master of the house is considered a guest." The child may be alluding to this tradition. Or he may be indicating that his mother is the mistress of the house. But then why aren't the rabbis guests? Perhaps he is hinting at the fantastic nature of the narrative. The child's true identity is soon revealed.

the cup of blessing   the cup of wine held during *Birkat ha-Mazon.*

"for the land and the food"   the conclusion of the second of the four blessings that constitute *Birkat ha-Mazon.*

May . . . life be extended to one of these . . .   When it was decreed that Rabbi Isaac was to die, Rabbi Shim'on interceded with God, saved his life, and became his surety below; see the account in Zohar 1:217b–218b.

who possesses all Shalom   following the reading of the Mantua and Cremona editions; later editions read: "who possesses the entire world"; see Tishby, *Mishnat ha-Zohar* 1:73, 500.

the son of Rav Hamnuna Sava!   Rabbi Hamnuna the Elder. The child hinted at this when he said that he was the "son of a great and precious fish [Aramaic, *nuna*]"; cf. Talmud, *Qiddushin* 25a; *Tosafot*, ad loc. On Rav Hamnuna see above, "Guests in the *Sukkah.*" In Talmud, *Shabbat* 119b, Rav Hamnuna says, "Jerusalem was destroyed only because they neglected the teaching of schoolchildren." In *Mo'ed Qatan* 25a–b both a *tayya'a* and a *yanuqa* are involved in the events following Rav Hamnuna's death. In Zohar 1:5a–7b, Rav Hamnuna appears to Rabbi El'azar and Rabbi Abba as a donkey driver, but they think that he is the son of Hamnuna; see Tishby, *Mishnat ha-Zohar* 1:44; cf. 1:238b–240b. The donkey driver who enlightens Rabbi Hiyya and Rabbi Yose (above, "The Old Man and the Beautiful Maiden") also fits the child's description; he even says that he has a small son in school. However, he identifies himself as Yeiva Sava.

The flowing light of his father shines upon him! following the reading of the Mantua, Cremona, and Constantinople editions: *meshikhu*, "flowing," rather than *meshibu*, "anointing." The secret is that the father's soul reappears in the son; see Cordovero, *Or ha-Hammah*, on this passage; Tishby, *Mishnat ha-Zohar* 1:73; Scholem, *Kabbalah*, pp. 348–9. On the Christological overtones cf. above, Introduction, §4.

Miracles

Rabbi Pinhas ... Pinhas son of Ya'ir lived in the second century in Palestine. He was renowned for his saintliness and his ability to work miracles; see Talmud, *Hullin* 7a; Jerusalem Talmud, *Demai* 1:3, 22a. The Zohar accords him special status. In recognition of his *hasidut* ("saintliness, piety, devotion, love of God"), Rabbi Shim'on affirms that Pinhas has attained the *sefirah* of *Hesed;* see 1:11b; 3:62a, 201a. In general he is in a class by himself among the Comrades; see 3:59b–60b, 62a–b, 203a, 225b, 288a, 296b (*Idra Zuta*); *Zohar Hadash, Bereshit,* 12b, 19a (*Midrash ha-Ne'elam*). It is reasonable to expect this special treatment since, according to Talmud, *Shabbat* 33b, Rabbi Pinhas was the son-in-law of Rabbi Shim'on. However, Moses de León elevates Pinhas further by transforming him into Rabbi Shim'on's father-in-law! This new role could be the result of a simple mistake made by Moses: confusing *hatan*, "son-in-law," and *hoten*, "father-in-law." However, the switch may have been made deliberately in order to create a fictional framework and stun or fool the reader; see above, Introduction, §5. The contexts in which the son-in-law appears as the father-in-law support this possibility. They are usually fantastic or contrived: Rabbi Rehumai delivers a turgid, mystical speech to Pinhas and alludes cryptically to the relationship (1:11a); Rabbi El'azar meets Pinhas on the road and quotes an appropriate verse (3:36a); Rabbi Shim'on quotes another verse to his son, El'azar, and interprets it as referring to El'azar's mother, Pinhas' daughter (3:240b, on the Torah portion *Pinhas*); the prophet Elijah appears and tells Rabbi Shim'on: "Today for your sake, your father-in-law, Rabbi Pinhas son of Ya'ir, has been crowned with fifty crowns!" (3:144b [*Idra Rabba*]). In this selection, "Miracles," the relationship is given narrative substance: Rabbi Pinhas is on his way to see his sick daughter, the wife of Rabbi Shim'on. Yet this setting is provided only to highlight the fabricated relationship and set the tone for a fantastic tale. Pinhas' daughter never appears in the story; cf. 3:64a.

You brought about this miracle for my sake ... It was Pinhas' donkey that brayed and saved the Jews, though Pinhas himself was unaware of the miracle happening. According to the Talmud, this donkey shared the piety of its master. Once captured by robbers, it refused to eat any of their untithed food; it even acted more strictly than the rabbis in observing the laws of tithing; see Talmud, *Hullin* 7a–b; Jerusalem Talmud, *Demai* 1:3, 21d–22a; *Bereshit Rabba* 60:8. Pinhas' donkey appears elsewhere in the Zohar and performs admirably; see 3:36a, 221b.

And no one knows except for Him! ... Cf. *Midrash Tehillim* 106:1; 136:2–3; Talmud, *Niddah* 31a. Rabbi Pinhas draws on the examples offered there but adds a dramatic touch.

as ransom Aramaic, *kufra*. Once an act of evil has been ordained, it must be executed, if not on the intended victim, then on a substitute. Cf. Isaiah 43:3–4; Zohar 1:174b (where Job 33:24 is cited); 3:204b (see Cordovero, *Or ha-Hammah*, ad loc.), 205a; *Zohar Hadash, Balaq*, 54a; Talmud, *Berakhot* 62b.

paved Aramaic, *mittaqqna*, "prepared, arrayed, established, mended, straightened, adorned"; the root *tqn* has a wide range of meaning in the Zohar. This phrase appears frequently: 1:89a (*Sitrei Torah*); 2:37a, 155b; 3:21b, 87b, 232b; *Zohar Hadash, Lekh Lekha*, 25c (*Midrash ha-Ne'elam*).

his donkey turned aside from the road This section of the Zohar corresponds to the Torah portion *Balaq*, which tells the story of Balaam and his ass. It is no accident that Pinhas' donkey appears so prominently. Cf. Numbers 22:23: "The ass saw the angel of *YHVH* standing in the road, with his sword drawn in his hand. The ass turned aside from the road and went into the field." In Zohar 3:201a–b Rabbi Shim'on contrasts Balaam's ass with Pinhas' donkey.

one mile Aramaic, *terein milin*, "two *mils*." A *mil* equals 2,000 cubits, approximately 3,000 feet. Two *mils* are approximately 1.1 miles. The phrase *terein millin*, "two things," appears several lines earlier.

the Countenance of Days the face of Rabbi Shim'on here associated with the Ancient of Days; cf. Tishby, *Mishnat ha-Zohar*, 1:12; Zohar 1:6a, 11a, 89b (*Sitrei Torah*), 130a; 3:132b (*Idra Rabba*), 265b; *Zohar Hadash, Bereshit*, 19a; *Lekh Lekha*, 25c (*Midrash ha-Ne'elam*).

the Great Face and the Small Face In Talmud, *Sukkah* 5b, these terms refer to the human and cherubic faces of the holy creatures described in Ezekiel 10:14. Cf. Zohar 1:18b; 3:60b, 217b, 274a. Here the terms signify Rabbi Shim'on and his son, Rabbi El'azar.

Hasid "devotee, pious one."

the mouth of YHVH As Rabbi Pinhas approached, Rabbi Shim'on was delivering a homily on different kinds of mouths that culminated in the mouth of *YHVH: Shekhinah;* see Zohar 3:201b; cf. 3:188b. Pinhas applies the phrase to Rabbi Shim'on; cf. 3:59b and above, "The Old Man and the Beautiful Maiden": "I am so glad to see the face of *Shekhinah!*" For other references to the divine nature of Rabbi Shim'on see 2:38a; 3:61b, 79b; cf. Talmud *Bava Batra* 75b; Jerusalem Talmud, *Bikkurim* 3:3, 65d; Bahya ben Asher on Exodus 33:7; above, Introduction, n. 84.

your Master standing here   apparently Rabbi Pinhas. Tishby interprets the phrase as applying to *Shekhinah;* see *Mishnat ha-Zohar,* 1:15.

him who is in charge of you   the power in charge of birds; cf. *Bereshit Rabba* 79:6. At first it was in his power to serve Rabbi Shim'on with his birds; now they must leave.

the Day of the Rock ...   the Day of Judgment. When *Tif'eret* and *Shekhinah,* the divine couple, are prevented from uniting by the dark cloud of human sin and demonic power, the world is judged harshly; see Zohar 3:59b.

for 'His compassion is upon all His works'   Cf. Talmud, *Shabbat* 133b: Abba Sha'ul said, "Just as He is gracious and compassionate, so you be gracious and compassionate." Cf. *Bava Mezi'a* 85a.

We have established ...   In *Shemot Rabbah* 20:3 this verse is applied to the people of Israel. Here Rabbi Pinhas applies it to *Keneset Yisra'el,* the Communion of Israel, their divine counterpart: *Shekhinah;* see above, "How to Look at Torah"; cf. Zohar 1:132a; 3:266a, 298a.

five gardens   five *sefirot: Hesed, Gevurah, Nezah, Hod,* and *Yesod. Tif'eret,* in the middle, is called the Blessed Holy One; cf. Tishby, *Mishnat ha-Zohar* 1:16.

one spring above ... secret and hidden   *Binah,* the Divine Mother, who nourishes the lower *sefirot* with the flow of emanation. She and *Shekhinah* are mother and daughter; both are referred to as springs.

one garden below them ...   *Shekhinah.* She contains all the fruits of the higher gardens and must be guarded from the evil powers lurking outside, eager to penetrate the divine realm.

other gardens   the lower worlds, fed by the emanation of *Shekhinah,* the garden who turns into a spring.

water flowing ... water drawn ...   The need and impulse arise from below. If human beings are living holy lives, *Shekhinah* becomes a spring, and blessings flow naturally. If life on earth is corrupt, *Shekhinah* turns into a well, and the water must be drawn by righteous heroes. Cf. Zohar 1:60a–b, 235a. On the concept of "arousal from below" see 1:35a, 77b, 82b; 2:256b, 265a, 267b; 3:31b, 38b.

'Flows from Lebanon'   Hebrew, *nozelim,* "flows," is a noun; cf. Isaiah 44:3; Psalms 78:16, 44; Proverbs 5:15.

Five sources   The five garden *sefirot* mentioned above are sources of emanation for *Shekhinah.*

Lebanon above *Hokhmah*, Wisdom, the primal point of emanation; cf. *Bahir*, §178; Zohar 1:29a.

when they turn into a spring ... pursued by the soul! As they flow into *Shekhinah* (the "spring of gardens"), water begins to trickle down to the human realm, and the soul responds. This is one interpretation. "A spring" could also refer to the flow of emanation from *Binah* (the "spring above ... secret and hidden"). "The soul" (*nafsha*) would then be *Shekhinah*, as in Zohar 1:87a; 2:142a. See Cordovero, *Or ha-Hammah*, on this passage; Tishby, loc. cit. The text is in disarray (see the variant readings in 3:202a); so it is difficult to determine the exact sense. Furthermore, the imagery is overflowing, intermingling, and multivalent; it defies simplistic correspondences. Its power lies in its capacity to stimulate the imagination; its inner meaning is an evocation of yearning for the divine flow.

The Wedding Celebration (Idra Zuta)

The other time I was ill The account of Rabbi Shim'on's earlier illness is found in *Zohar Hadash, Bereshit*, 18d–19a (*Midrash ha-Ne'elam*).

Rabbi Pinhas son of Ya'ir the son-in-law of Rabbi Shim'on, promoted by Moses de León to the rank of his father-in-law; see above, "Miracles."

selecting my place in Paradise next to Ahiyah of Shiloh On this reading see *Or ha-Hammah*, ad loc.; Scholem, *Tarbiz* 3 (1932): 183, n. 6; cf. *Zohar Hadash* 19a. Ahiyah was the prophet who revealed to Jeroboam that Solomon's kingdom would be divided; see 1 Kings 11:29–39. According to rabbinic tradition, he was a master of the secrets of Torah (Talmud, *Sanhedrin* 102a; *Midrash Tehillim* 5:8) and the teacher of Elijah (Jerusalem Talmud, *Eruvin* 5:1, 22b). Later, Hasidic legend portrays him as the mentor of Israel Ba'al Shem Tov, the founder of Hasidism; see Jacob Joseph of Polonnoye, *Toledot Ya'aqov Yosef* (Koretz, 1780), p. 156a. Rabbi Shim'on associates himself with Ahiyah in *Bereshit Rabba* 35:2; cf. Zohar 1:4b. Hayyim Vital cites a tradition in the name of Cordovero that Rabbi Shim'on was a reincarnation of Ahiyah; see *Or ha-Hammah*, loc. cit.

they extended my life until now to purify the Comrades and others who drew near to him (Isaac Luria, cited in *Nizozei Orot* on this passage). For a different reading see Tishby, *Mishnat ha-Zohar*, 1:33, 499.

saw what he saw This phrase appears frequently in the Zohar in the context of mystical or prophetic vision. Here it conveys the image of seeing *Shekhinah* before one's death; see *Tanhuma, Huqqat*, §16; Zohar 1:65b, 79a, 226a, 245a; 3:88a. Cf. above, "The Old Man and the Beautiful Maiden"; 1:149a, 172a; 2:2b, 13b, 81a, 112b, 136a, 211a.

for I have been surety for him When it was decreed that Rabbi Isaac was to die, Rabbi Shim'on interceded with God and saved his life, pledging himself as surety; see the account in Zohar 1:217b–218b, and the wonder child's prayer, above, "The Rabbis Encounter a Child." Now it is time for Rabbi Isaac to depart along with Rabbi Shim'on.

the threshing house Aramaic, *bei idra.* For the various associations of *idra* see above, "Threshing Out the Secrets." During the assembly at the threshing house, six of the Comrades proved their mystical ability and stamina. Three others died from the overwhelming power of the revelations. Now the experienced Comrades are invited to hear Rabbi Shim'on's final words. This section of the Zohar (3:287b–296b) forms the bulk of the Zohar's commentary on the Torah portion *Ha'azinu* (Deuteronomy 32), which contains Moses' farewell song to the people of Israel. The parallel between Moses and Rabbi Shim'on is alluded to several times before and after this section; see 3:286b–287a, 297a, 298a; cf. above, loc. cit.; 1:236a; 2:149a; 3:15a, 22b–23a. The early kabbalists called this section *Idra de-Ha'azinu;* later it was called *Idra Zuta,* "The Small *Idra,*" to distinguish it from *Idra Rabba,* "The Great *Idra,*" (3:127b–145a), the assembly at the threshing house.

to enter without shame into the world that is coming Displaying the knowledge of secrets removes the feeling of shame, Aramaic, *kissufa.* Cf. *Zohar Ḥadash, Shir ha-Shirim,* 70d: "Teach me the secrets of wisdom that I have not known and have not learned until now, so that I will not be in shame within those high levels that I am about to enter. For until now I have not reflected on them." The phrase recurs twice below; cf. 1:4a; 2:123b; 3:144a (*Idra Rabba*); also 3:46a; and above, "The Old Man and the Beautiful Maiden." In *Zohar Ḥadash, Shir ha-Shirim,* 67d *kissufa* is said to be essential for admission into the world that is coming! In Hebrew the root *ksf* means "to yearn, long for, desire." The Zohar employs it to describe *Shekhinah* (see above, "God, Israel, and *Shekhinah*": "His most precious possession [*kissufa dileih*]"); the precious worlds of the Blessed Holy One (1:19a; *Zohar Ḥadash, Bereshit* 9d, 13b, 18a; *Noaḥ* 22a [*Midrash ha-Ne'elam*]); and the pleasures awaiting the righteous in the world that is coming (above, "The Gift of Dwelling"; 1:124b [*Midrash ha-Ne'elam*]; 3:178a, 288a [*Idra Zuta*]; *Zohar Ḥadash, Noaḥ* 22a [*Midrash ha-Ne'elam*]). The root *ksf* exhibits what Freud called "the antithetical sense of primal words" (see his essay by this title, *Complete Works* 11:153–61). On "the world that is coming," see above, "*Qorban* and *Olah.*"

as a password to the world that is coming literally, "to enter with them into the world that is coming." Cf. Zohar 3:144a (*Idra Rabba*); 3:291a (*Idra Zuta*): "All these words have been hidden in my heart until now. I wanted to hide them for the world that is coming, for there they ask us a question . . . and require wisdom of me. But now it is the will of the Blessed Holy One [that I reveal these words]. Behold, without shame I will enter His palace!" Cf. Talmud, *Shabbat* 31a.

will meditate within Aramaic, *yirḥashun be-libbaihu. Rḥsh* means "to move, be moved, feel, think"; *lev* means "heart" and "mind."

Yah a short form of *YHVH* that appears in poetry.

Dumah "silence," the silence of death; cf. Psalms 94:17. In the Talmud Dumah is the name of the angel in charge of souls after death; see *Berakhot* 18b, *Shabbat* 152b, *Sanhedrin* 94a. In the Zohar he sometimes retains this function but also appears as the Prince of Hell; see Margaliot, *Mal'akhei Elyon*, pp. 225–9.

those called 'dead' ... those called 'living' Cf. *Berakhot* 18a–b: Rabbi Hiyya said, "These are the righteous, who even in death are called 'living.'" ... These are the wicked, who even in life are called 'dead.' " Cf. Zohar 1:132a, 164a, 207b; 2:106b; 3:182b; *Zohar Hadash, Bereshit* 18b (*Midrash ha-Ne'elam*), in the name of Rabbi Hiyya.

at the threshing house ... chariots See above, "Thresing Out the Secrets"; Zohar 3:135a (*Idra Rabba*).

Jeroboam the first king of the northern kingdom of Israel, who had golden calves built in Bethel and Dan to dissuade the people from going to the Temple in Jerusalem in the southern kingdom of Judah; see 1 Kings 12:25–33.

Ido the prophet According to 1 Kings 13, a prophet from Judah came to Bethel and prophesied the destruction of the altar. "When the king heard the word that the man of *Elohim* had proclaimed against the altar in Bethel, Jerobaom stretched out his hand above the altar and cried, 'Seize him!' But his hand that he stretched out against him dried up; he could not draw it back" (verse 4). The name of the prophet is not mentioned, but he is traditionally identified as Ido; see 2 Chronicles 9:29; Talmud, *Sanhedrin* 89b; *Sifrei*, Deuteronomy, §342; *Tanhuma, Toledot*, §12; *Pesiqta de-Rav Kahana* 2:6; Rashi and Radaq on 1 Kings 13:1.

Rav Hamnuna Sava On this figure see above, "Guests in the *Sukkah*," "The Rabbis Encounter a Child." Rav Hamnuna missed the assembly at the threshing house because he was being held captive in a tower; see Zohar 3:144b (*Idra Rabba*). Rabbi Shim'on had once been promised that he and Rav Hamnuna would be neighbors in Paradise; see 1:7b.

adorned with crowns literally, "engraved [*gelifan*] with crowns."

the Holy Ancient One the primal and most ancient manifestation of *Ein Sof,* the Infinite, through *Keter,* Its Crown.

Look! Here is Rabbi Pinhas son of Ya'ir! ... See above, the beginning of the selection. Historically, Rabbi Pinhas outlived Rabbi Shim'on, but according to the account here, Pinhas has already died; cf. Zohar 3:144b (*Idra Rabba*); Tishby, *Mishnat ha-Zohar* 1:71 (Introduction). "Prepare his place!" may indicate that Pinhas will accompany Rabbi Shim'on to the world beyond; cf. the final words of Rabbi Yohanan son of Zakkai: "Prepare a throne for Hezekiah, king of Judah, who is coming!" (Talmud, *Berakhot* 28b; see Rashi, ad loc.).

the outskirts of the house Aramaic, *shippulei beita. Shippula* means "lower part, extremity, skirt, train of a dress, train of a tent."

all the Comrades speaking ... In the *Idra Rabba* (3:127b–145a) all the

Comrades participated in revealing mystical secrets. (The selection above, "Threshing Out the Secrets," includes just a portion of Rabbi Shim'on's words.) In this assembly the Comrades listen as Rabbi Shim'on expounds.

the Blessed Holy One *Tif'eret*, the central *sefirah*, less concealed than the Holy Ancient One.

nine lights the nine *sefirot* that emanate from the Holy Ancient One. On the *sefirot* see above, Introduction, §6.

I have not acted for my own honor ... Is Moses de León alluding to the pseudepigraphic style of the Zohar? Cf. above, Introduction, nn. 61, 107; Zohar 2:102a, 104a; 3:144a (*Idra Rabba*). The same expression appears in Talmud, *Ta'anit* 20a, *Megillah* 3a, *Bava Mezi'a* 59b.

wedding celebration Aramaic, *hillula*. In the Talmud the word means "wedding celebration"; see, e.g., *Berakhot* 30b–31a. In the Zohar this literal meaning recurs (e.g., 3:94b). The word is also applied to a circumcision celebration (1:93a), perhaps because circumcision initiates the male into an intimate relationship with *Shekhinah*; see 1:8a–b, 216a. In a number of passages *hillula* describes the *hieros gamos*, the sacred marriage between *Tif'eret* and *Shekhinah*; see 1:10a; 3:66b, 87b, 105a, 118a. The occasion of Rabbi Shim'on's death is also a wedding celebration: his soul is about to ascend and unite with *Shekhinah*; cf. 1:218a, where Song of Songs 3:11 is cited; Tishby, *Mishnat ha-Zohar* 1:10. By the sixteenth century, it was customary to visit the grave of Rabbi Shim'on at Meron in the Galilee on *Lag ba-'Omer*. This was a ritual of celebration, not mourning, and became known as *Hillula de-Rabbi Shim'on bar Yohai*; see Avraham Yaari, *Tarbiz* 31 (1962): 72–101.

the Holy Spark Aramaic, *bozina qaddisha*, "the holy lamp," Rabbi Shim'on's honorific title; see above, "The Golden Calf." In the Zohar *bozina* means "spark, light" as well as "lamp"; see Liebes, *"Peraqim,"* pp. 136–60.

permission to reveal it.

"A river issues from Eden" ... "Like a spring ..." Both of these verses appear elsewhere in the Zohar to describe the flow of emanation. The first one is cited over fifty times, e.g., 1:34a, 35b; 2:83a; 3:65b. The second appears in 2:55a, 83a; 3:266a, 290b (*Idra Zuta*).

adorning my head like a crown A similar expression appears in Zohar 2:123b.

will not miss its mark like the other day at the threshing house, when the Comrades participated in revealing secrets. Cf. above, "Jacob's Garment of Days."

I have begun! I will speak! For other examples of overcoming the hesitation to reveal secrets see above, "The Old Man and the Beautiful Maiden," "The Golden Calf," "Threshing Out the Secrets."

the High Spark Aramaic, *bozina ila'ah*. Above, this phrase denotes Rabbi Shim'on. Here it denotes the Holy Ancient One, the primal manifestation of *Ein Sof* through *Keter*, the highest *sefirah*. All the other *sefirot* ("sparks, levels") emanate from this High Spark. Cf. above, "The Creation of *Elohim*," "Threshing Out the Secrets."

Adornments of the King, Crowns of the King   Aramaic, *tiqqunei malka, kitrei malka*. The Zohar carefully avoids the common kabbalistic term *sefirot;* see Scholem, *Kabbalah*, p. 229; above, Introduction, §6.

It and Its Name is one   The *sefirot* are God's Name, the expression of Its being. Cf. Zohar 3:288a (*Idra Zuta*): "They are called the Holy Name; therefore all is one." Cf. 3:11b: "They are Its Name, and It is they." Cf. *Pirqei de-Rabbi Eli'ezer*, Chap. 3: "Before the world was created, there was only the Blessed Holy One and His great Name."

the Garment of the King   another metaphor for the *sefirot;* cf. *Shir ha-Shirim Rabbah* 4:21; Zohar 3:7b; Altmann, *Studies*, p. 134.

Ineffable   Aramaic, *de-la itperash*, "not expressed," inexpressible. The reference is to *Ein Sof,* the Infinite.

the Holy Ancient One   *Ein Sof* manifesting through *Keter.*

Upon reflecting   Aramaic, *kad mistakkalan;* see above, "The Binding of Abraham and Isaac," note on "reflect."

there is nothing but the High Spark   Through meditation, one discovers the ultimate reality of the High Spark. The *sefirot,* levels of enlightenment, are stages on the path to this realization and are finally seen to have no independent existence. Cf. Zohar 3:288a (*Idra Zuta*), the continuation of the passage translated above: "When arrayed, It [the Holy Ancient One] generates nine lights, flaming from It, from Its array. Those lights, sparkling, flashing, radiate, emanate to all sides. Like a spark [or "lamp," *bozina*] from which lights emanate to all sides. Those lights emanating, when one draws near to know them, there is nothing but the spark alone. So it is with the Holy Ancient One, the High Spark, Concealed of all Concealed: there is nothing but those lights emanating, revealing themselves—and hidden away. They are called the Holy Name; therefore all is one." The analogy does not reach its logical conclusion. The passage should end by saying: "there is nothing but the High Spark," which is what our passage finally does say. Rabbi Shim'on leaves the reader suspended and perplexed, forces him to question the logic and to wonder; cf. above, "God, Israel, and *Shekhinah*," note on "So, with Israel. . . ." Even now when he finally spells out the mystical truth that all is one, he immediately adds: "hidden and unrevealed!" The sensitive reader is drawn into the search.

'life'   Rabbi Shim'on was expounding the verse: "There *YHVH* ordained blessing, life forever" (Psalms 133:3). Cf. Liebes, *"Ha-Mashiah shel ha-Zohar,"* pp. 191–4.

'He asked you for life . . .   You granted it; length of days everlasting.'

Three there were! Turned back into one!   One interpretation is that Rabbi Shim'on, Rabbi Pinhas, and Rabbi El'azar were a triad of holy Comrades; cf. Zohar 2:14b (*Midrash ha-Ne'elam*); 3:203a; Cordovero, *Or ha-Hammah,* ad loc.; *Zohar Hadash, Bereshit* 19a (*Midrash ha-Ne'elam*); Tishby, *Mishnat ha-Zohar* 1:36. Now only Rabbi El'azar, the son, remains in the world.

the animals will wander off! . . . Rabbi Shim'on's death has thrown all of nature into chaos; cf. Zohar 3:296a (*Idra Zuta*). Rabbi El'azar may also be alluding to the holy animals carrying the divine throne and the birdlike angels who will flee to the Great Sea of *Shekhinah;* see Zohar 2:48b–49a; Tishby, loc. cit.

drinking blood! Aramaic, *shatyan dema.* This bizarre image is apparently meant to convey the Comrades' misery. Tishby considers emending the text to: *shotetin dema,* "dripping blood"; cf. Talmud, *Sanhedrin,* 68a; Zohar 2:16b, 17b (*Midrash ha-Ne'elam*). An allusion to Christian beliefs should also be considered; the doctrine of transubstantiation had been defined at the Fourth Lateran Council in 1215. Cf. Rabbi El'azar's opening words; and above, the conclusion of "The Rabbis Encounter a Child."

a truckle made out of a gangplank—Who has seen the confusion of the Comrades? The Comrades carry Rabbi Shim'on in a *tiqra de-siqla. Tiqra* is a neologism constructed from three of Moses de León's favorite letters: *t, q, r.* Its meaning is unknown; I have rendered it semiphonetically and contextually; cf. Zohar 3:59b. *Siqla* appears in Tosefta, *Shabbat* 13:14, where it means "a ship's ladder" used to disembark; cf. Latin, *scala,* "ladder"; *Arukh,* s.v. *siqla;* Mishnah, *Shabbat* 16:8: *kevesh.* Tishby, *Mishnat ha-Zohar* 1:36, renders the phrase: "a canopy," which reads well but does not do justice to these unusual words. "Confusion" describes not only the Comrades' state of mind following Rabbi Shim'on's death, but also Moses de León's deliberately confusing vocabulary and chaotic creativity. A number of words in the following lines are anagrams of *tiqra* and *siqla;* see below. Cf. *Zohar Hadash, Bereshit,* 12a (*Midrash ha-Ne'elam*), where it is said that King David must have been "confounded" when he wrote an illogical word in Psalms 46:9. The same question, "Who has seen the confusion?" appears in a positive sense in *Zohar Hadash, Rut* 90d (*Midrash ha-Ne'elam*), where it parallels "Who has seen the joy?"

lifted Aramaic, *seliqu,* containing the same root letters as *siqla.* The root *slq* appears twice again in the vicinity.

Truculent stingers . . . Aramaic, *teriqin,* containing the same letters as the neologism *tiqra.* The root *trq* means "to sting, bite"; in the Zohar it usually describes powers of harsh judgment; see 2:244a; 3:291b (*Idra Zuta*). The shield-bearing warriors are of a similar nature; see 1:43a, 229b, 249a; 2:147b; 3:231a. Here the warriors are not powers from the beyond but rather mighty Torah scholars from Sepphoris who want Rabbi Shim'on buried in their city, famed for its learning; cf. Talmud, *Berakhot* 27b; Zohar 2:38b, 145b; Scholem *Ziyyon* (*Me'assef*) 1 (1926): 44, n. 2; above, "Threshing Out the Secrets," note on "wearing coats of mail." A variant reading substitutes "the village" for "Sepphoris."

Meron   the traditional site of Rabbi Shim'on's grave; see *Pesiqta de-Rav Kahana* 11:23.

ganged together   Aramaic, *bi-qetirin*, "in knots, bands"; again the same three letters: *q, t, r.*

the wedding celebration   see above.

the cave   in Meron.

"This is the man . . ."   a rephrasing of Isaiah 14:16: "Is this the man who made the earth tremble, who shook kingdoms?" There the words are spoken derisively by those who witness the fallen condition of the king of Babylon. Here the mockery is transformed into praise for Rabbi Shim'on.

open mouths of accusation   Aramaic, *pitrin*, "openings," short for *pitrin de-fuma*, modeled after Hebrew, *pithon peh*, "opening of the mouth," opportunity for fault-finding, accusation by the powers above. Cf. Zohar 1:89a (*Sitrei Torah*); 2:14b (*Midrash ha-Ne'elam*), 262a.

'As for you . . .'   the last verse in the Book of Daniel: 12:13.

APPENDIX

GLOSSARY

[Most Hebrew words and kabbalistic terms are explained in the notes. The Glossary includes those that are not and those mentioned frequently.]

alef: the first letter of the Hebrew alphabet; the beginning of divine and human speech.

Ba'al Shem Tov: Master of the Good Name; the title of Israel son of Eli'ezer, charismatic founder of Hasidism (ca. 1700–1760).

Bahir: *Sefer ha-Bahir,* Book of Brightness; an early kabbalistic work, edited in southern France late in the twelfth century.

Binah: Understanding; the third *sefirah;* the Divine Mother who gives birth to the seven lower *sefirot.*

Blessed Holy One: common rabbinic name for God; in the Zohar it is often associated with *Tif'eret.*

Din: Judgment; the fifth *sefirah;* the left arm of the divine body counterbalancing *Hesed;* the roots of evil lie here; also called *Gevurah.*

Ein Sof: there is no end, that which is boundless, the Infinite; the ultimate reality of God beyond all specific qualities of the *sefirot.*

Elohim: God, gods, a biblical name for God; in the Zohar it has various sefirotic associations: *Binah, Gevurah, Shekhinah.*

Gedullah: Greatness; the fourth *sefirah;* the outpouring of God's great goodness; also called *Hesed.*

Gevurah: Power; the fifth *sefirah;* also called *Din.*

gimatriyya: the numerical value of Hebrew letters, employed as a technique of interpretation.

hasid: devotee, pious one.

Hasidism: popular religious movement that emerged in the second half of the eighteenth century in Eastern Europe.

Hesed: Love, the fourth *sefirah;* the right arm of the divine body counterbalancing *Din:* also called *Gedullah.*

Hod: Majesty; the eighth *sefirah;* the left leg of the divine body; source of prophecy along with *Nezah.*

Hokhmah: Wisdom; the second *sefirah;* the primal point of emanation.

GLOSSARY

Holy Ancient One: the most ancient manifestation of *Ein Sof* through *Keter*, Its Crown.

idra: threshing floor, assembly.

Idra Rabba: The Great *Idra;* a description of the gathering of Rabbi Shim'on and the Comrades at the threshing house, where secrets of God's inner being are expounded; Zohar 3:127b–145a; selections: above, "Threshing Out the Secrets."

Idra Zuta: The Small *Idra;* a description of the death of Rabbi Shim'on and his final teachings; Zohar 3:287b–296b; selections: above, "The Wedding Celebration."

Kabbalah: receiving, that which is handed down by tradition; the esoteric teachings of Judaism.

Keter: Crown; the first *sefirah;* coeternal with *Ein Sof;* also called *Razon,* Divine Will, and *Ayin,* Nothingness.

Malkhut: Kingdom; the tenth *sefirah,* administering divine justice to the lower worlds; also called *Shekhinah.*

Matnitin: Our Mishnah; short pieces scattered through the Zohar; most of them appear as utterances of a heavenly voice urging the Comrades to open their hearts to the mysteries.

menorah: candelabrum of seven branches; a prominent feature of the *mishkan.*

mezuzah: parchment scroll affixed to the doorpost.

midrash (pl. **midrashim**); legal or homiletical interpretation of the Bible.

Midrash: a collection of *midrashim;* the midrashic literature.

Midrash ha-Ne'elam: The Concealed Midrash, The Esoteric Midrash; the earliest stratum of the Zohar.

mishkan: God's dwelling in the desert; the tabernacle constructed by Moses and the Children of Israel.

Mishnah: collection of oral teachings redacted, arranged, and revised around the beginning of the third century by Rabbi Judah ha-Nasi; the earliest codification of Jewish Oral Law.

mizvah (pl. **mizvot**): divine commandment; one of the 613 precepts of the Torah; by extension: good deed.

Nezah: Endurance; the seventh *sefirah;* the right leg of the divine body; source of prophecy along with *Hod.*

nishmato eden: May his soul abide in the Garden of Eden.

Oral Torah: the interpretation of the Written Torah; in Kabbalah a symbol of *Shekhinah.*

GLOSSARY

Qav ha-Middah: The Standard of Measure; a detailed explanation of the process of emanation delivered by Rabbi Shim'on; *Zohar Hadash* 56d–58d.

Ra'aya Meheimna: The Faithful Shepherd; an early imitation of the Zohar, so successful that it was printed as part of the work; it expounds the mystical significance of the *mizvot*.

Rahamim: Compassion; the sixth *sefirah*, balancing *Hesed* and *Din*; also called *Tif'eret.*

Rashi: Rabbi Solomon son of Isaac (1040–1105); French commentator on the Bible and Talmud.

Raza de-Razin: The Mystery of Mysteries; an anonymous piece of physiognomy and chiromancy; Zohar 2:70a–75a; *Zohar Hadash* 35b–37c.

Rut: The Book of Ruth.

Sava de-Mishpatim: The Old Man of [Torah portion] *Mishpatim*; an account of the Comrades' encounter with a donkey driver who turns out to be a master of wisdom; Zohar 2:94b–114a; selections: above, "The Old Man and the Beautiful Maiden."

sefirah (pl. **sefirot**): one of ten aspects of God, nine of which emanate from *Ein Sof* and *Keter*; see above, Introduction, §6.

shalom: peace, well-being, completeness.

Shekhinah: Divine Presence; the tenth *sefirah*; female partner of *Tif'eret*; also called *Malkhut.*

Shir ha-Shirim: Song of Songs.

Sifra di-Zeni'uta: The Book of Concealment; a fragmented commentary on the beginning of the Torah in short obscure sentences, divided into five chapters; it deals with the secrets of divinity; Zohar 2:176b–179a.

Sitrei Torah: Secrets of Torah; pieces on verses from Genesis, printed in separate columns, parallel to the main text of the Zohar; they contain allegories of the soul and secrets of the divine and the demonic.

sukkah (pl. **sukkot**): booth.

Sukkot: Festival of Booths; a celebration of the harvest and a commemoration of the Children of Israel's dwelling in booths in the desert after the Exodus from Egypt.

Talmud: the body of teaching comprising commentary and discussions on the Mishnah by scholars of the third to sixth centuries.

Targum: translation, translation of the Bible into Aramaic.

Targum Onqelos: a Targum on the Torah composed by a proselyte named Onqelos in the second century.

tav: the last letter of the Hebrew alphabet.

Tif'eret: Beauty; the sixth *sefirah*; male partner of *Shekhinah*; the trunk of the divine body; also called *Rahamim.*

305

GLOSSARY

Tiqqunei Zohar: Embellishments on the Zohar; an early imitation of the Zohar; a wide-ranging commentary on the first portion of the Torah.

Torah: Teaching; the first five books of the Bible; by extension: all religious teaching.

Tosafot: collections of comments on the Talmud and on Rashi's commentary on the Talmud, composed between the twelfth and fourteenth centuries in France and Germany.

Tosefta: Addenda; short pieces scattered through the Zohar; most of them appear as utterances of a heavenly voice urging the Comrades to open their hearts to the mysteries.

the world that is coming: see above, end of notes to "*Qorban* and *Olah*."

Written Torah: the first five books of the Bible; in Kabbalah a symbol of *Tif'eret*.

Yanuqa: The Child; the story of a wonder child who teaches the Comrades profound secrets; Zohar 3:186a–192a; selections: above, "The Rabbis Encounter a Child."

Yesod: Foundation; the ninth *sefirah*, who channels the flow of emanation to *Shekhinah*; also called *Zaddiq*.

YH, Yah: a short form of *YHVH* that appears in poetry.

YHVH: the ineffable name of God; in the Zohar it is often associated with *Tif'eret*.

Zaddiq: Righteous One; the ninth *sefirah*; *Yesod*.

zohar: splendor, radiance; see above, note to Foreword.

Zohar Hadash: New Zohar; a collection of zoharic texts found in manuscripts of the Safed kabbalists after the printing of the bulk of the Zohar; the title is misleading since the volume contains much of *Midrash ha-Ne'elam*, the oldest stratum of the Zohar.

BIBLIOGRAPHY

1. Zohar

Margaliot, Re'uven, ed. *Sefer ha-Zohar.* 3 vols. 4th edition. Jerusalem, 1964.
———, ed. *Zohar Hadash.* Jerusalem, 1953, 1978.
Scholem, Gershom. *Zohar, The Book of Splendor: Basic Readings from the Kabbalah.* New York, 1949.
Sperling, Harry, and Simon, Maurice, trans. *The Zohar.* 5 vols. London, 1931–1934.
Tishby, Isaiah, and Lachover, Fishel. *Mishnat ha-Zohar.* 2 vols. Jerusalem, 1961, 1971.

2. Hebrew Works by Moses de León

Or Zaru'a. Edited by Alexander Altmann. *Qovez al Yad,* n.s. 9 (1980): 219–93.
Sefer ha-Mishqal. Edited by Jochanan H. A. Wijnhoven. Ph.D. dissertation, Brandeis University, 1964. (Earlier, corrupt edition: *Ha-Nefesh ha-Hakhamah.* Basle, 1608.)
She'elot u-Teshuvot be-'Inyenei Qabbalah. Edited by Isaiah Tishby. *Qovez al Yad,* n.s. 4 (1950): 15–38.
Sheqel ha-Qodesh. Edited by A. W. Greenup. London, 1911.
Shushan Edut. Edited by Gershom Scholem. *Qovez al Yad,* n.s. 8 (1975): 325–70.
Sod Eser Sefirot Belimah. Edited by Gershom Scholem. *Qovez al Yad,* n.s. 8 (1975): 371–84.

3. Other Works of Kabbalah

Azri'el of Gerona. *Perush ha-'Aggadot le-Rabbi Azri'el.* Edited by Isaiah Tishby. Jerusalem, 1945.
Azulai, Avraham, ed. *Or ha-Hammah.* 4 vols. Przemysl, 1896–1898. Reprint (3 vols.). Benei-Berak, 1973.
David ben Yehudah he-Hasid. *The Book of Mirrors: Sefer Mar'ot ha-Zove'ot.* Edited by Daniel Chanan Matt. Chico, California: Scholars Press, 1982.
Ezra of Gerona. *Le Commentaire d'Ezra de Gérone sur le Cantique des Cantiques.* Translated and edited by Georges Vajda. Paris, 1969.
Gikatilla, Yosef. *Sha'arei Orah.* Warsaw, 1883. Reprint. Jerusalem, 1960.
Ibn Gabbai, Me'ir. *Avodat ha-Qodesh.* Jerusalem, 1973.
Labi, Shim'on. *Ketem Paz.* 2 vols. Leghorn, 1795. Djerba, 1940.

BIBLIOGRAPHY

Ma'arekhet ha-'Elohut. Mantua, 1558. Reprint. Jerusalem, 1963.

Margaliot, Re'uven, ed. *Sefer ha-Bahir*. Jerusalem, 1951, 1978.

————, ed. *Tiqqunei Zohar*. Jerusalem, 1948, 1978.

Recanati, Menahem. *Perush al ha-Torah*. Jerusalem, 1961.

Scholem, Gershom, trans. and ed. *Das Buch Bahir*. Leipzig, 1923. Reprint. Darmstadt, 1970.

Zavva'at Rabbi Eli'ezer. In *Beit ha-Midrash*, edited by Adolf Jellinek, 3:131–40. Jerusalem, 1938.

4. Secondary Literature

Altmann, Alexander. *Studies in Religious Philosophy and Mysticism*. Ithaca, 1969.

Bacher, Wilhelm. "L'exégèse biblique dans le Zohar." *Revue des Études Juives* 22 (1891): 33–46, 219–29.

————. "Judaeo-Christian Polemics in the Zohar." *Jewish Quarterly Review* 3 (1891): 781–4.

Baer, Yitzhak. *A History of the Jews in Christian Spain*. 2 vols. Translated by Louis Schoffman. Philadelphia, 1978.

————. "*Ha-Reqa ha-histori shel ha-Ra'aya Meheimna*." *Zion* 5 (1940): 1–44.

Bension, Ariel. *The Zohar in Moslem and Christian Spain*. London, 1932. Reprint. New York, 1974.

Biale, David. *Gershom Scholem: Kabbalah and Counter-History*. 2d ed., rev. Cambridge, Mass., 1982.

Blumenthal, David R. "Maimonides' Intellectualist Mysticism and the Superiority of the Prophecy of Moses." *Studies in Medieval Culture* 10 (1977): 51–67.

————. *Understanding Jewish Mysticism: A Source Reader*. New York. 1978.

Emden, Jacob. *Mitpahat Sefarim*. Lvov, 1870. Reprint. Jerusalem, 1970.

Epstein, Perle. *Kabbalah: The Way of the Jewish Mystic*. New York, 1978.

Farber, Asi. "*Iqvotav shel Sefer ha-Zohar be-khitvei R. Yosef Gikatilla*." *Alei Sefer* 9 (1981): 40–53.

————. "*Li-Ve'ayat meqoroteha shel torato ha-qabbalit ha-muqdemet shel R. Mosheh de León*." In press.

————. In *Mehqerei Yerushalayim be-Mahshevet Yisra'el* 1 (1981): 158–76.

Ginzberg, Louis. *The Legends of the Jews*. 7 vols. Translated by Henrietta Szold and Paul Radin. Philadelphia, 1968.

Gottlieb, Efraim. *Mehqarim be-Sifrut ha-Qabbalah*. Edited by Joseph Hacker. Tel Aviv, 1976.

————. *Ha-Qabbalah be-Khitvei Rabbenu Bahya ben Asher*. Jerusalem, 1970.

Graetz, Heinrich. *History of the Jews*. 6 vols. Translated by Bella Löwy. Philadelphia, 1891–98.

Heschel, Abraham J. "The Mystical Element in Judaism." In *The Jews: Their*

BIBLIOGRAPHY

History, Culture, and Religion, edited by Louis Finkelstein. Philadelphia, 1966.

Idel, Moshe. *"Ha-Mahshavah ha-ra'ah shel ha-'el." Tarbiz* 49 (1980): 356–64.

———. *"Ha-Shimmush be-'orot u-zeva'im bi-tefillat ha-mequbbalim."* In press.

———. *"Targumo shel R. David ben Yehudah he-Hasid le-Sefer ha-Zohar u-ferushav la-'alfa beita." Alei Sefer* 8 (1980); 60–73; 9 (1981): 84–98; 10 (1982): 25–35.

Jacobs, Louis. *Jewish Mystical Testimonies.* New York, 1977.

Jellinek, Adolf. *Beiträge zur Geschichte der Kabbala.* 2 vols. Leipzig, 1852.

———. *Moses ben Schem-Tob de Leon und sein Verhältniss zum Sohar.* Leipzig, 1851.

Kaddari, Menahem Z. *Diqduq ha-Lashon ha-'Aramit shel ha-Zohar.* Jerusalem, 1971.

Kaplan, Aryeh. *Meditation and Kabbalah.* York Beach, Maine: Samuel Weiser, 1982.

Kushner, Lawrence. *Honey from the Rock.* New York, 1977.

———. *The River of Light.* San Francisco, 1981.

Labi, Shim'on. *"Be'ur miqzat millot zarot she-be-Sefer ha-Zohar."* In *Qevuzat Hakhamim,* edited by Solomon Stern. Vienna, 1861. Reprint. Jerusalem, 1970.

Levine, Lee. "R. Simeon b. Yohai and the Purification of Tiberias: History and Tradition." *Hebrew Union College Annual* 49 (1978): 143–85.

Liebes, Yehuda. *"Hashpa'ot nozriyyot al Sefer ha-Zohar." Mehqerei Yerushalayim be-Mahshevet Yisra'el* 2 (1983): 43–74.

———. *"Ha-Mashiah shel ha-Zohar."* In *Ha-Ra'yon ha-Meshihi be-Yisra'-el,* pp. 87–236. Jerusalem. 1982.

———. *"Peraqim be-Millon Sefer ha-Zohar."* Ph.D. dissertation, Hebrew University, 1976. (Jerusalem: Hebrew University, 1982.)

Margaliot, Re'uven. *Sha'arei Zohar.* Jerusalem, 1956.

Matt, Daniel. "David ben Yehudah he-Hasid and His *Book of Mirrors." Hebrew Union College Annual* 51 (1980): 129–72.

Patai, Raphael. *The Hebrew Goddess.* 2d ed., rev. New York, 1978.

Scholem, Gershom. *"Ha-'Im hibber R. Mosheh de León et Sefer ha-Zohar?" Madda'ei ha-Yahadut* 1 (1926): 16–29.

———. *Jewish Gnosticism, Merkabah Mysticism, and Talmudic Tradition.* New York, 1960.

———. *Kabbalah.* Jerusalem, 1974.

———. *Major Trends in Jewish Mysticism.* 3d ed., rev. New York, 1961.

———. *The Messianic Idea in Judaism.* New York, 1971.

———. *On the Kabbalah and Its Symbolism.* Translated by Ralph Manheim. New York, 1965.

———. *"Parashah hadashah min ha-Midrash ha-Ne'elam she-ba-Zohar."* In *Sefer ha-Yovel li-Khevod Levi Ginzberg,* pp. 425–46. New York, 1946.

———. *Pirqei Yesod be-Havanat ha-Qabbalah u-Semaleha.* Translated by Joseph Ben-Shlomo. Jerusalem, 1976.

BIBLIOGRAPHY

——. *Reshit ha-Qabbalah.* Jerusalem, 1948.

——. "She'elot be-viqqoret ha-Zohar mi-tokh yedi'otav al erez yisra'el." *Ziyyon* (Me'assef) 1 (1926): 40–55.

——. *Über einige Grundbegriffe des Judentums.* Frankfurt am Main, 1970.

——. "Eine unbekannte mystische Schrift des Mose de Leon." *Monatsschrift für Geschichte und Wissenschaft des Judentums* 71 (1927): 109–23.

——. *Ursprung und Anfänge der Kabbala.* Berlin, 1962.

——. *Von der mystischen Gestalt der Gottheit.* Zurich, 1962.

——. "Ha-Zitat ha-rishon min ha-Midrash ha-Ne'elam." *Tarbiz* 3 (1932): 181–3.

Silver, Daniel J. *Maimonidean Criticism and the Maimonidean Controversy, 1180–1240.* Leiden, 1965.

Singer, June. *Androgyny.* New York, 1977.

Steinsaltz, Adin. *The Thirteen Petalled Rose.* Translated by Yehuda Hanegbi. New York, 1980.

Stern, Samuel M. "Rationalists and Kabbalists in Medieval Allegory." *Journal of Jewish Studies* 6 (1955): 73–86.

Tishby, Isaiah. "Ha-Pulmus al Sefer ha-Zohar be-me'ah ha-shesh-'esreh." *Peraqim* 1 (1967–68): 131–82.

Urbach, Ephraim E. *Hazal: Pirqei Emunot ve-De'ot.* Jerusalem, 1971.

Werblowsky, R. J. Zwi. "Philo and the Zohar." *Journal of Jewish Studies* 10 (1959): 25–44, 112–35.

INDEX TO ZOHAR PASSAGES

---

*References are to the standard editions of the Zohar in three volumes: 1: Genesis; 2: Exodus; 3: Leviticus, Numbers, Deuteronomy. *Zohar Hadash* is cited according to Re'uven Margaliot's edition (Jerusalem, 1978).

INDEX

INDEX TO PREFACE,
FOREWORD,
INTRODUCTION
AND NOTES

313

INDEX

INDEX

315

INDEX TO TEXT

INDEX

INDEX

Holy of Holies, the, 147, 187
Holy Spark, the, 185, 187
Hosea, the Book of: 1:2, 228; 9:4, 270

Ibn Sahula, Isaac, 204
Ido the Prophet, 184, 295
Idra, 278, 279
Idra Rabba, 277, 278
Idra Zuta, 278
Impatient One, the, 166–167, 282
Infinite, the, 49, 208
Infinity, 147
Isaac, Rabbi: on the Deviser of Evil, 61,
    90; encounters a child, 170–176; on
    Jacob, 94; on light, 52; mentioned,
    100, 118, 155–156, 164; as Rabbi
    Shim'on leaves the world, 182–183,
    293–294
Isaac son of Abraham: Abraham's
    offering of, 72–74, 225; mentioned,
    70, 76, 77, 106, 107, 108, 134, 151;
    tested, 72–73
Isaac son of Jacob Kohen, 282
Isaiah, the Book of: 3:10, 100; 6:13, 50;
    10:5, 245; 11:2, 67; 14:16, 299; 25:8,
    232; 26:16, 111, 245; 26:19, 166; 27:13,
    232; 28:8, 151; 30:22, 89; 34:14, 260;
    41:8, 71, 75; 42:5, 211; 42:18, 91;
    43:21, 136; 44:3, 292; 50:1, 160; 50:2,
    129; 51:4, 260; 54:9, 218; 54:17, 151;
    57:2, 188; 58:8, 151; 58:11, 94, 151;
    186; 58:14, 151; 60:21, 254, 271
Israel: the Beauty of, 44, 206; the
    Communion of, 44, 99, 148, 180, 206,
    235–236; in exile, 67, 222; and God,
    111–112, 153–162; and Pharaoh,
    111–112, 244–245; and *Shekhinah*,
    153–162, 275–277
Israel the Patriarch. *See* Jacob the
    Patriarch

Jacob son of Idi, Rabbi, 60–62
Jacob the Patriarch: his garment of days,
    91–95; as Israel, 75, 226, 228; the
    Journey of, 75–79, 226–229;
    mentioned, 74, 106, 107, 108, 134,
    139, 151; as *Tif'eret*, 225; the Voice
    of, 75, 227
Jeremiah, the Book of: 2:2, 148; 17:6, 94;
    31:33, 262; 49:19, 260
Jeroboam, 184, 293, 295
Jethro, 102
Job, 86, 93, 235

Job, the Book of: 1:6–12, 232; 1:21, 93;
    2:1–6, 232; 20:14, 228; 28:12, 249;
    33:15–16, 81; 33:24, 291; 38:14, 94;
    38:15, 211
Joseph: attempted seduction of, 84–90,
    231–234; his dream, 80–83, 229–231;
    mentioned, 91, 174; as *Yesod*, 233
Joshua, the Book of: 6:26, 167; 13:22, 103
Joshua son of Levi, Rabbi, 277, 280
Joshua son of Nun, 155, 273
Judah, Rabbi: encounters a child,
    170–176; on the garment of days,
    91–95; on the hidden light, 52; on
    Joseph's dream, 81–82; mentioned,
    65, 102, 155, 164, 169; on Moses, 101,
    102, 104
Judges, the Book of: 13:25, 251

Keter, 209, 210, 226, 278, 280, 281, 282,
    297
Kingdom of Heaven, the, 81, 230
1 Kings: 6:38, 76; 8:56, 137; 11:29–39, 293;
    12:25–33, 295; 13:1, 295; 13:4, 184

Levi, the House of, 99
Leviticus, the Book of: 1:1–2, 145; 1:9,
    266, 268; 5:7, 223; 6:1–2, 147; 11:44,
    100; 15:33, 88; 16:2, 245; 16:7–22, 232;
    19:18, 281; 23:33–34, 148; 23:39–43,
    148; Ch. 26, 153; 26:11, 256; 26:16,
    275; 26:44, 277
Lilit, 227, 228, 232–233
Lot, 59, 60, 61–62
Luke, the Gospel of: 10:2, 277

Malachi, the Book of: 1:2, 158, 281; 1:3,
    158; 2:3, 150
Malkhut, 233
Manna, 113–116, 245–247
Mark, the Gospel of, 286
Masters of Judgment, the, 159
Matthew, the Gospel of: 9:37, 277; Ch.
    15, 286
Menorah, the, 255
Meshaḥta, the, 249
Meshal ha-Qadmoni, 204
Messiah, King, 67, 131
Micah, the Book of: 6:7, 224
Michael, 229
Mighty Voice, the, 76, 227
Mishkan, 254
Mizvah, 170, 286
Moriah, Mt., 72

318

INDEX

Moses: the birth of, 99–101, 235–238; and the blazing bush, 102–104, 238–240; the Bride of, 130, 256; and colors and enlightenment, 107–110, 243–244; and the golden calf, 133–141, 258–265; and the light, 51, 211–212; mentioned, 72, 123, 130, 155–156, 167, 171, 211; and *Shekhinah*, 99–101, 236–242, 252, 255–256; shielded his generation, 59, 218; and Torah, 51, 76; the wisdom of, 141, 264; and *YHVH*, 105–106, 113, 117–118, 127, 145, 148

Mt. Sinai, 44, 51, 167, 206

Neshamah, 66, 221
Neshamah of *neshamah*, 66, 222
Nezah, 229, 230, 279
Noah: after the Flood, 57–59, 218; became drunk, 63, 76; mentioned, 218; and *Shekhinah*, 220
Nothingness, 147, 267
Numbers, the Book of: 7:1, 130: 9:6–14, 205; 11:12, 280; 11:25, 245; 12:6, 80; 12:7, 103; 12:8, 242; 15:32–36, 205; 15:37–41, 285; 15:41, 260; 16:26, 150; 22:21–35, 239; 22:23, 291; 27:1–11, 205; 28:2, 57

Other Side, the, 89, 100, 132, 172, 220, 222, 257

Palanquin, the, 128, 255
Patient One, the 166–167, 282–283
Patriarchs, the, 94, 107–108, 235, 243
Pharaoh, 111–112, 244–245
Pinḥas, Rabbi, 177–181, 184, 290–293, 295
Proverbs, the Book of: 3:2, 185, 187; 3:11, 157; 3:12, 158; 3:16, 84; 3:17, 87; 3:18, 273; 3:34, 248; 4:18, 254; 5:5, 86; 5:15, 292; 6:23, 86; 6:24, 84; 7:13, 228; 7:16, 228; 8:17, 128; 9:4, 125; 10:25, 213; 12:19, 135; 13:24, 274; 13:25, 151; 14:17, 245; 22:9, 174; 23:6, 150; 23:8, 151; 31:10–31, 221; 31:23, 65
Psalms, the Book of: 18:31, 120; 21:5, 187; 24:7, 66; 25:14, 164; 27:4, 254; 31:20, 51; 34:19, 223; 42:9, 53; 45:4, 278; 57:12, 65; 65:5, 118; 69:14, 283; 78:16, 292; 78:25, 113; 78:44, 292; 85:12, 261; 89:3, 69; 94:17, 295; 97:11, 52, 211; 104:2, 52; 104:4, 43; 106:20, 139, 264; 106:23, 59; 112:2–3, 151; 113:4, 65; 115:17, 183; 116:13, 175; 118:19, 67; 118:24, 157; 119:18, 44; 119:126, 163; 130:3, 159; 133:3, 297; 135:4, 226; 136:4, 177; 139:16, 93; 140:14, 90; 145: 9, 180

Qav ha-Middah, 208, 249
Qorban, 145–146, 265–268

Rainbow, the, 123, 251–252
Reapers of the Field, the, 163, 277
Rosh ha-Shanah, 86, 232

Sabbath, 132, 169, 257–258
Sama'el, 77–78, 228, 232–233
1 Samuel: 4:22, 139
Sarah, 65–68, 70, 71, 221–222
Satan, 69, 70–71, 223. *See also* Deviser of Evil, the
Sava, Rav Hamnuna, 175, 184, 269
Sava de-Mishpatim, 249
Sea of Ginnosar, the, 127, 254
Sea of Tiberias, the, 155, 272
Seduction, 63, 76, 84–90, 226–229, 231–234
Sefirot, the, 216, 221, 222, 229
Shekhinah: and Adam's sin, 215–216; and Amram and Yocheved, 99–100, 236; as the End of Thought, 226–227; with Israel, 153–162, 275–277; and *Mazzah*, 245–247; mentioned, 121, 137, 139, 173, 206, 215–216, 224, 229, 242, 282; and Moses, 99–101, 236–242, 252, 255–256; as the Mouth of *Sefirot*, 249; and Noah, 220; and the poor, 223; as Rabbi Shim'on leaves the world, 183; and Sabbath, 257–258; and Speech, 230, 249; and *Tif'eret*, 206, 217; 219, 221, 228, 235, 236–237, 270, 274, 296; as "word" of God, 224
Shema, the, 170, 286
Shema'yah the *Hasid*, Rabbi, 170–171, 286
Sheva, the, 76
Shim'on, Rabbi: on Abraham's offering of Isaac, 72–74; on Abram's descent into Egypt, 63–64; on Balaam, 103; on colors and enlightenment, 107–110; on the creation of Adam, 55–56; and the donkey driver, 126; on the gift of dwelling, 127–131; as the Holy Light, 138; leaves the